UNIVERSITY OF NORTH CAROLINA AT CHAPEL HILL
DEPARTMENT OF ROMANCE LANGUAGES

NORTH CAROLINA STUDIES
IN THE ROMANCE LANGUAGES AND LITERATURES

ESSAYS; TEXTS, TEXTUAL STUDIES AND TRANSLATIONS; SYMPOSIA

Founder: URBAN TIGNER HOLMES

Distributed by:

UNIVERSITY OF NORTH CAROLINA PRESS
CHAPEL HILL
North Carolina 27514
U.S.A.

NORTH CAROLINA STUDIES IN THE
ROMANCE LANGUAGES AND LITERATURES

Essays

Number 16

AN ANATOMY OF POESIS:
THE PROSE POEMS OF STÉPHANE MALLARMÉ

AN ANATOMY OF POESIS:
THE PROSE POEMS
OF
STÉPHANE MALLARMÉ

BY

URSULA FRANKLIN
Grand Valley State Colleges

CHAPEL HILL

NORTH CAROLINA STUDIES IN THE ROMANCE
LANGUAGES AND LITERATURES
U.N.C. DEPARTMENT OF ROMANCE LANGUAGES
1976

Library of Congress Cataloging in Publication Data

Franklin, Ursula.
  An anatomy of poesis.

  (North Carolina studies in the Romance language and literature: Essays; 16)
  "Appendix" (p.   ) consists of Mallarmé's Anecdotes ou poèmes (first published together in 1897 as part of his collection entitled Divagations) in French and English.
  1. Mallarmé, Stéphane, 1842-1898. Divagations. 2. Mallarmé, Stéphane, 1842-1898—Criticism and interpretation. I. Mallarmé, Stéphane, 1842-1898. Divagations. Selections. English & French. 1975. II. Title. III. Series.

PQ2344.D53F7   841'.8   75-29040
ISBN 9780807891674

DEPÓSITO LEGAL: V. 281 - 1976

ARTES GRÁFICAS SOLER, S. A. - JÁVEA, 28 - VALENCIA (8) - 1976

TABLE OF CONTENTS

	Page
Preface	8
Introduction	9
Le Phénomène Futur	18
Plainte d'Automne	29
Frisson d'Hiver	40
Le Démon de l'Analogie	52
Pauvre Enfant Pâle	67
La Pipe	82
Un Spectacle Interrompu	93
Réminiscence	109
La Déclaration Foraine	119
Le Nénuphar Blanc	136
L'Ecclésiastique	150
La Gloire	160
Conflit	172
Conclusion	195
Appendix	210
A List of Works Cited	265

PREFACE

Stéphane Mallarmé's verse and prose has produced a considerable volume of perceptive and sometimes exciting criticism and interpretation. However, the poet's important prose poems have for the most part escaped the attention of scholars. This study, a detailed analysis of each prose poem, following the order established by Mallarmé himself, addresses itself to filling this gap.

I am indebted to Professor Laurence M. Porter who drew my attention to Mallarmé's prose poems a few years ago and directed an earlier version of this study. He has taught me much about literary scholarship. My reading of Mallarmé owes much to his previous commentators: to Haskell M. Block, Gardner Davies, Wallace Fowlie, Emilie Noulet, Jean-Pierre Richard, Kurt Wais and others; but especially to Robert Greer Cohn, I am grateful for guidance in my exploration of the Mallarméan universe.

I regret that the important recent studies of the poet by Jacques Derrida and Julia Kristeva were not available to me during the time that this book was being written.

I thank the editors of *The French Review, Nineteenth-Century French Studies* and *The Romanic Review* for their kind permission to use material which first appeared in their journals.

Finally I wish to express my deepest gratitude to my friend and teacher Professor John A. Yunck who first introduced me to poetry. His constant encouragement, his criticism and untiring advice, made this study possible.

Grand Valley
April 8, 1974

INTRODUCTION

Mallarmé's monumental literary significance, both historical and intrinsic, has produced an abundance of excellent critical scholarship devoted to his work during the past fifty years. Attention has been focused, however, almost wholly on his verse;[1] his prose — a substantial and artistically important part of his work — has only recently begun to receive attention. Dieter Steland[2] has pointed out that Mallarmé's prose works cannot be indiscriminately designated as *kritische Schriften,* for even his critical prose, like that represented in "Symphonie Littéraire," is a special type of poetry.[3] The *Divagations,*[4] Mallarmé's collected prose work, published under his supervision in 1897, introduces a new prose genre, the "poème critique," which term appears in the "Bibliographie" of the *Divagations,* where the poet explains:

> Les cassures du texte, on se tranquillisera, observent de concorder, avec sens et n'inscrivant d'espace nu que jusqu'à leurs points d'illumination: une forme, peut-être,

---

[1] Mallarmé's verse attracted critical attention during his lifetime, and more intensively since the publication of Albert Thibaudet's *La Poésie de Stéphane Mallarmé* (Paris: Gallimard, 1912; 2e ed., 1926).

[2] Dieter Steland, *Dialektische Gedanken in Stéphane Mallarmés "Divagations"* (München: Wilhelm Fink Verlag, 1965).

[3] Henri Mondor, *Stéphane Mallarmé: Correspondance 1862-1871 I* (Paris: Gallimard, 1959), p. 113; in a letter to Albert Collignon, of April 11, 1864, Mallarmé writes:

> Je vous envoie aujourd'hui quelques poèmes en prose dont vous aimez les *inspirateurs.*

The "inspirateurs" are Gautier, Banville, and Baudelaire.

[4] Stéphane Mallarmé, *Divagations* (Paris: Bibliothèque Charpentier, 1897).

en sort, actuelle, permettant, à ce qui fut longtemps le poème en prose et notre recherche, d'aboutir, en tant, si l'on joint mieux les mots, que poème critique. Mobiliser, autour d'une idée, les lueurs diverses de l'esprit, à distance voulue, par phrases ... [5]

In this study I will examine a body of prose which stands between Mallarmé's verse and the poème critique: his prose poems, which are not critically interpretive in the manner of the poetic essay. The term "prose poems" refers here to the thirteen prose pieces first published separately in various reviews from 1864 to 1895, and finally grouped together as the "Anecdotes ou Poèmes" of *Divagations,* a book which reflects the author's own structural determination of his prose work a year before his death. [6]

The prose poem did not appear suddenly in the nineteenth century. Rather it grew out of the much earlier concept of poetic prose, whose basic idea — simply stated, that prose can be poetic — represented a striking revolt against the formalism of the seventeenth century. Classicism's most typical spokesmen, grammarians and critics like Vaugelas and Bouhours, insisted on rigorous distinctions among genres, and specifically between prose and verse. Nevertheless, the revolt was already voiced by La Bruyère, and was manifest, moreover, in many a page of Bossuet. But it is with Fénelon's *Télémaque* that poetry most obviously invades the prose of the classical century. [7]

Poetic prose came into its own in the following century, in the pages of two of the Enlightenment's greatest representatives: Diderot and Rousseau. Hence the nineteenth century inherited a long tradition of poetic prose which it developed richly. Mme de Staël,

---

[5] Mallarmé, *Divagations,* p. 373.

[6] The first twelve of these poems had been gathered together in *Pages* of 1891, and common editorial practice tends misleadingly to follow this early grouping, despite Mallarmé's own later addition. Cf., e.g., H. Mondor and G. Jean-Aubry, *Œuvres complètes de Stéphane Mallarmé* (Paris: Gallimard, 1945). The editors indicate in a note, p. 1573, the appearance of "Conflit" as the closing piece of the "Anecdotes ou Poèmes" of *Divagations.* All quotations are from this *Pléiade* edition, unless otherwise indicated.

[7] The origin of the prose poem in reaction against the classical tradition is traced thoroughly in Vista Clayton, *The Prose Poem in French Literature of the Eighteenth Century* (New York: Columbia Univ., 1936). See especially pp. 181 ff.

INTRODUCTION

enthusiast of the "souffle lyrique" of German Romanticism, notes in *De l'Allemagne* that France's best lyric poets are perhaps her great *prosateurs,* Bossuet, Pascal, Fénelon, Buffon and Jean-Jacques.[8] In Chateaubriand poetic prose finds its great master; and it is in Chateaubriand also that the first signs of the prose poem begin to appear, in the form of his "beaux morceaux" dispersed here and there in his work, which seem like lyric songs — in prose — interpolated in his *romans.* Thus, the early nineteenth century in France represents a literary terrain and climate propitious for the birth of the new genre, "le poème en prose." The genre's earliest representative is Alphonse Rabbe, whose "La Pipe"[9] constitutes one of its significant early examples. The first recueil of prose poems is the "Gaspard de la Nuit" (1842) of Aloysius Bertrand — much admired by Baudelaire and Mallarmé — whom literary historians generally consider to be the originator of the new genre.

From this point on, many poets venture into the new form which, according to the young Mallarmé's master, Baudelaire, introduces a modern accent into lyricism:

> Quel est celui de nous qui n'a pas, dans ses jours d'ambition, rêvé le miracle d'une prose poétique, musicale sans rythme et sans rime, assez souple et assez heurtée pour s'adapter aux mouvements lyriques de l'âme, aux ondulations de la rêverie, aux soubresauts de la conscience?[10]

The present study is not concerned with Mallarmé's prose poems as representative of the development of the genre, nor as product of the Symbolist movement. These aspects of his work have been dealt with by others;[11] but the best modern Mallarmists

---

[8] Madame de Staël, *De l'Allemagne* (ed. by the Countess Jean de Pange, "Les grands écrivains de la France," 5 vols. (Paris: Hachette, 1958-60), Vol. 2, p. 108.

[9] "La Pipe," written in 1825, is quoted in full in note 4, of our chapter "La Pipe."

[10] Charles Baudelaire, *Petits Poèmes en Prose (Le Spleen de Paris)* (Paris: Garnier, 1962), p. 7.

[11] Suzanne Bernard, *Le poème en prose de Baudelaire jusqu'à nos jours* (Paris: Nizet, 1959), devotes a substantial chapter, pp. 252-330, to Mallarmé's work as a manifestation of the genre, but necessarily views it only as a stage in a historical process. Guy Michaud, *Message poétique du symbolisme* (Paris: Nizet, 1966), devotes a chapter, pp. 159-98, to Mallarmé's work in general as a part of the movement.

have been very sparing in their analyses of the prose poems, either individually or as a unified grouping. Kurt Wais has commented brilliantly on some of them, but without giving them a strictly analytical reading, nor considering them as a group.[12] Jean-Pierre Richard touches upon each prose poem in the course of his "global" discussion of the poet's major themes and motifs, but without discussing any single poem as an organic whole.[13] The poet's most significant critic, Robert Greer Cohn, whose work has given a decisive orientation to the interpretation of all of Mallarmé's poetry,[14] does not discuss them specifically. And Frederic Chase St. Aubyn, in the most recent full-length study of Mallarmé in English,[15] limits himself sharply by his brevity, merely touching on twelve of the prose poems in the first part of a short chapter devoted to Mallarmé's prose.

Our attempt, then, in the discussions which follow, will be to provide readers of Mallarmé with the first full exegesis of each prose poem. A significant and innovative part of our analysis, however, will be to examine these prose poems as a *recueil,* in the order determined by the poet himself. In this we are heeding Mallarmé's own suggestion, since the choice and grouping of the pieces in *Divagations* was his own, thus inviting us to consider them not as a conglomeration of separate elements, but as a structure. Yet this suggestion — and the poet always preferred suggestion over statement — intimated by the most structured of poetic minds, has never been heeded. Moreover, while each poem individually may have revealed one meaning, it might — like *les mots* — take on an infinitely enriched one in the specific context furnished by Mallarmé, a more complex significance which will illuminate each piece beyond its original radiance, as if by "reciprocal reflection:"

---

[12] Kurt Wais, *Mallarmé* (München: Beckshe Verlagsbuchhandlung, 1938 and 1952).

[13] Jean-Paul Richard, *L'Univers imaginaire de Mallarmé* (Paris: Ed. du Seuil, 1961).

[14] Robert Greer Cohn, *L'Œuvre de Mallarmé: Un Coup de Dés* (Paris: Librairie Les Lettres, 1951) and *Toward the Poems of Mallarmé* (Berkeley: Univ. of California Press, 1965).

[15] Frederic Chase St. Aubyn, *Stéphane Mallarmé* (New York: Twayne Publishers Inc., 1969).

INTRODUCTION 13

> L'œuvre pure implique la disparition élocutoire du poëte, qui cède l'initiative aux mots, par le heurt de leur inégalité mobilisés; ils s'allument de reflets réciproques comme une virtuelle traînée de feux sur des pierreries, remplaçant la respiration perceptible en l'ancien souffle lyrique ou la direction personnelle enthousiaste de la phrase (OC p. 366).

As these poems represent almost the whole span of the poet's productive life, our reading — aside from dealing with thematic aspects — has to account for the marked stylistic break, even more apparent in Mallarmé's prose than in his verse, which separates his early from his mature work. And we will find the mature prose style of the *Divagations* to be related to the thematic development of the prose poems. However, as our reading reveals the very close interrelationship of style and theme, or form and function, in the thirteen pieces, they are not anywhere discussed from a purely stylistic point of view.[16] Our principal aim, rather, is to explore the significance of the prose poems in Mallarmé's poetic universe, in order to make those poems and that universe more accessible to the careful reader. The writer's English renditions of the prose poems including "Conflit," which has not before been translated into English, are to be found in the Appendix.[17] Any exegesis of poetry, however, necessarily modifies and qualifies "translation" — since it attempts to elucidate poetic by discursive language — and particularly in the case of Mallarmé, who constructed a new idiom which became increasingly remote from the clarity, accessibility, and order of the customary French language.

---

[16] Mallarmé's typical stylistic devices have been identified by Jacques Scherer, *L'Expression littéraire dans l'œuvre de Mallarmé* (Paris: Droz, 1947). More recent stylistic approaches are Norman Paxton, *The Development of Mallarmé's Prose Style* (Genève: Droz, 1968) and Monique Parent, *Saint-John Perse et quelques devanciers, étude sur le poème en prose* (Paris: Belles Lettres, 1960).

[17] We refer the reader, moreover, to Bradford Cook's translations of four of the prose poems in *Mallarmé: selected prose poems, essays and letters*, translated by (Baltimore: Johns Hopkins Univ. Press, 1956). The twelve prose poems, with the exception of "Conflit," have been translated by Anthony Hartley, *Mallarmé,* prose translations by (Baltimore: Penguin, 1965).

Our reading will involve us in the examination of imagery not only within each poem individually, but also with reference to that of the other prose poems as well as the verse and the critical prose. For just as Mallarmé believed that all myths can be reduced to the solar drama, so he was drawn to a form of composition made up of a few carefully selected patterns of imagery; as Gardner Davies and others have pointed out, he uses a fairly limited number of terms repeatedly to create his symbolic language. This highly closed and synthetic aspect of the *œuvre* is, moreover, emphasized by Mallarmé himself:

> Jamais pensée ne se présenta à moi, détachée, je n'en ai pas de cette sorte et reste ici dans l'embarras; les miennes forment le train, musicalement placées, d'un ensemble et, à s'isoler, je les sens perdre jusqu'à leur vérité et sonner faux; après tout, cet aveu, peut-être, en figure-t-il une, propre au feuillet blanc d'un album (OC p. 883).

To form his symbolic system, Mallarmé not only unhinged the syntax of the language of communication, but also scrutinized most minutely its fundamental elements, the words themselves. For, as he reminded his friend Manet, *les mots* are the poet's primary working material; and hence he meditated upon them, from their multiple meanings to their etymological heritage, from their outer appearance (that is their sound-look) to their very anatomy, the flesh and bones of vowels and consonants:

> A toute la nature apparenté et se rapprochant ainsi de l'organisme dépositaire de la vie, le Mot présente, dans ses voyelles et ses diphtongues, comme une chair; et, dans ses consonnes, comme une ossature délicate à disséquer (OC p. 901).

The word is — as a microcosm to the poem — a multifaceted gem, scintillating with both spiritual and sensual fire, out of which the poet forges his delicate jewelry:

> —Les mots, d'eux-mêmes, s'exaltent à mainte facette reconnue la plus rare ou valant pour l'esprit, centre de suspens vibratoire: qui les perçoit indépendamment de la suite ordinaire, projetés, en parois de grotte, tant que dure leur mobilité ou principe, étant ce qui ne se dit pas du

discours: prompts tous, avant extinction, à une réciprocité de feux distante ou présentée de biais comme contingence (OC p. 386).

And so our venture into the prose poems is grounded on a careful examination of their supremely self-conscious diction.[18]

Although we necessarily begin with the poet's language, this examination reveals that there is a thematic unity and progression within the collection itself relating the prose poems to each other and thus constituting an artistic unity. The principal theme which emerges is the Poet's story: on the one hand his relation to the contingent phenomena of human experience and on the other the transformation of that experience into an ordered artistic universe through the poetic vision. And here we encounter a paradox in this work, which becomes progressively more impersonal — "L'œuvre pure implique la disparition élocutoire du poëte" — for it tells both the story of the Poet *par excellence* and that of a particular individual, Mallarmé, who sacrificed the man in himself for the sake of the poet. One of the primary structural tensions of the whole *recueil* is that fundamental one of Life and Death, that is the dying of a man and the becoming of the Poet.

Furthermore, though it is clear that we are dealing with a writer who is primarily a great poet, and not even secondarily a philosopher, it is nevertheless true that the *œuvre* is chronologically bracketed by two works of an overwhelmingly metaphysical significance; the body of Mallarmé's mature work begins with *Igitur* and ends with "Un Coup de Dés." Therefore our reading of the prose poems will also show how they reflect Mallarmé's philosophic stance. *Igitur* has come down to us in fragmentary

---

[18] Here we base ourselves on the contemporary dictionary of Emile Littré, which we are now certain that the poet utilized in order to give "un sens plus pur aux mots de la tribu," to create a language whose words are carefully chosen and polished not only for their sound-look aspect and customary significance, but also for their less apparent and often completely unfamiliar meanings. Particular attention has been paid to the etymological wealth of his vocabulary for which Mallarmé consulted Littré. Charles Chassé has devoted an entire book, *Les clefs de Mallarmé* (Paris: Aubier, 1954), to Littré's influence on Mallarmé's poetry, revealing it as an indispensable key to both his verse and prose. The poet himself mentions it in LA DERNIÈRE MODE: "... grand Dictionnaire de la Langue Française par Littré dans toute bibliothèque sérieuse..." (OC p. 282).

form, but the poet's last and most significant work, the "Coup de Dés," might itself be considered the culminating achievement of the prose poem, while at the same time constituting a radical departure not only from that genre, but from all poetry or prose preceding it.

The influence of *Igitur,* which constitutes the purgation of the metaphysical crisis undergone by the young poet, the "crise de Tournon," already appears in some of the early prose poems, written several years before. These poems reflect Mallarmé's ontological questioning, directly revealed in the *Igitur* fragment, and seen indirectly through the veil of anecdote in the prose poems. They presage then, as early as 1864, some of the existential anguish which caused that crisis to erupt a few years later in Mallarmé's life. We will find that many of the key images and symbols of *Igitur,* such as the room, the mirror, the clock, and most of all the solitary anguished hero, hesitating before life and his calling and tempted by suicide and madness, are identical with those of some of the early prose poems. Moreover, *Igitur* is a dramatic fragment, addressing itself "à l'Intelligence du lecteur qui met les choses en scène, elle-même" (OC p. 433), and Mallarmé's life-long preoccupation with the theatre, and its attendant themes of the poet as performer and his relationship with *la foule,* the audience, pervades the prose poems. For in the *recueil,* whose central theme is *poesis,* we follow the development of the poet-persona from harlequin and showman to consecrated poet-priest; we see likewise his paradoxical love and hate for the crowd, and yet his need for Mankind, whom it will be the poet's ideal function to serve.

Even after the early Descent and Return reflected in *Igitur,* however — the death of the persona's former self and his rebirth as atheist and poet — the human personality which emerges from the mature prose poems, as well as from the verse poetry, is that of a man tortured by a nostalgia for an Eden which he now knows not to exist. And so Mallarmé's final and culminating poetic venture, the "Coup de Dés," again, like the dramatic *Igitur,* expresses both Man's metaphysical yearnings and the ultimate futility and failure of a quest which must end in annihilation. The threat both of the early voyage into the inner depths of the self, and of the final one into cosmic space, is already vaguely foreshadowed in an early prose poem, "Frisson d'Hiver," whose hero dares not look into the deep mirror of his soul, nor through the windows which shield him from the vast spaces beyond. Nevertheless, the search for transcendent meaning is carried on through the stormiest seas: the poetic venture is not abandoned until ultimate shipwreck and extinction. The undertaking is hopeless, and the poet knows this, but he perseveres *as if* it were not. And as the early prose poems reflect *Igitur* and the poet's inner drama, so the late ones move progressively toward the outside, toward an acceptance of both life and nature. But this acceptance is on the poet's terms: he transforms the world and confers necessity and meaning on contingency and chaos by means of his Art. In a nihilistic age which has lost its faith, the heroic Poet attempts to save humanity by the supreme *fiction* of the Orphic, that is the Poetic, explanation of the universe, "qui est le seul devoir du poëte et le jeu littéraire par excellence" (OC p. 663).

LE PHÉNOMÈNE FUTUR

"Le Phénomène Futur" occupies the first place in all the editions of the collected prose poems, though it was one of the latest in order of composition of the six poems written in 1864.[1] Mallarmé probably always placed the piece at the head of the *recueil* because of its prophetic character, for it presages and announces in a blinding vision his own unique poetry. Though the poem's impact is primarily that of an impressionistic *Stimmungsgedicht,* setting forth that instantaneous vision of a flaming Beauty amidst night, decay and death, it narrates a coherent anecdote. This tells about a showman who displays before a dull audience, representing a tired and late civilization, a feminine marvel, a wonder of by-gone times preserved by "la science souveraine." And her fresh and brilliant beauty contrasts with the decadence and bleakness of the world in which she appears, while in the audience only the poets have the wisdom to understand what they are contemplating.

To readers of Mallarmé, "phénomène" might suggest the terminology of Hegelian philosophy,[2] to which he was initiated

---

[1] The three publications of the *recueil* are *Pages* (Bruxelles: Deman, 1891); *Vers et Prose* (Paris: Perrin, 1893); *Divagations* (Paris: Charpentier, 1897). The order of composition of the early prose poems is set forth in OC pp. 1548-49.

[2] A contemporary article by Edmond Scherer, "Hegel et l'hegélianisme," *Revue des deux mondes,* January, 1861, which might have been read by the young Mallarmé, gives a summary *vulgarisation* of Hegel's system. The following section might conceivably have influenced our poem:

> ... Hegel a parlé à sa manière, en symboles, et formules; il a été obscur comme les prophètes, mais comme eux il a eu le regard qui va au fond des choses ... Il a reconnu que si l'univers dit quelque chose à l'homme, c'est qu'il a quelque chose de

through Villiers de l'Isle-Adam, whom he met in 1864. And while Hegel certainly has influenced some of Mallarmé's early poetry, above all the *Igitur* fragment, the "Phénomène" brings to mind also another cosmos of ideas, the Kantian one with its *noumena* beyond the reach of man and yet preeminently dominating his world. Thus the phenomenon's antonym suggests both itself and the tension between the Ideal-Idea on the one hand and its realization on the other. For the future phenomenon unveiled in the anecdote will be the incarnation of Ideal Beauty, its noumenal essence made flesh as it were, created by the supreme science of the "Montreur." On the narrative level, "phénomène" as "chose ou personne extraordinaire qu'on montre à la foire; phénomène vivant" sets the scene of the fairground which emerges, however, only gradually.

At first we find ourselves in the vaguely dream-like setting of sky, a dying sun, water, a slow agony of the elements which announces that the earth approaches its final hour; we perceive somewhat unstable colors and tones, with Mallarmé's two most important ones, white and red — though here reduced to "pâle" and "pourpre usée" — predominating. The pale sky has lost its freshness, and in a dying world where miracles are no longer understood, the very concept of "sky" has paled also, with the splendor of ancient astronomy irretrievably lost to a modern and progressive *Weltanschauung*. In its sophistication, the world has turned senile; the pale sky might not only disappear behind the clouds, but vanish along with them, for darkness is impending. The violence of the sun's bloody death, "lambeaux de la pourpre usée," is but a dim memory, with the crimson and royal splendor of by-gone sunsets faded along with everything else in this tired world. And as a worn sun, weakened by too many deaths, sinks into a watery extinction, the erstwhile fervor of that consummation — the male fire immersed and quenched in the female water — has withered into a vague fusion of elements dormant at the horizon.

Of the four elements of ancient philosophy, fire, air, water, and earth, the poet has used the first three to paint the sunset, one of

---

commun avec l'homme; en un mot, que la vraie réalité, la première, ce n'est pas la matière, mais l'esprit. La chose n'est que le corps de l'idée, le phénomène n'est que l'expression de la loi.

the pervasive motifs in these prose poems and indeed in this total poetic universe.[3] And as our eyes now turn to the earth we encounter night and darkness, for we can barely make out the foliage of the trees, no longer green but faded out, on this earth so old that it is reduced to dust — the very symbol of dissolution. Not the dust of the roads, but that of time and age, "la poussière des siècles," has turned those senile trees white. With the word "siècles" time, already alluded to in the title, is reintroduced into the piece, where it will play a part throughout, juxtaposing that which is limited with that which is unlimited, perhaps eternal — *ars longa, vita brevis*. Just as the day is ending, the dust on the foliage suggests the end of summer, and this double impact of the solar drama reflects the human one: sickness and sin announce the end of the human race, for with the next generation the earth will die. This obsession with devouring time is reminiscent of Baudelaire — "horreur, horreur, le temps mange la vie" — as is the poem's setting, which recalls "Le Vieux Saltimbanque." And Baudelairean also is the fundamental opposition of Art and Nature, as well as the antithetical tension of the *jeu de contrastes* employed throughout the piece.

As the streetlights gradually illuminate the scene in the falling dusk, we recognize the fairground with canvas tent and showman, familiar from "Le Pitre Châtié," and which we will encounter in other prose poems. The sky's vault is now replaced by that of the tent, and the sun — source of its own light, but now extinguished — by the derivative light of gaslamps, an image of modernity frequently used by Mallarmé, which also reappears later in the *recueil*. Now humanity comes into sight: an anonymous showman and an anonymous crowd, with time irrupting again: the showman specializes in curiosities of the past. Lamplit dusk momentarily revives the faces of a vulgar, death-bound throng, whose only claim to immortality is its sickness, "vaincu par la maladie immortelle." But the showman rises out of that crowd, like the poets of "Le Guignon" who towered "au-dessus du bétail ahuri des humains."

The "péché des siècles," the very sin of perpetuating the human race, echoes both Baudelaire and Schopenhauer, for whom the

---

[3] For an extensive treatment of the theme in Mallarmé's verse poetry, see Gardner Davies, *Mallarmé et le Drame Solaire* (Paris: Corti, 1959).

reproductive function is one of the most powerful and pernicious manifestations of the Will's endless and blind striving. It is the basic life-drive which has become the source of conflict and corruption in a fallen world, and from which the only possible escape is aesthetic contemplation — and is it not that which the "Montreur" will offer the uncomprehending throng? This notion reflects a dominating literary mood — as well as a philosophical one — of the century, from Musset's "Rolla" to Rimbaud's "Soleil et Chair," finally taken up by such late figures as Laforgue. But it is Baudelaire who probably inspired the young Mallarmé's vision with a poem in which he not only contrasts a former golden age with present misery but also expresses his horror of the sin of perpetuating a fallen humanity:

> J'aime le souvenir de ces époques nues,
> . . . .
> Et vous, femmes, hélas! pâles comme des cierges,
> Que ronge et que nourrit la débauche, et vous, vierges,
> Du vice maternel traînant l'hérédité
> Et toutes les hideurs de la fécondité! [4]

The women in the crowd are their mates' "accomplices," thus participants in a crime; "chétives," sickly, they are by the term's etymological association, *captivus,* at the same time the slaves of their men, whose miserable offspring they bear: that last generation of mankind. And the image of these "hommes près de leurs chétives complices enceintes des fruits misérables avec lesquels périra la terre" recalls the verse poem "Sonnet" preceding our prose piece by two years, where we also find the echo of this Schopenhauerian contempt for the flesh, and particularly woman in her reproductive function.

The imminent catastrophe presaged by a perishing sun is reflected by the anguished silence, now broken by "le simple boniment" of the Showman. Significantly "Montreur" is capitalized: he not only rises above the dumb crowd, but he alone speaks at this last silent hour of humanity. Yet there is a highly derogatory note in "boniment," a "parade de charlatan" and "mot très

---

[4] Charles Baudelaire, *Les Fleurs du Mal* (Paris: Garnier, 1961), pp. 13-14.

vulgaire." Is the poet, then, undercutting the "Phénomène" by presenting her in a "boniment," or is it that humanity at this point no longer listens to any language but "salestalk?" While the setting had been supplied by an omniscient author, we see the "Femme d'autrefois" by means of the Showman's words alone; as he proclaims, no painter could give even a sad reflection of the marvel, his words alone being able to render her. In this dying world, he has a "phénomène vivant" to show, a living woman, not of this age indeed, but of a golden age long past, which seems to echo Baudelaire's *mystique* of "La Vie Antérieure." The marvel has been preserved mysteriously, over the centuries; she alone is not subject to time in this death-bound world, but capable of survival, and eternally young, for she is not a natural wonder at all and thus not subject to the laws of nature: she is the product and creature of "la science souveraine," which, on the narrative level, is to be accepted as part of the Showman's magic.

The woman's description introduces a series of images which are basic and recurring in Mallarmé's poetic universe, above all that of the golden hair, which will be celebrated also in the much later prose poem, "La Déclaration Foraine." [5] Here it appears like living gold, recalling "l'or vivant" of the alchemists: fire imprisoned in matter — one of Mallarmé's constant symbols for feminine beauty and the passion it inspires. "Originelle et naïve," the latter an etymological doublet of "native," this hair is not of this age, is even hardly recognizable at first, and so the Showman, impressionistically, describes its properties first, culminating in the "extase d'or," which the woman then identifies as her hair. "Extase," in suggesting the supernatural, points to the preternatural character of the apparition. Now the blood imagery of the poem's sunset opening is taken up again with the red lips, "la nudité sanglante des lèvres," which is then juxtaposed with the gleaming white of the nude body. The very opposite of *fané*, this woman — both virginal and maternal — with her eyes sparkling like precious gems, her lithe legs still moist from the sea, her virginally hard and pointed breasts which at the same time are pregnant with maternal

---

[5] For a study of the motif of *la chevelure* in Mallarmé's verse poetry, see C. Soula, *La Poésie et la pensée de Stéphane Mallarmé, essai sur le symbole de la chevelure* (Paris: Champion, 1929).

milk, brings before the mind's eye Botticelli's Aphrodite at the moment of her birth, and this ideal image of love and fecundity — Aphrodite and Cybele — stands in diametrical opposition to the senile decadence of the "real" world in which it appears.

After the "boniment" which has cut through the night like a flash of lightning, the omniscient author's willfully anecdotical ending, which brings us back into the here and now, underlines its contrast with the overwhelming vision, further emphasized by the juxtaposition of that image of eternal youth with flaming hair and the "pauvres épouses, chauves, morbides, et pleines d'horreur."

The concluding paragraph breaks sharply with the body of the poem by shifting to the future perfect tense, thereby abandoning the predominantly descriptive mode for a prophetic tone in harmony with the poem's apocalyptic ambiance. For when humanity will have contemplated the miracle of the Showman, most men will merely return to looking at the shadows in the Cave. Yet there will be some observers vaguely moved by a mysterious force, and they shall weep. But even in these last days, there shall be poets, who will feel a glory mysteriously — an intoxication: the breath of Terpsichore. Haunted by the vision, they shall forget their doomed age and turn to their lamp — the light of art replacing that of nature — one of Mallarmé's key symbols of the poet's isolation: "Et ma lampe qui sait pourtant mon agonie" (OC p. 35).

One of Mallarmé's much later and most poetic prose pieces beautifully shows how this vision of "les poètes de ces temps" — embodied magnificently for him in Villiers de l'Isle-Adam — persisted unchanged throughout his life; in his commemorative lecture for his friend, the poet says:

> ... Une question d'heure, en effet, étrange et de grand intérêt mais qu'ont occasion de se poser peu d'hommes ici-bas, à savoir que peut-être lui ne serait point venu à la sienne, pour que le conflit fut tel. Si! à considérer l'Histoire il avait été ponctuel, devant l'assignation du sort, nullement intempestif, ni répréhensible: car ce n'est pas contemporainement à une époque, aucunement, que doivent, pour exalter le sens, advenir ceux que leur destin chargea d'en être à nu l'expression; ils sont projetés maint siècle au-delà, stupéfaits, à témoigner de ce qui, normal à l'instant même, vit tard magnifiquement par le regret,

et trouvera dans l'exil de leur nostalgique esprit tourné vers le passé, sa vision pure (OC pp. 495-96).

The echoes of imagery of "Le Phénomène Futur" in the early verse poetry are too abundant to be quoted: the bleeding sunsets, as well as the poet-persona's disgust with the human throng surrounding him, and his isolation, appear again and again. Of that early verse poetry, "Le Pitre Châtié," of the same year as the prose poem, shows the most striking kinship with it; for not only does it have the fairground setting and show tent, but also a poet-persona in the role of a showman, "l'histrion" — reminiscent of the "literary *histrio*" of Poe's "Philosophy of Composition" — who resembles our "Montreur." But the most significant work which Mallarmé undertook in 1864, "Hérodiade," reveals many imagistic similarities with "Le Phénomène Futur." The opening of "Hérodiade," also celebrates the solar drama, autumn, the purple sky — though of a sunrise rather than a sunset — evoking crime and blood and death:

> Crime! bucher! aurore ancienne! supplice!
> Pourpre d'un ciel! Etang de la pourpre complice! (OC p. 41)

And this sky's purple, reflected in the water, recalls the sun drowning on the horizon of our poem; the white chastity of Hérodiade's room, "le neigeux jadis" and the nurse's gown, "ma robe blanchie," contrast with this red violence. Again there is an evocation of the last hour, "...l'heure d'agonie et de luttes funèbres!," and of the end of the world, "Lever du jour dernier qui vient tout achever." The most striking similarity, however, is that of the two main symbols, the golden-haired women — "Le blond torrent de mes cheveux immaculés" — whose eyes resemble precious gems, the Phénomène's "semblables aux pierres rares," and "Hérodiade au clair regard de diamant." And in both poems, the heroine's youth is juxtaposed with senility, embodied in "Hérodiade" by the old nurse: "Calme, toi, les frissons de ta sénile chair." Yet the two figures are not identical, for the sterile splendor of Hérodiade in her stiff, jewel-encrusted gown, shielding a body which is seen only at the cost of death, contrasts strikingly with that of the Phénomène so proudly displaying her jubilant nakedness: the Phénomène has just emerged from the sea, while Hérodiade has not yet entered it.

While in some of the other early, more anecdotical, prose poems the theme emerges naturally from the reading, in a truly symbolist poem, like "Le Phénomène Futur," the notion symbolized will have to be inferred from the main symbol itself, and from other signs in the poem. By a truly symbolist poem I mean one in which only one term of the principal metaphor is developed throughout without any explicit identification of the thing or idea to which this first term stands in an analogical relationship.[6] Contemporary commentaries on the poem do not reveal its meaning, for even Baudelaire, to whom it owes so much, refrains from interpreting while discussing it;[7] and Mallarmé's close friend of those years, Cazalis, acknowledging receipt of the poem with a warm letter of admiration, limits himself to very general remarks.[8]

The pervading mood of the poem is one of despair with the state of the world, also reflected in much of Mallarmé's correspondence of that time, as well as in most of his contemporary verse poetry. From Baudelaire's time onward, nineteenth-century poets despaired of curing the ills of their positivist age through their involvement, poetic or otherwise; they "turned their back to life," as Mallarmé puts it in "Les Fenêtres." From Baudelaire, again, who had admired Rousseauists like Bernardin de Saint-Pierre and occultists like Eliphas Levi, came the inheritance of what we might

---

[6] For an exposition of 19th-century Symbolist technique, see Bernard Weinberg, *The Limits of Symbolism* (Chicago: Univ. of Chicago Press, 1966), pp. 34-35.

[7] Mondor, *Correspondance* I, p. 201, quotes Baudelaire's comments:

> Un jeune écrivain a eu récemment une conception ingénieuse, mais non absolument juste. Le monde va finir. L'humanité est décrépite. Un Barnum de l'avenir montre aux hommes dégradés de son temps une belle femme des anciens âges artificiellement conservée. "Eh! quoi! disent-ils, l'humanité a-t-elle pu être aussi belle que cela." Je dis que cela n'est pas vrai. *L'homme dégradé s'admirerait et appellerait la beauté la laideur.* (*Pauvre Belgique, Œuvres posthumes*, t. III, p. 35.)

[8] Bernard, *Le Poème en Prose*, p. 260, reproduces a section of this letter in a note:

> Tu m'envoies ... un poème en prose qui m'a fait jaloux, qui est d'une couleur splendide; le grand couchant avec ses reflets rouges et rayé de bandes noires, sur lequel se dessinent, pâles, étirés, longs et maigres, les squelettes à peine vêtus de nos petits enfants, ce dernier saltimbanque et ce dernier débris des vieux âges, tout cela forme un tableau étrange d'une vraie et rare beauté, un de tes chefs-d'œuvre...

call a rejection of history, accompanied by *le regard en arrière,* towards a lost Eden. The consequent notion that the very perpetuation of the race removes humanity *ipso facto* farther from the source and thus towards evil, and that only art is capable of reflecting some of the lost glory, naturally leads to the opposition of Art and Nature, fully developed by the Symbolists. This antinaturalist stance, that art rather than imitating nature must conquer and defeat it, is also the principal theme of Villiers de l'Isle-Adam's almost contemporary *Eve Future,* whose title expresses that nostalgia for the past while the book conveys the idea that only an artificially created woman, and not the real one of our day, may reflect some of that original harmony now irretrievably lost. This work and our similarly named prose poem do not show any mutual, influence, but both develop a common theme: that nature has fallen into decay, and that only by means of some supreme science — or supreme art — a memory of what we have lost might be *artificially* restored. And in the creation of the Beautiful, its creator breaks beyond the limits of his time.

Our Montreur is connected to the past Golden Age by the vision which inspires him — much like a Platonic Reminiscence of the pure Form or Idea — and projected into the future by his immortal creation. And the isolation of this creator is reinforced by the fact that most of humanity is incapable of comprehending his creation, just as it has lost the memory of Eden. But, upon his return to the Cave, he who has beheld the true light risks blindness and even the loss of his reason among his fellow man. In our poem, then, the Showman is the creator of the marvel. That his "act" is the poetic one is revealed in the closing lines; thus the Phénomène is probably the Idea of a poem, of poetry, personified. For Mallarmé the most perfect expression of Beauty is poetry: "... Il n'y a que la Beauté, — et elle n'a qu'une expression parfaite: la Poésie." [9]

Though wary of the current critical predilection for interpreting poetry as "poetry about poetry," in the case of Mallarmé we know that one of the pervading themes of his work is that of *poesis* and its attendant problems. The poet himself implies this for his prose

---

[9] Henri Mondor, *Propos sur la Poésie* (Monaco: Ed. du Rocher, 1953), p. 79.

pieces, for he comments about the Divagations: "Les Divagations apparentes traitent un sujet, de pensée, unique," [10] his "doctrine," which is his poetic theory. And although in the same preface he seems to restrict this statement to the articles of that book, this study will show that its prose poems are concerned with the same theme. As for Mallarmé's verse poetry, Thibaudet has long ago observed that it also is dominated by the theme of poetic creation. [11]

The Montreur's "boniment," that he alone can show the marvel, no painter these days being capable of giving a sad shadow of it, emphasizes the notion of the verbal as the supreme art form, but also announces a new aesthetic. For the new poetic language — on the narrative level the "boniment" — does not "describe" the marvel, but creates it. The "boniment's" very substance, its words and rhythm, is that of the vision unfolding before our glance: we do not behold a living woman, but a statue coming to life in and with the self-creating word. The language of the poetry of the future — "le Phénomène Futur" — will no longer serve to form or convey an idea or content, for there shall be no longer a distinction between content and form.

The belief that poetry surpasses all other forms of art, even its greatest rivals music and dance, is the subject of many a Divagation. The Phénomène has been "préservé à travers les ans par la science souveraine," and this supreme science is that of language, for language is the memory of the human race. Although for the young poet of the early prose poems this is again partly a Baudelairean inspiration — the "sorcellerie évocatoire" — Mallarmé continued to explore the mysterious resources of language all his life. [12] Both he and his great predecessor might well have been influenced by the Kabala through such figures as the already mentioned Eliphas Levi, whose *Dogmes et Rituel de haute Magie* was published in 1861. [13] In a late essay of *Divagations*, appropriately called

---

[10] Mallarmé, *Divagations*, p. 1.
[11] Thibaudet, at the end of *La Poésie*, p. 466, comes to this conclusion:
> Aussi, chez lui, le sujet de l'écrit est ordinairement, par un jeu d'allusions plus ou moins complexes, l'écrit lui-même.

[12] An examination of *Les Mots Anglais* of 1877 bears this out.
[13] For the influence of occultists on Mallarmé, see Alain Mercier, *Les Sources ésotériques et occultes de la poésie symboliste (1870-1914) I Le Symbolisme français* (Paris: Nizet, 1969), pp. 123-145.

"Magie," Mallarmé still repeatedly uses terms of alchemy to designate the poetic art.

On the narrative level, the poem's closing gives the clearest sign for the interpretation of its major symbol: most of mankind will remain indifferent at beholding the marvel, because they will not have the wisdom to understand what they are contemplating; but others will be "navrés," broken-hearted, that is emotionally responsive to a poetry which they will nevertheless not really understand; finally the poets alone will "comprehend" the apparition, that is in the etymological sense of the word be able to take into themselves that which renders them "ivre un instant d'une gloire confuse." And this is indeed prophetic of the reception of Mallarmé's own later poetry among his contemporaries.

The poet as Showman, a most important and constant image in this poetic universe, makes his earliest appearance, then, in our prose poem and the contemporary "Le Pitre Châtié." The spectacle which the poet-showman offers, the Birth of Venus, is the poem's central symbol, which figures in a blinding vision the mature poetry anticipated but yet to be created. Ideal Beauty, once lost but now remembered and recreated, embodies the motif of the return to the source, as well as that of Paradise regained through Art. These motifs, together with the figure of the poet, will be progressively developed throughout the prose poems, as they also reappear in other sections of the *Divagations,* ultimately to reflect Mallarmé's confident, mature affirmation of the importance of the poet's role.

PLAINTE D'AUTOMNE

One of Mallarmé's two earliest prose poems, this piece was originally called "L'Orgue de Barbarie" and published several times under that name. Its present title, which it also bears in the three *recueils* of the prose poems, appears for the first time in 1875. The change is significant, for it reflects one of the fundamental principles of Mallarmé's new poetics, already announced in a letter of the same year as our poem:

> ... car j'invente une langue qui doit nécessairement jaillir d'une poétique très nouvelle, que je pourrais définir en ces deux mots: *Peindre, non la chose, mais l'effet qu'elle produit.* [1]

While the former title names "la chose" as it were, the new one suggests "l'effet qu'elle produit." Moreover, as this poem like the preceding one is influenced by Baudelaire, it is possible that two titles of *Les Fleurs du Mal*, "Chant d'automne" and "Sonnet d'automne," helped determine the poet's choice. "Plainte," a mood-setting noun, is at the same time a term of poetics, a "complaint" being the formal designation of a lyric poem, frequent in both French and English medieval and Renaissance literature, which generally bemoaned the poet's unhappy lot, or expressed his regret at the unhappy state of the world. So the association of literature as well as an orientation toward the past are brought into play by the multivalence of the very first word, while the title's second term reintroduces the motif of the solar drama, which will be richly developed in the poem.

---

[1] Mondor, *Correspondance* I, p. 137.

"Plainte d'Automne" tells about the solitary narrator's reveries on an autumn evening which he spends alone with his cat in a room visited by memories of his dead sister. And as he meditates on those memories of the past and also on his literary taste, which is likewise directed toward the past, he hears playing under his window a barrel organ, whose melancholy tune is in harmony with the lonely listener's somewhat voluptuous sadness.

The opening sentence of this poem — which in its anecdotal and narrative tone contrasts with "Le Phénomène Futur" — introduces a first-person narrator musing about the stars: to which one did Maria go? This highly subjective beginning barely veils an important biographical event, the death of Mallarmé's sister in 1857, which not only exerted a dominating influence on most of the poet's juvenilia, but also left its mark on much of the later poetry. The persona's reveries on Maria's Ascension take him on a cosmic voyage.[2] "Orion" recalls the Latin *orior,* to arise, which suggests in our poem's context the resurrection motif, while "Altaïr," the first magnitude star whose Arabic name means "flier" or "bird," brings to mind the traditional bird or wing symbol for the poet and poetic creation so frequently elaborated by Mallarmé. "Verte Venus" evokes the image of an antique statue of the goddess with its verdigris patina — thus vaguely recalling "Le Phénomène Futur" — and also suggests the idea of rebirth and spring; and youth and age will be contrasted throughout the poem. Venus, moreover, is the name of copper in alchemy, and "cuivre" appears twice in this paragraph as the predominant tone of the atmosphere enveloping the hour.

"J'ai toujours chéri la solitude" reintroduces the motif of solitude familiar from the Montreur and poets of "Le Phénomène Futur," and which is part of the theme of the poet's isolation developed in the *recueil*; "solitude" is immediately reinforced in the second sentence with "seul," repeated in the third and fourth

---

[2] The complete original version of "Plainte d'Automne" is reproduced in Adile Ayda, *Le Drame intérieur de Mallarmé* (Istanbul: Ed. de la Turquie Moderne, 1955), pp. 29-30. This highly biographical study "explains" much of Mallarmé's poetry, and particularly his early work, in the light of the deaths of the poet's mother, sister, and young friend, Harriet Smythe. Cf. also Léon Cellier, *Mallarmé et la morte qui parle* (Paris: Presses Universitaires de France, 1959).

sentences, and finally the last word of the piece. Originally another sentence was added to that ending: "Oh! l'orgue de Barbarie, la veille de l'automne à cinq heures, sous les peupliers jaunis, Maria!", which linked the image of the barrel organ, evoked once more, to the memory of Maria and with the precise indication of the time of day ended the poem on a more anecdotal note. The change indicates that while Mallarmé initially might have felt the poem to be mainly about Maria, he subsequently rendered it more general by subduing the personal occasion in order to emphasize a deeper and more universal significance. The image of the solitary narrator with his cat recalls Baudelaire, and it is not unlikely that Mallarmé's admiration for cats was, at least originally, due to his master's repeatedly and poetically expressed fascination with them. [8]

"Longues journées" and "alanguis," as well as the long mood-setting adverbs, "étrangement," "singulièrement," "languissamment," "mélancoliquement" and "désespérément," tend to slow the passage of time in this piece, while the device of repeating not only words but whole phrases contributes to the effect of isolating and insulating space and time — the world — of the narrator's reveries from the general flow of the world outside. Yet in this early piece, the poet frequently still resorts to "telling" rather than "imaging" this effect of silent solitude with expressions such as "par seul j'entends" or "je peux donc dire." The "compagnon mystique," contrasting with "un être matériel," evokes an occultism reminiscent of the tone of "Hérésies Artistiques" written two years before our poem, and which begins:

> Toute chose sacrée et qui veut demeurer sacrée s'enveloppe de mystère. Les religious se retranchent à l'abri

---

[8] Cats were throughout Mallarmé's life members of his little family. Geneviève Mallarmé recalls in "Mallarmé par sa fille," *La Nouvelle Revue Française*, XXVII (July-December, 1926), p. 519:

> La maison était toujours fleurie et jamais elle ne fut vide de quelque bestiole. Ces petites présences vivantes et naïves lui étaient nécessaires. Voici pour vous faire sourire et venant en ordre: l'oiseau bleu et le bengali, la chatte angora blanche Neige et son fils blanc, Frimas.

Cf. also Henri Mondor, *Autres Précisions sur Mallarmé et inédits* (Paris: Gallimard, 1961), p. 218.

d'arcanes dévoilés au seul prédestiné: l'art a les siens (OC p. 257).

For the young poet, the religion of art is clearly distinct from religion, from which, however, it borrows its vocabulary. And in that mode the cat has been transformed by and in our narrator's reveries into "un esprit" from the other world, that of the artistic imagination.

The "derniers auteurs de la décadence latine" reintroduces the subject of literature already announced by the title: the persona, if not yet a poet, is nevertheless a reader of poetry or literature, and his literary taste presages the artistic climate of the closing nineteenth century. A des Esseintes before the hour, he isolates himself from the world of the living to pursue *entre quatre murs* the divagations of his mind, turned inward and toward the past. [4] Decadence as a literary movement both in France and England will elaborate not only the superiority of art over nature — the theme underlying "Le Phénomène Futur" — but also the other Baudelairean one of the beauty of dying and decaying things, which recalls the literary hero of both Baudelaire and the young Mallarmé,

---

[4] The vogue of the Latin writers at the end of the century is reflected in J.-K. Huysmans' *A Rebours,* which may even have been influenced by the prose poem, for not only is Decadence a theme of both that book and our poem, but Huysmans admired Mallarmé's work, and his hero, des Esseintes, loved particularly these early prose poems. *A Rebours* (Paris: Ed. Fasquette, 1968), p. 244:

> Mais dans ce recueil, avaient été colligés certains poèmes sauvés de revues mortes: le Démon de l'analogie, la Pipe, le Pauvre Enfant pâle, le Spectacle interrompu, le Phénomène futur, et surtout Plaintes [sic] d'automne et Frisson d'hiver, qui étaient les chefs-d'œuvre du poème en prose, car ils unissaient une langue si magnifiquement ordonnée qu'elle berçait, par elle-même, ainsi qu'une mélancolique incantation, qu'une énivrante mélodie à des pulsations d'âme de sensitif dont les nerfs en émoi vibrent avec une acuïté qui vous pénètre jusqu'au ravissement, jusqu'à la douleur.

And not only the love for art, but also the turning away from life will be epitomized by des Esseintes:

> Ses idées de se blottir, loin du monde, de se calfeutrer dans une retraite, d'assourdir, ainsi que pour ces malades dont on couvre la rue de paille, le vacarme roulant de l'inflexible vie, se renforcèrent (p. 35).

Edgar Allen Poe.[5] Did Poe not say in his "Philosophy of Composition" that "melancholy is the most legitimate of all poetic tones," and that "the death ... of a woman is, unquestionably, the most poetic topic in the world —"? "Plainte d'Automne" celebrates the death of a woman, the Decadence of a decaying literature, the agonizing sun of a dying day in the late, the Fall, season of the year — all of which the poet sums up with the word "chute." The "blanche créature" who is no more sets the poem's melancholy tone and gives it its death-direction, out of and away from the real world.

White, one of Mallarmé's two dominant colors — which like the black of mourning is more precisely the absence of color — is Maria's, whose very absence constitutes her only presence. The significance of this example of evocation by negation cannot be stressed too strongly, for it is an early revelation of one of the secrets of Mallarmé's future poetics: ideal and essential presence is at the cost of real and existential absence — a death to be suffered before the resurrection. Only by abolishing the real — "Abolie, et son aile affreuse dans les larmes / Du bassin, aboli, qui mire les alarmes" (OC p. 4) — can the ideal be created, so that "le creux néant musicien" alone renders the mandola's essential musicality.

The virginal white evokes the paraphernalia of the funeral, the crown of white roses and the winding sheet, Maria's last image; and the vocabulary cluster of the "last and languid" days of summer, the "fainting" of the sun, and the "agonizing" literature reinforces this moribund ambiance. The copper-red sunset — somewhat weakened with "jaune" — contrasts with the white as blood with pallor, and a similar contrast is produced by "derniers moments de Rome" and the "approche rajeunissante des Barbares," while in the same sentence "esprit" and "volupté" are juxtaposed to suggest a sublimation of the sensuous or physical to the mental or spiritual. But the young narrator's intellectual "volupté" is death-directed, preferring a moribund, rather than a rejuvenating, tradition and moment of art.

---

[5] In his famous "biographical" letter to Verlaine, Mallarmé says:
    Ayant appris l'anglais simplement pour mieux lire Poe, je suis parti à vingt ans en Angleterre (OC p. 662).

"Les carreaux" introduces an important image frequently occurring in Mallarmé's verse and also in several of the prose poems, that of the window, which here physically fixes the rather mental setting. In the scene which unfolds, the window divides the phenomenal world into an "inside" and an "outside"; on the inside is the musing narrator with his dreams, for whom the window is the threshold to the outside, a sunset and a city setting reminiscent of both the *Spleen de Paris* and a considerable part of *Les Fleurs du Mal*. The persona's posture of solitude — remaining alone behind the window — is in harmony with his choice of literature. Moreover, in preferring Latin over French he chooses a dead over a living language, thus shielding himself mentally from his own time and world by removing himself into that of the past. His association with decrepitude rather than with rebirth is further emphasized by his rejecting the "proses chrétiennes," those early Latin Church hymns, because their Latin is "enfantin."

At the half-way point of the poem, a break occurs, for while the first paragraph was principally concerned with the narrator's thoughts, the second one is dominated by sensations: the sound of the street organ and the images of the funeral procession in the street below. But as the first part ended, so the second one begins with a discussion of poetry, this subject linking the two. Even the poetry now seems to take on concrete form in the personification of the old *filles*. Once again, decrepitude and youth are contrasted in the worn-out old women, whose "plaques de fard" the persona prefers to "l'incarnat de la jeunesse," and so the artificial and the faded are juxtaposed with, and exalted over, nature and youth. To reinforce the contrast, the image of the old women follows almost immediately upon the personification of the early Christian hymns stuttering their child-like Latin.

The cat, too, has taken on concrete form; no longer merely a spirit, it now lets the narrator plunge his hand into its fur. And while in its purity it still recalls the "compagnon mystique," "pure" here somehow also evokes the image of a white cat, a truly visual one, whereas in the first part the whiteness was that of a sublimated memory — "blanche créature" — of the virginal and seraphic Maria. The tactile sensation of stroking the animal's fur is followed by the auditory one of the barrel organ's singing below the window.[6] "Orgue de Barbarie," echoing "barbares" above, by association reaches back to a far-away past and the center of the Decadence, for its invention is attributed to a mathematician of Alexandria, some 120 years before the Christian era. And the mood evoked by the ancient instrument — that barrel organ which cannot renew itself but is eternally condemned to repeat — recalls the tone of sickness and mourning of the poem's first part, with its singing "languissamment" and "mélancoliquement" echoing "alanguis" and "agonisante." The street's old trees — recalling the tired, dusty trees of "Le Phénomène Futur" — have lost their freshness, their leaves seeming even in springtime "mornes." Mallarmé, an English teacher, was certainly aware of the English "to mourn" and added this association to the adjective, for immediately upon "mornes" follows the evocation of the funeral procession.

"Depuis que Maria a passé là avec des cierges, une dernière fois" not only evokes the image of the procession, but rhythmically conveys its slow and solemn movement, while at the same time echoing the opening words of the piece: "Depuis que Maria m'a quitté..." "Cierges," phonetically evocative of "vierges" and resonating in "dernière," stresses once again virginal whiteness: the slim white wax tapers of the funeral procession, the pale young girl in the casket wearing the customary "couronne des mortes" of white roses; and "une dernière fois" marks not only her last passing, but the last mention of Maria in this poem.

Musical instruments occur frequently in Mallarmé's verse — long before he becomes interested in music as a rival to poetry — due to the traditional Orphic association of poetry and music, represented in our piece by the Latin poetry and the barrel organ. The additional piano which "sparkles," and the violin's giving "aux fibres déchirées la lumière," constitute rather Baudelairean synes-

---

[6] This predilection for the street organ is again a biographical detail, revealed in a letter of 1862, Mondor, *Correspondance* I, p. 58:
> Je me suis arrêté un instant pour jeter un sou à un pauvre orgue qui se lamente dans le square. ... Le pauvre hère attend peut-être encore son déjeuner... Non vraiment. Cet homme fait de la musique dans les rues, c'est un métier comme celui de notaire, et qui a sur ce dernier l'avantage d'être inutile. Peut-on rêver une vie plus belle que celle qui consiste à errer par les chemins et à faire l'aumône d'un air triste ou gai à la première fenêtre qu'on voit, ... à jouer pour les pavés, pour les moineaux, pour les arbres maladifs des squares.

thesias, also common in the poet's verse of those years; one recalls the example of "de blancs sanglots" of "Apparition" of 1863. Music carries the persona again into a timeless inner and spiritual realm, the "crépuscule du souvenir." This twilight zone of memory, where past becomes present and the departed souls are with us again, suggests one of the young Mallarmé's obsessive themes, that of the return of the dead. The *revenant* dominates much of his adolescent poetry, like the early poetic prose composition "Ce que disaient les trois cigognes"; and it is many years later still beautifully celebrated in the sonnet "Sur les bois oubliés."

Is the narrator's dreaming "despairing" because he cannot reach the ideal — Maria — whose calling, however, isolates him in the world of the living? And that world, the "outside," interrupts the reverie, for the "maintenant" pulls the narrator back from his dreams into the here and now where he has no sense of belonging. The contrast of his sadness with the instrument's joyous vulgarity, which gladdens not his but the suburb's heart, emphasizes his alienation. He is thus doubly isolated from his fellow men, physically by the window and spiritually by their happy unconcern for his tears. For the human world outside is as indifferent to the narrator's melancholy as is the barrel organ itself, the cyclic recurrence of whose melody reflects that of nature: in this world there is only endless Sisyphean repetition, whereas his aspiration draws him to the spheres beyond — the stars were Maria beckons. And yet he loves the banal melody — as he does his very sadness, one feels — because it is old-fashioned, "come une ballade romantique." The quaint and moreover foreign literary genre, which suggests itself by association, might here vaguely presage that other Marie, Mallarmé's young German wife, who will be celebrated in the following prose poem, "Frisson d'Hiver." The rather discursive closing sentence of our piece, which "explains" the narrator's refusal to go to the window to throw the customary alms to the street musician, might well already reflect a turning away from experience. Rather than being lived, it will be transmuted into art. For it appears that if the musing listener stirred, a kind of spell might be broken; moreover this enchantment of the old-fashioned melody might be dispelled if he saw its human agent, the poor barrel organ man.

The variants reveal that in the revisions Mallarmé tends to suppress the sentimentally-seraphic flavor which characterized much of his adolescent poetry, though the subjective and confiding tone, as well as a certain sentimentality, still permeate the definitive version. Much of the verse poetry contemporary with "Plainte d' Automne," such as "Angoisse," "Las de l'amer repos," "Le Sonneur," and "Tristesse d'Éte," is dominated also by funereal images; the poet-persona is haunted by his winding sheet — white as the page on which the poem cannot be born — and the death wish becomes a hallucination nearly driving him into suicide. At the same time, and in seeming opposition to this weary sinking down into death, there is the soul's elevation toward its ideal: the sister who has reentered paradise, or an anima who remembers it. And so the death wish becomes an upward inspiration and aspiration — in paradoxical contradiction with the love for dying and decaying things, for "chute" — to the innocence before the Fall.

The mood of "Plainte d'Automne," that nostalgia for a release from earthly bounds so that the self may freely soar, and sink, as in a dream, is most strongly reflected in a similarly named verse poem, "Soupir." It also celebrates autumn, and "l'azur," that is the Ideal, is "attendri" as the persona's soul strives to rise toward its ideal sister — animus to anima — in nature's gentle Fall:

> Mon âme vers ton front où rêve, ô calme sœur,
> Un automne jonché de taches de rousseur,
> Et vers le ciel errant de ton œil angélique
> Monte, comme dans un jardin mélancolique,
> Fidèle, un blanc jet d'eau soupire vers l'Azur!
> —Vers l'Azur attendri d'Octobre pâle et pur
> Qui mire aux grands bassins sa langueur infinie
> Et laisse, sur l'eau morte où la fauve agonie
> Des feuilles erre au vent et creuse un froid sillon,
> Se traîner le soleil jaune d'un long rayon (OC p. 39).

"Soupir," of the same year as "Plainte d'Automne," not only renders a very similar theme, but in its total tonality corresponds exactly to that of the prose poem.

This rising and falling, the simultaneously ascending and descending movement and direction — so reminiscent of Baudelaire's "double postulation" — confers a distinctive tension on "Plainte d'Automne," one of whose themes is the "complaint" bemoaning the Fall from Eden.[7] The occasion of the fall from childhood's innocence and the oneness of paradise is Maria's death, for throughout the poem the persona's separateness and loneliness is stressed and linked to that event. But "Plainte d'Automne" is not merely a commemorative poem, because the theme of art, of literature, is of equal importance. Both the themes of the memory of Eden and of the resurrective power of art link this piece to the preceding one.

"Plainte d'Automne" celebrates the Orphic function of poetry and music in bringing back the dead and thus asserts the victory of art over nature. Orpheus was both poet and musician, and our narrator reads poetry and listens to music; and while in this early piece he does not yet directly assume the Orphic role, his marked withdrawal from the world of the living already portends the traditional Orphic descent into the other world. Moreover, by reading and listening the persona does participate in the magical act of resurrection, and in another prose poem of the same year, "Le Démon de l'Analogie," we will see him fall under the artistic demon's spell.

Maria is not only the remembered sister, but becomes the personification of an ideal, and her death is at once a descent and an ascension, an *envol* to the stars, so that the unconsoled young narrator who dreams of her is both in love with death and at the same time with the elevation to the ideal to which he aspires. Torn between these polar opposites, on the one hand a refusal of and turning away from life and on the other the acceptance of the ideal vocation, he vacillates. "Plainte d'Automne" marks the moment when the young poet hesitates to follow his privileged calling.

---

[7] Thomas Williams, *Mallarmé and the Language of Mysticism* (Athens: Univ. of Georgia Press, 1970), pp. 31-32, considers "Plainte d'Automne" a "falling away from the divine after the deaths of Maria and Harriet Smythe" and sees in the piece the first of five stages in Mallarmé's rebirth cycle as a mystic. The author bases his hypothesis on the correspondence and does not discuss the poem itself.

Both his refusal of life and his love for art are reflected in the decadent posture.[8] Decadence, as a moment in the history of art and as an attitude of this poem's narrator, is a rejection of the world of matter, materialistic and historical progress, and of nature, whose every spring is born only to decay in the end. In celebrating decay and death itself, the Decadent refuses the enchantment of youth, which he knows to be an illusion.

---

[8] That the decadent posture represents but a moment in the young poet's development is evident in the mature Mallarmé's refusal to be identified with the Decadent movement. Cf. Mondor, *Correspondance* III, p. 62, (letter of 1886 to Orfer, co-editor of LA DÉCADENCE):

> Certainement, prenez ces deux petits poëmes, ["Placet" and "La Pipe"] pour votre publication: mais quel titre abominable que *La Décadence* et comme il serait temps de renoncer à tout ce qui y ressemble!

FRISSON D'HIVER

"Frisson d'Hiver" appeared twice under the title "Causerie d'Hiver," before receiving its definitive name in subsequent publications. As in "Plainte d'Automne," its anecdote is about the reveries of the narrator in his room; but the narrator is now a poet, and the room is painstakingly elaborated into one of the poem's major symbols. The poet-persona is no longer alone, but addresses his musings to his silent companion, a poetic transposition of Mallarmé's young German wife. [1]

Its title, like that of the preceding piece, also identifies the poem with one of the year's seasons: winter, "L'hiver, saison de l'art serein, l'hiver lucide," as the poet had said two years earlier in "Renouveau." But winter is also the old age and death of the year, its cold whiteness the non-color of absence — recalling the ambiance of the preceding piece — and for the poet the *ennui* of sterility. [2] "Frisson" harmonizes with this atmosphere more than the original title, for it suggests trembling from cold and fear, as well as implying fragility by its sound-look, so similar to the other word of the title; and Mallarmé also suggests the bi-lingual "shiver"-"hiver" association. Moreover, while "causerie" pointed to the narrative tone of the piece, "frisson" announces at the outset

---

[1] Mallarmé had married Maria-Christine Gerhard, a German girl, on August 10, 1863.

[2] The same winter, Mallarmé writes to Cazalis, Mondor, *Correspondance* I, p. 150:

> ... et [je] pleure quand je me sens vide et ne puis jeter un mot sur mon papier implacablement blanc. "Sur le vide papier que la blancheur défend."

And in "Brise Marine," of 1865, the white page haunts the poet: "Sur le vide papier que la blancheur défend."

one of its principal recurring images, the trembling spiders' webs. Finally, "frisson," conveying a sense of expectancy and potentiality, is rich with tension, for it combines the notions of movement and stasis; and while in this winter poem the latter predominates — for life and movement seem arrested as if frozen — there is at the same time the promise of hidden life, the life of poetry to be realized. In the contemporary "Hérodiade," the princess' essence similarly appears both hidden and paralyzed in white virginal coldness, while the promise of her nubility manifests itself in a shiver:

> De mes robes, arôme aux farouches délices
> Sortirait le frisson blanc de ma nudité (OC p. 47).

In Mallarmé's later verse "frisson" will designate the very rhythm of poetic creation, as in "Toast Funèbre," where the role of the ideal poet, Gautier, is described:

> Le Maître, par un œil profond, a sur ses pas,
> Apaisé de l'eden l'inquiète merveille
> Dont le frisson final, dans sa voix seule, éveille
> Pour la Rose et le Lys le mystère d'un nom (OC p. 55).[3]

But in "Frisson d'Hiver," this poetic rhythm is still hidden, like a secret well-spring, under a blanket of ice.

Although we hear only the voice of the poet-persona throughout, we are aware of another presence in the room, that of the silent woman for whom he lovingly paints each of its cherished objects. The first of these, the "pendule de Saxe" evocative of both Time and Space — not only does it count hours, but it is old and from far away — suggests fragility: it is a Dresden china clock, white and fragile, with gods and flowers painted on its delicate house of porcelain.[4] This clock, which is behind time,

---

[3] Mallarmé later again uses "frisson" in a similar sense in "Hommage":
> Hiéroglyphes dont s'exalte le millier
> A propager de l'aile un frisson familier!

[4] René Ghil, *Les Dates et les Œuvres* (Paris: Crès, 1923), p. 25, describes Mallarmé's room at Valvins:
> Bureau ancien, et la pendule de Sèvres inspiratrice de l'exquis poème en prose que l'on sait: "Frisson d'Hiver."

fits well into the room whose objects are all of the past, and its striking the thirteenth hour constitutes, moreover, a symbolic value, aside from its descriptive function. Not only does it strike an hour "out of time," but like the barrel organ of the preceding piece, it symbolizes the cyclical nature of the solar drama, one of whose moments provides the atmosphere and setting of the poem: the winter room. [5] The far-away country from which the clock came, "Pense qu'elle est venue de Saxe par les longues diligences d'autrefois," is also that of the narrator's companion, whom we will see later reading her outdated German almanac. And while there might be an underlying Freudian symbolic correspondance of clock and woman, on the narrative level both are precious ornaments of the persona's world, mysterious, fragile and out of step with their time. So the china clock is a richly multivalent symbol as well as a mood-setting image which suggests evasion from the here and now, back to a deep past, far away — recalling the mood of "Plainte d'Automne."

Now the persona's glance falls on the room's windows whose worn panes have lost their transparency and polish, so that they no longer serve as a threshold to the outside, nor to reflect the interior of the room. These dull, lusterless, windows rather shield the inside from the outside, while at the same time threatening to

---

Whether Dresden (Meissen) or Sèvres, it is a painted *porcelain* clock. As some of the other early prose poems, this one is highly biographical. For the Bengal birds, see note 3 of "Plainte d'Automne"; in a letter of the same year as these poems, Mallarmé again mentions his white cat, the birds, and, above all, Marie Gerhard, and our Saxony clock. Mondor, *Correspondance* I, pp. 133-34:

> ... si tu voyais comme nous sommes d'une façon charmante avec nos délicieux oiseaux, les poissons d'or et la chatte blanche, et parmi tout cela, ma douce Allemande, qui va des uns aux autres. Elle a été éblouie des belles choses que j'ai rapportées, de bien loin, et ne cesse de contempler la belle petite pendule de Saxe.
> J'ai repris courage et, grâce à ce qui m'entoure, j'espère que je ne retomberai pas de sitôt dans les lourdes ténèbres où j'ai si longtemps vécu.

Cf. *ibid.*, p. 136.

[5] This old Dresden clock striking the thirteenth hour is reminiscent of Nerval's "Artemis," where "la treizième revient ... encore la première," and where the poet celebrates the themes of life and death with imagery of flowers, gods and phantoms.

expose the former to the latter. The narrator keeps looking anxiously at, but never through or into them, his eye being caught by those shadows hanging there. Are they the spiders' webs which he will recognize later or are they imaginary phantoms? For while refusing to look through the windows at an outside, the persona's glance seems turned inward, so that "the curious shades" might be phantoms of his mind, those ghosts of the past which this setting — almost identical with that of "Sur les bois oubliés" — invites: the winter night outside, the lonely room with its sad fire and antique furnishings, and the introspective dreamer in a state of expectancy. Thus, by the merest suggestion, the two Marias appear to be present: the dead sister of "Plainte d'Automne" and the silent, pale companion, addressed as "ma sœur au regard de jadis," with which the poet seems to speak to them both.

The Venetian mirror [6] introduces one of the key symbols of the Mallarméan universe, and one of the most precious objects of the room. "Glace," which, aside from the traditional mirror-water association carries the additional one of mirror-frozen water, is in harmony with the atmosphere of "Frisson d'Hiver." For ice suggests not only the mirror's impassibility, but also its virginal fragility and frigidity. Finally the mirror intimates the "frisson" of recognition experienced at the revelation of one's image. "De Venise," echoing "de Saxe," again evokes the far-away while, like the china clock, producing a precise image: a mirror with an ornate gilt frame which recalls the aristocratic elegance of a by-gone "grand siècle." And while both mirror and window function as virtual doors from — or into — the room, the mirror in contrast to the dull panes is smooth and clear, like the watery surface imaged by "froide fontaine," which combines the clearness of water with the coldness of ice. The fountain's depth — "profonde" — suggests its mystery. At the same time, as with the notion of "frisson," the fountain image encompasses the notions both of movement and immobility; however, in our poem im-

---

[6] This mirror is likewise a biographical detail. In his famous letter to Cazalis of 1867, describing his spiritual crisis, Mallarmé says, Mondor, *Correspondance* I, p. 242:

> ... enfin je me sois revu un jour devant ma glace de Venise, tel que je m'étais oublié plusieurs mois auparavant.

mobility is again stressed, for its coldness freezes that fountain. "Rivage" superimposes the images of the fountain's border and the mirror's frame; for this fountain is not a natural running spring, but an artificial one with its smooth, almost frozen, surface bordered by an ornately sculptured edge. Its stone and marble wiverns are the same that are carved into the mirror's tarnished old gilt frame, "guivres dédorées," by their etymological association with "givre," hoar-froast, once more echoing the winter theme. And so the mirror has become a fountain decorating a park, the latter being but the extension of the artificial and artistic environment of the room. In a single sentence, then, the poet has magnificently developed and superimposed two images: the ornate Venetian mirror in a carefully constructed room, and the richly embellished fountain of a park by Le Nôtre: Nature subjugated by Art.

As with the clock, so with the mirror the poet first introduces the image and then muses about it; and his questions — "à qui a-t-elle été?" "qui s'y est miré?" — intimate the mysterious origin of the treasures. But the mirror question also points to its function, and the ideal function of a luxurious mirror is to reflect an image of Beauty. "Mirer" invites the association with Narcissus and his fountain, further developed with "baigner," which extends the mirror-fountain analogy, recalling the contemporary "Le Pitre Châtié," where the reflecting also becomes a bathing. The association of looking into and bathing in the mirror-fountain leads to the nude, "un fantôme nu," bringing to mind the Aphrodite-like "Phénomène Futur" stepping out of the sea. "Le péché de sa beauté" is not the sin of nudity, but that of nudity seen, which motif links "Frisson d'Hiver" to "Hérodiade," begun in the same winter. In that poem the mirror-fountain image and the theme of narcissistic introspection are elaborated in a similar setting of cold, white, and virginal sterility:

> ... Tiens devant moi ce miroir.
>   O miroir!
> Eau froide par l'ennui dans ton cadre gelée
> Que de fois et pendant des heures, désolée
> Des songes et cherchant mes souvenirs qui sont
> Comme des feuilles sous ta glace au trou profond,
> Je m'apparus en toi comme une ombre lointaine,
> Mais, horreur! des soirs, dans ta sévère fontaine,
> J'ai de mon rêve épars connu la nudité (OC p. 45)!

Hérodiade's mirror, then, is also the frozen and motionless fountain of a sterile winter world, corresponding to that of "Frisson d'Hiver."

The phantom is but the illusory image evoked — like the shades by the window — by the persona's reverie, so that the apparitions of his mind come to people the room in a curious fusion of inner and outer worlds. [7] Moreover the "fantôme nu" in the Venetian mirror recalls Hérodiade's naked "ombre lointaine" in her own mirror; and both already prefigure the nymph which will appear many years later in "Ses purs ongles," where "Elle défunte nue en le miroir" will symbolize death and night, the *néant* presaged here. But whose is the voice which now interrupts the poet's meditations? Since the poet's companion remains silent throughout the poem, is it not his own, the phantom's, — who becomes a Psyche beckoning and at the same time warning him to look no further into this deep fountain in which the self might drown? Hérodiade was horrified by her mirror's revelation of nothingness, that impassible "Néant," which threatens from without and from within and which also makes our young poet hesitate before both, those windows and that mirror.

The threat from the outside is concretized in the recurring window motif, and as the persona now recognizes "des toiles d'araignées au haut des grandes croisées," the "vitres" have changed to "croisées," no longer alluding to the window's transparency, but emphasizing the solidity of the frame, that is an extension of the room's protective walls. Again, the poet turns his eyes away from the windows and to the inside, where they fall on "notre bahut encore très vieux," an object again evocative of the far-away and a distant past. Its wood is "triste," even as it is struck by the light of the fire which fails to impart any warmth to the faded objects of the winter room. This fire is, moreover, not directly seen but present by its reflection only, like that pale beam of a distant sun in the contemporary "Soupir":

---

[7] In a letter of 1865 to Lefébure, *ibid.*, p. 176, Mallarmé says:
   Ma chambre est si grande, et haute, que j'y suis encore un étranger et ne l'ai pas peuplée de ma pensée et de mes paroles.

> ...
> Et laisse, sur l'eau morte où la fauve agonie
> Des feuilles erre au vent et creuse un froid sillon,
> Se trainer le soleil jaune d'un long rayon (OC p. 39).

The narrator fittingly invites his companion to "contemplate" their treasures, for she is the personification of the contemplative life. Mary, and not Martha; one of those "qui ne goûtent pas l'action." And as he sums up his catalog of all that is cherished in the room — the faded curtains, as old as the chest with its sad wood, the antique chairs with their paled tapestry and frames, the engravings on the wall — with "toutes nos vieilleries," even the living presences — the colorful waxbill and the bluebird — seem to have faded with time, for the poet's animals, like the white cat of "Plainte d'Automne," assume and reflect their owner's mood.

The window motif which now interrupts the narrator's meditations for the third time becomes haunting by its very insistence, and he directs both his and his companion's eyes and thoughts away from those spiders' webs which have begun to tremble, and whose "frisson" suggests stirrings, perhaps, of a mere idea caught in their lace.

The poem's tone becomes more discursive with "... et voilà pourquoi je peux vivre auprès de toi," which identifies the woman as the narrator's wife. But the bond uniting them appears more spiritual than conjugal, the erotic not even being suggested; when it had been distantly evoked with the naked mirror phantom, the persona had immediately turned away. Here, in the winter room, both Marias seem present, the dead one come to life, and the living one remote as a ghost in this "sœur au regard de jadis." The sister-beloved association is, moreover, again highly reminiscent of Baudelaire, and the whole sentence — "N'as-tu pas désiré, ma sœur au regard de jadis, qu'en un de mes poëmes apparussent ces mots 'la grâce des choses fanées'?" — is a kind of homage to the older poet, whose celebration of "la grâce des choses fanées" certainly influenced this and the preceding prose poem. The narrator also identifies himself as a poet here, and we recall that the phrase "la grâce des choses fanées" did, in fact, appear in one of Mallarmé's poems, the poetic prose piece "Symphonie Littéraire II," [8] also of 1864, which is the younger poet's formal tribute to his master:

> L'hiver, quand ma torpeur me lasse, je me plonge avec délices dans les chères pages des *Fleurs du Mal.* Mon Baudelaire à peine ouvert, je suis attiré dans un paysage surprenant qui vit au regard avec l'intensité de ceux que crée le profond opium. ... Arrivé, je vois de mornes bassins disposés comme les plates-bandes d'un éternel jardin: dans le granit noir de leurs bords, enchassant les pierres précieuses de l'Inde, dort une eau morte et métallique, avec de lourdes fontaines en cuivre où tombe tristement un rayon bizarre et plein de la grâce des choses fanées...
> (OC p. 263).

We find here already then some symbols and themes of our prose poem which were later to become characteristic of much symbolist poetry: winter, escape into the exotic, the park and its fountain with its still water, the melancholy reflection of the distant winter sun on the mirror-fountain surface, and the obsession with death, for "où tombe tristement" is certainly meant to evoke "triste tombe," all summed up in "la grâce des choses fanées." [9]

The jarring tone of the paragraph's remainder with its lack of imagery is surely intended, for now the ugliness of new objects — symbolizing progress and materialism — irrupts into this secluded world: "Les objets neufs" sounds and looks hard, while the discord is accentuated with the onomatopoetic "leur hardiesse criarde" with its offensive alliteration. In the following section, the image of Maria reading — in harmony with her contemplative nature — recalls that other portrait of a lady holding a book, the silent saint of the stained glass window, "...la Sainte pâle, étalant/Le livre vieux qui se déplie" of the verse poem of 1865. Our

---

[8] This composition found its way, in a much shorter version, into *Divagations* under the title "Autrefois, en Marge d'un Baudelaire."

[9] Noel Richard, *Le Mouvement décadent* (Paris: Nizet, 1968), p. 51, cites part of a poem which one of Mallarmé's admirers, Albert Aurier, published in 1886 in LE DÉCADENT, and in which the phrase, "la grâce des choses fanées" reappears: "Poète Mallarmé, toi qui chantas sur ton / Luth mystique, la grâce des choses fanées." Be it again recalled that while the young Mallarmé had anticipated a literary mood, the mature poet has passed beyond the Decadent stance long before it becomes fashionable.

lady's book, the outdated almanac, like the clock also from Germany — home of by-gone Romanticism — is behind the time also; moreover the very type of calendar, "almanach," is an old-fashioned one. Like the clock, originally designated to measure time, it now merely recalls the past, for it appeared "il y a plus de cent ans," and the future it presages is dead, with the kings it announces all gone to their graves. This lost past is again evoked with "il n'y a plus de champs," for these fields have now become the city with its empty evening streets.

Not of the world outside, but of that inner one which is their home, will the poet speak to the "calme enfant" in her faded dress, his head resting on her "genoux charitables." This is the same Marie who will be celebrated also in the last of the prose poems of 1864, "La Pipe," and in the verse poem "Don du Poëme" of 1865, when the poet will bring his new-born "Hérodiade" to her so that she may nourish it. The poet will speak to her, his soul's sister and companion, for hours of their treasures, hours which are out of time — fictitious as that thirteenth hour of the old china clock. For "Frisson d'Hiver" is about itself: the introspective poet's fragile and narcissistic reveries threatened by chaos, and symbolized by the delicate spiderwebbing, which now shivers high up on the casement windows.

The only significant variant of the piece, which stylistically resembles the others of that year, is that of the title. However the young Mallarmé's predilection for repetition, which had already manifested itself in "Plainte d'Automne," has in "Frisson d'Hiver" become a major structural device, evidencing the influence of Poe, [10] and also that of Baudelaire in his prose poems. For the recurrence of the obsessive window-spiderweb image is the equivalent of a Wagnerian *leit-motif,* a melodic figure playing repeatedly into the main narrative theme. We find Mallarmé utilizing the same

---

[10] In 1864, Mallarmé writes to Cazalis, *ibid.,* p. 104:
>Toutefois, plus j'irai, plus je serai fidèle à ces sévères idées que m'a leguées mon grand maître Poe.

In 1853 Baudelaire had translated the "Philosophy of Composition" which, whether in jest or in earnest, discusses the use of repetition at length.

musical device in his verse of those years, as for example in the "Ouverture" of "Hérodiade," which he himself called "musical": [11]

> Une Aurore a, plumage héraldique, choisi
> Notre tour cinéraire et sacrificatrice,
> ...
> Un arôme qui porte, ô roses! un arôme
> Loin du lit vide qu'un cierge soufflé cachait,
> Un arôme, d'ors froids rodant sur le sachet,
> ...
> Une Aurore traînait ses ailes dans les larmes!
> ...
> Comme un cygne cachant en sa plume ses yeux,
> Comme les mit le vieux cygne en sa plume, allée
> De la plume détresse, en l'éternelle allée (OC pp. 41-43).

There is then a correspondence of both imagery and style between Mallarmé's early prose and verse poetry. Moreover, in both "Frisson d'Hiver" and "Hérodiade" this specific stylistic device is so inextricably linked to the theme that form and function become inseparable, style not merely expressing, but objectifying the idea.

"Frisson d'Hiver," then, introduces some of the major symbols of the prose poems, and indeed this whole poetic universe. The room itself — which emerges as the symbol of the poet's mind or consciousness — will be the setting also of some of Mallarmé's late sonnets, where we meet the familiar objects: the mirror, the window, the lace, and the clock. At the same time, this poem is still under the influence of Baudelaire, and the winter room itself might owe part of its inspiration to "Paysage":

> Et quand viendra l'hiver aux neiges monotones
> Je fermerai partout portières et volets
> Pour bâtir dans la nuit mes féeriques palais [12]

The need to close off the mind from what threatens it reflects two important aspects of this moment in the poet's development, both

---

[11] In a letter to Cazalis of 1866, *ibid.*, p. 207, Mallarmé says:
> J'ai donc a te raconter trois mois, à bien grands traits; ... je les ai passés, acharné sur *Hérodiade*, ma lampe le sait! j'ai écrit l'ouverture musicale, ...

[12] Baudelaire, *Fleurs*, p. 91. Also, of course, the prose poem, "La Chambre Double" of the *Spleen de Paris* comes to mind.

revealed by the correspondence of those years: Mallarmé's desire for solitude and withdrawal to hear the melody within, and also the approaching mental crisis of 1866,[13] which will influence the next prose poem of the cycle even more strongly. The emerging poet is already beginning to suffer the existential anguish whose full force will be rendered dramatically in *Igitur* by means of these same symbols: the room and its furnishings, and above all the mirror — into which the hero must now look — and the clock, objectification of the obsession with Time and reminder of the ephemeral in human existence:

> J'ai toujours vécu mon âme fixée sur l'horloge. Certes j'ai tout fait pour que le temps qu'elle sonna *restât* présent dans la chambre ... j'ai épaissi les rideaux, et comme j'étais obligé pour ne pas douter de moi de m'assoir en face de cette glace, j'ai recueilli précieusement les moindres atomes du temps. ...
> Et quand je rouvrais les yeux au fond du miroir, je voyais le personnage d'horreur, le fantôme de l'horreur absorber peu à peu ce qui restait de sentiment et de douleur dans la glace, nourrir son horreur des suprêmes frissons des chimères et de l'instabilité des tentures, et se former en raréfiant la glace jusqu'à une pureté innouie, — jusqu'à ce qu'il se détachent, permanent, de la glace absolument pure, comme pris dans son froid, — jusqu'à ce qu'enfin les meubles, leurs monstres ayant succombé avec leurs anneaux convulsifs, fussent morts ... et que les rideaux cessant d'être inquiets tombassent, avec une attitude qu'ils devaient conserver à jamais (OC pp. 439-41).

The delicate cobwebs, still shivering by the windows, will later become Mallarmé's image for the Orphic explanation of the earth,

---

[13] In the letter already quoted from above (Note 6), about this crisis, Mallarmé relates this experience in rather Hegelian terms:
> Je viens de passer une année effrayante: ma Pensée s'est pensée, et est arrivée à une Conception pure. Tout ce que, par contrecoup, mon être a souffert, pendant cette longue agonie, est inénarrable, mais, heureusement, je suis parfaitement mort, et la région la plus impure où mon Esprit puisse s'aventurer est l'Eternité, mon Esprit, ce solitaire habituel de sa propre Pureté, que n'obscurcit plus même le reflet du Temps.

which it is the poet's function to reveal: the relation between all parts — the universal analogy — of an artistic universe imposed on chaos:

> ... je venais de jeter le plan de mon œuvre entier, après avoir trouvé la clef de moi-même, clef de voûte, ou centre, si tu veux, pour ne pas nous brouiller de métaphores, —centre de moi-même, où je me tiens comme une araignée sacrée, sur les principaux fils déjà sortis de mon esprit, et à l'aide desquels je tisserais *aux points de rencontre* de merveilleuses dentelles, que je devine, et qui existent déjà dans le sein de la Beauté.[14]

---

[14] Mondor, *Correspondance* I, pp. 224-225.

LE DÉMON DE L'ANALOGIE

The anecdote of "Le Démon de l'Analogie" tells about the narrator's obsession with a phrase which haunts him as he is walking in the streets, and which he vainly tries to exorcise. The poet-persona ultimately finds himself in front of a store window which reflects his image, and upon looking through that window discovers that this is a lutemaker's shop, with old stringed instruments hanging on the wall, precisely the kind of instruments he had been thinking about in connection with the haunting phrase. At this point he is overcome by the strange and unexplainable correspondence between the images of his imagination and those of the phenomenal world. [1]

The piece had appeared several times under the title "La Pénultième," its definitive one appearing for the first time in *Pages* of 1891 and again in *Divagations*. As in the case of "Plainte d'Automne" the change in title again reflects Mallarmé's principle of painting no longer "la chose," but the effect produced. "La Pénultième" is part of "la chose," that is of the haunting phrase itself, whereas its demonic power is the effect it has on the poet-persona. Further, the identification of this demon as that of analogy places the piece in the domain of poetics. [2] That analogy was the underly-

---

[1] The first and only full *analyse* of the poem known to me is Thibaudet's (*Poésie*, pp. 184-88), but it is essentially descriptive, rather than analytic. A. R. Chisholm takes issue with Thibaudet's treatment in a short article, "Le Démon de l'Analogie," ESSAYS IN FRENCH LITERATURE, 1 (Nov., 1964), 106, Univ. of West Australia Press, which though interpreting the prose poem does not attempt to explain its multiple levels of meaning.

[2] Gardner Davies in "The Demon of Analogy," FRENCH STUDIES, IV, 3 & 4 (July and October, 1955) 197-211 and 326-347, analyzes the different figures of discourse, commonly called analogies, which Mallarmé employs most often.

ing logic of Mallarmé's *Weltanschauung* not only strikes the reader of his poetry, but also struck those who knew him.[3] And as the spider-web image of "Frisson d'Hiver" already presaged an order which the poet creates out of his own substance and imposes on chaos, so many years later in "Le Livre, instrument spirituel" Mallarmé reaffirms that the perception and creation of analogies is the structural basis for his poetic universe, that universal Analogy which reveals the relation between all parts of an artistic cosmos: "l'hymne, harmonie et joie, comme pur ensemble groupé dans quelque circonstance fulgurante, des relations entre tout" (OC p. 378).

This discovering and creating of correspondences recalls Baudelaire, in whose translation of Poe's prose Mallarmé might have come upon a title, "Le Démon de la Perversité," which could have influenced his own choice.[4] The word "démon," originally a spirit, good or bad, points to the role which the supernatural plays in this piece, while figuratively it stands for poetic inspiration, compulsive in the manner of Socrates' private *daemon*.[5]

Many words of the poem's vocabulary fall, in at least one of their significations, in the domains of rhetoric and music. Consider, for example, the opening single-sentence paragraph: "Des paroles inconnues chantèrent-elles sur vos lèvres, lambeaux maudits d'une

---

[3] Camille Mauclair in *Princes de l'esprit* (Paris: Ollendorf, 1931), p. 116, remembers of the poet:

> ... une faculté personnelle qu'il possédait à un degré incroyable: celle de l'analogie. Stéphane Mallarmé eut le sens des analogies développé jusqu'à stupéfier quiconque parlait avec lui. Il surprenait entre les objets ou les actes les plus disparates d'un œil infaillible, le point de contact et de comparaison. Il concevait si nativement et avec une si grande force la plénitude indéfinie de l'univers, qu'à son esprit rien ne se présentait isolément, et que tout était système de signes cohérents et solidaires.

[4] *Œuvres Complètes de Charles Baudelaire*, Traductions, "Histoires Extraordinaires" par Edgar Poe (Paris: Conard, 1932), pp. 1-9. In "Le Démon de la Perversité" we also find a narrator haunted by words as he is walking in the city streets, though aside from that there are no other similarities, the tale being a rather typical Poesque psycho-horror story which has nothing to do with the theme of poetry.

[5] Many years later, in his commemorative lecture for Villiers de l'Isle-Adam, Mallarmé will again use this term for inspiration: "Le démon littéraire qui inspira Villiers de l'Isle-Adam, à ce point fut-il conscient?" (OC p. 481).

phrase absurde?" "Paroles," literally signifying simply "words," the poet's raw material, etymologically points to "parable," a figure whose functional similarity to analogy is obvious. But used in the plural, as it is here, the term may also refer to the words of a song, and "chantèrent-elles" reinforces this association. Again, "phrase" is a term both grammatical and musical, in each case signifying a unit. But here unity has been destroyed, only shreds of it remaining, and "maudits" endows these shreds of words with a magical quality, as with a charm. The alliterating juxtaposition of "lèvres" and "lambeaux" invites the image association of red lips and "lambeaux de chair," the torn shreds of the phrase bleeding red, and this surrealistic image is reinforced with "absurde." The "torn" phrase introduces a whole vocabulary cluster in this piece, namely that of something broken, ruptured: "interrompre," "détacher," "descendre," "casser," "discontinuer," "désespérer," which accompanies the death motif throughout the poem.

The following sentence introduces a first-person narrator in a city setting and, with the factual banality of "je sortis de mon appartement," contrasts for a moment with the mood produced by the images of the opening paragraph. But then, with the narrator's curious sensation, the first manifestation of the demon, we reenter the realm of the mysterious, where all perceptions seem curiously related and intertwined: "La sensation... d'une aile glissant sur les cordes d'un instrument, traînante et légère, que remplaça une voix prononçant les mots sur un ton descendant...." Is the sensation first visual, tactile, or auditory, or is it all of these at once? This phrase gives a purely poetic sensation, where the repetition of the "l," that of the "-ent" sound, the "r," and finally that of the "o," produces an incantatory effect, so that the cluster of images named is also suggested by the sound, not so much of individual words, but of the whole phrase.

The very first image, "aile," is so rich in multivalent suggestiveness that it produces a sort of expectant confusion: "d'une aile" sounds like a feminine presence, "une elle," and as the image of the soft wing comes before the mind's eye, it evokes the picture of a white angel; and in these prose poems the white angel is Maria. At the same time the wing, synecdoche for bird, is also a symbol for poetic inspiration and *envol*. "Glissant sur les cordes d'un instrument" evokes the lyre, traditional symbol for poetry, and the Orphic association of poetry and music. And then the music suggested by the wing's gliding over the instrument becomes, in fact, "une voix." The voice is born out of the wing's contact with the instrument, suggesting the mandola's belly rendered fruitful by inspiration.

These associations are not confined to "Le Démon de l'Analogie" or to the prose poems in general. All of them are reflected in Mallarmé's verse poetry, where the force of poetic *envol* is likened to the powerful wing beat of the swan:

> Va-t-il nous déchirer avec un coup d'aile ivre (OC p. 67).

And the wing-angel-music association is harmoniously synthesized in the Saint Cecilia poem:

> Que frôle une harpe par l'Ange
> Formée avec son vol du soir
> Pour la délicate phalange (OC p. 54).

The birth of art, of song, out of the mandola's belly, a womb waiting sadly for its fulfillment, is suggested in the last sonnet of the triptych:

> Mais, chez qui du rêve se dore
> Tristement dort une mandore
> Au creux néant musicien
>
> Telle que vers quelque fenêtre
> Selon nul ventre que le sien
> Filial on aurait pu naître (OC p. 74).

So this one rich phrase, with its sudden release of blending sensations and images and sounds is so many-faceted and mobile that we are taken as by a spell of vertigo, until we can make out the words of the falling voice: "La Pénultième est morte."

Out of sensations, created by the sound of words in a falling intonation, emerges a phrase, detached from any conscious context like a lonely leaf fallen from a tree: "La Pénultième est morte." Almost immediately the words arrange themselves in a rhythmic pattern, but then the intonation and pattern are not merely heard, but visualized, with the noun at the end of a line and the verb and predicate adjective spilling over into the following verse in a run-on line. The poet-persona not merely tells us about this arrangement, but shows it to us:

> "La Pénultième est morte," de facon que
>
> > *La Pénultième*
>
> finit le vers et
>
> > *Est morte*
>
> > > se détache de la suspension fatidique plus inutilement en le vide de signification.

Poetry is for Mallarmé as much visual as it is auditory, and the schematic presentation of but one "absurd phrase" in this early poem already foreshadows that growing preoccupation with the visual design of his poetry which will culminate in the "Coup de Dés."

The "pénultième," whose lexical definition the poet himself explains further on, suggests something I have mentioned above, namely something broken, discontinued, cut short before its end. Not the last, with which phenomena naturally come to an end, but the one before the last; and the penult of the very word "Pénultième" is precisely the "nul" syllable over which the instrument's strings will break. "Nul," denoting the absence of being, "qui, pour ainsi dire, en parlant des personnes, n'a pas d'existence," suggests the death of a person. I purposely quote Littré's definition of this term as it refers to "personnes," rather than to "choses," for the word "pénultième," from its very first appearance, is personified in such a way that one forgets that it is "quelque chose" rather than "quelqu'un," or, I should say, "quelqu'une." The word's feminine gender plays into the poet's hands; moreover, this notion of a feminine presence — evoked as so often in Mallarmé by its absence — is reinforced by the capitalization of the first letter, making a proper noun out of it, a woman's name.

And this "Pénultième" is dead; thus, from the outset, two antithetical forces are at work: a phrase is born, but in a dying fall it tells of a death. The "est morte," with its double designation of "has died" and "is dead," is detached from the line, again reinforcing the notion of rupture and cessation. "Suspension" is again both a rhetorical and a musical term, i.e. "temporary cessation," and it is "fatidique," one that was fated to be, with the notion of the fates suggesting ultimate disaster. Just as at this initial stage of inspiration the verse pattern seems inexplicable, so does the "fateful suspension," this death. And the feeling of absurdity which necessarily accompanies the mind's reflections upon its own approaching and inevitable nonexistence is reinforced by "le vide de signification," with its typically Mallarméan nominalization of the adjective and the use of a prepositional phrase. This stylistic device is significant here, as it couples the opposing concepts in a single phrase, raising the notion of the void and of emptiness so that it predominates over its very opposite, namely meaning.

Again, the anecdotal "je fis des pas dans la rue" seems to put us back into the realm of the ordinary, but only briefly so, for now the penultimate syllable of "La Pénultième," the "nul," associates itself onomatopoetically with the image of a taut string of the musical instrument evoked above and forgotten again, but now recalled once more. But there is here so mighty a sweep of Memory, that it must refer to more than merely the recall of the image of the instrument; "le glorieux Souvenir," with its significant capitalization, surges out of a deeper past, and this vast sweeping movement is beautifully rendered with "venait de visiter de son aile ou d'une palme," again recalling the wing image above and adding that of the "palme." Memory and Penult are the only two words capitalized in the poem; Memory is the prime inspiration of the Penult's monody, this song commemorating one departed.

The wing symbol in this connection suggests the poet's Orphic function of resurrecting the past and bringing back the dead, while "palme," somehow blending with wing in "de son aile ou d'une palme," a symbol of triumph, intimates the triumph of the poetic quest. But the palm branch is also the sign of the martyrs, thus conveying the notion of the poet not only as Orpheus who triumphs over nature and death, but as the Promethean giver of life, fire, who is sacrificed, martyred — a motif taken up again in the following prose poem. At the same time, both images, wing and palm, evoke again angels and saints, the blessed beyond the tomb, and the white figure of Maria. In "Symphonie Littéraire II," the palm-saint association was explicitly stated with "les saintes ont des palmes . . ." (OC p. 264).

"Je fis des pas dans la rue et reconnus en le son *nul* la corde tendue de l'instrument de musique," with its fourfold repetition of the stressed "u" sound and its short, almost shrill, syllables conveys an obsessive effect. The merciless insistance of these sounds, and their association with the tension of taut strings, creates an indeed mysteriously demonic quality. "Le doigt sur l'artifice du mystère" indicates the persona's cognizance of the mechanism of Memory inspiring song, or poetry. But "artifice" and "je sortis" somehow also point, by the merest hint, to something else. Does the persona here momentarily step beyond and out of the poem, so as to fuse and identify with the poet? For "artifice," etymologically related to "art," could also refer to the poetic artifice just described, which produced so mysterious an effect. Further, it could well describe Poe's poetic theory which, as we have seen, influenced some of these early prose poems. However, this suggestion, if it is one, is so well hidden behind the primary level of meaning, that the illusion of the poem is not destroyed, the spell not broken, as the persona now tries by any means, natural or supernatural — "implorer" and "vœux" having religious, "speculation" and "intellectuelle" rational, undertones — to escape the demon who drives him relentlessly from sounds to images, to rhythmic patterns, to thoughts, and even into the realm of the dead.

The obsessiveness of the *furor poeticus* is rendered doubly, in the persona's telling us that the phrase keeps coming back to him, and, at the same time, in the very repetition of the same images and phrases throughout the poem. When the phrase returns "virtuelle," it has something menacing about it, a self-contained, so far unreleased, energy and force. Now it is finally freed, "dégagée d'une chute antérieure de plume ou de rameau." What is this "chute," a world used so weightily by Mallarmé in "Plainte d'Automne?" The whole phrase had come in a falling tone, and this obsession with falling and fall must point to a former, higher state. "Chute antérieure" curiously combines both the notions of a former state and the fall from it, just as the very notion of the Fall implies a lost Eden, or, inversely, the very idea of Paradise implies a state now lost. Again, Baudelaire comes to mind, and his "La Vie Antérieure" complex, so well expressed in the poem of that title.

And looking once more at "Symphonie Littéraire II," Mallarmé's Baudelairean prose poem, we find there the images of our poem: "Nulles fleurs, à terre, alentour — seulement, de loin en loin quelques plumes d'aile d'âmes déchues" (OC p. 263), which renders explicit the association of "aile" and "chute" with the idea of the Fall from Eden — also one of the basic themes of "Les Fleurs du Mal."

"De plume ou de rameau," by the conjunction "ou" superimposes and thus deliberately obscures the images, so that they appear to be almost identical. The phrase is now freed from "une chute antérieure de plume ou de rameau," that is, literally freed from the earlier sensation of wing touching instrument. It has now definitely become a voice. But "aile" has changed to "plume ... ou ... rameau." The feather is a synecdoche for the wing it now replaces, but at the same time it evokes the poet's pen which traces the poem on the white page. "Rameau" evokes both classical and Christian mythology, "rameau-palme" recalling the "dimanche de Rameaux," and also the "rameau d'or" without which the realm of the dead could not be entered.

Henceforth the new-born phrase, no longer merely vaguely felt, but finally articulated by the voice, become *logos,* will live its own life, no longer living of the poet's substance but of its own. The formerly vague, subjective perceptions of the persona have grown into an objective entity, no longer dependent on him. This is the very birth of poetry, the process of creation itself, in which subjective experience is objectified.

Now the poet, no longer content merely to perceive it, toys experimentally with this phrase. Again, characteristically, he first sees it, "la lisant en fin de vers," then speaks and hears it, "l'adaptant à mon parler." As in the beginning, the Penult will come at the end of the line, the rest run over into the following, with the string so stretched in forgetfulness over the penultimate syllable, "nul," that it breaks. And this breaking, this dying, is then rendered in the manner of a lament: "est morte." "Si tendue en l'oubli" seems strange as applied to the string of a musical instrument; but it must here refer to the poet's "oubli," for above we read: "la corde tendue de l'instrument de musique, qui était oublié," which means that the poet-persona had forgotten his lyre, now visited by memory. And "pénible jouissance" reflects at once the poet's joy at the recreation of a remembered past and the regret over its loss; moreover, this antithetical feeling of both joy and pain, which accompanies the natural process of birth, is also characteristic of the artistic one.

The poet now tries again to escape and to calm his obsession by speculating on the cause of the Penult's apparition. He considers that, after all, this is but a lexical term, whose definition is simple enough, but he fails, of course, to apprehend the word's deeper significance.

Critics have speculated vainly in trying to define, without analyzing the rest of the piece, what Mallarmé might have alluded to with "le reste mal abjuré d'un labeur de linguistique par lequel quotidiennement sanglote de s'interrompre ma noble faculté poétique." Whether it alludes to Mallarmé's work as a language teacher or to his researches into the secrets of language in the service of poetry (I hold to the former),[6] it again clearly and explicitly establishes the narrator as a poet, a fact, of course, implicit throughout the poem. But what is interesting above all is the ironic tone of the sentence: the "noble faculté poétique," which "sanglote de s'interrompre," can be read as an undercutting of the poet's own sense of mission, still threatened by doubts about his ability, which implies his fear of the poetic vocation at the beginning of his career.

The facile "explaining away" of the haunting Penult does not succeed, but only increases the persona's torment. "Tourment" is immediately reinforced with "harcelé"; conquered, he gives in to the demon of words, letting them play over his lips, surrendering to them. This surrendering "l'initiative aux mots" is many years later described in a passage of "Crise de Vers":

> L'œuvre pure implique la disparition élocutoire du poëte, qui cède l'initiative aux mots, par le heurt de leur inégalité mobilisés; ils s'allument de reflets réciproques comme une virtuelle traînée de feux sur des pierreries, remplaçant la respiration perceptible en l'ancien souffle lyrique

---

[6] One should recall, at any rate, that *Les Mots Anglais* does not preoccupy Mallarmé until several years later; it is not until 1868 that he begins to think of undertaking linguistic studies, as indicated by his correspondence.

ou la direction personnelle enthousiaste de la phrase (OC p. 366).

So the dirge for the Penult intones itself with the appropriate note of condolence, and in this murmured incantation, with its repetition of "morte ... morte ... morte," the persona hopes to sing himself to peace. But here more than ever does this inexplicable Penult seem to become a woman, a dead woman whose desperate ghost haunts the poet. Wishing to lay this ghost and rid himself of the spell of the phrase, he tries to bury her once more, that shade, and the haunting phrase with her, in the "amplification" of the "psalmodie," a kind of *placandis Mariae manibus*.

But the demon will not let him go, pursuing him from the mind's recesses out into the world of the city streets, for now the narrator sees himself, reflected in a shop window, caressing something with his hand — in a descending motion, which corresponds to the "ton descendant" of the voice. The window, here functioning as a mirror, provides an entry into the visible manifestation of the mystery, not to be explained away as "une magie aisément déductible et nerveuse." A very similar distillation of the creative process, both a birth and a dying, occurs in a verse poem of those years, "Les Fenêtres":

> Je me mire et me vois ange! et je meurs, et j'aime
> — Que la vitre soit l'art, soit la mysticité —
> A renaître, portant mon rêve en diadème,
> Au ciel antérieur où fleurit la Beauté! (OC p. 33).

The poet recognizes in the voice now the voice which first intoned the obsessive phrase, and it must be this one which he is caressing, that song which originated in him and has now been born into a life of its own, but which is always the same. And so the poem points back to its beginning: "une voix prononçant les mots sur un ton descendant: 'La Pénultième est morte.'" In a strange fusion of the visual and the auditory, the reflected image of the poet caressing his own voice becomes a symbol for a vocation which seems to condemn to solitude and narcissism: the poet, Pygmalion-like, himself creates the object of his love.[7]

---

[7] In a letter to Cazalis of 1867, *Correspondance* I, p. 243, Mallarmé writes: "Pour moi, la Poésie me tient lieu de l'amour parce qu'elle est

The poem might have ended here, with the ring of its circular structure closed. But the final paragraph, taking up once again the key images of the piece, underlines the demonic and inexplicable nature of poetic passion. Yet the intervention of the supernatural, as well as the narrator's anguish, do not really begin here, with the marvelous anecdote. They have prevailed throughout the piece.

The persona now remains standing in front of the shop window which has just reflected his image. What changes is his "regard," for now he looks no longer merely at, but through, the window. There is again a tone of irony in "l'angoisse sous laquelle agonise mon esprit naguère seigneur," but what is undercut is not the anguish of the obsession, but the rational mind, "naguère seigneur," which has become its victim. "Angoisse" and "agonise," though ironically used, reinforce the *Angst* atmosphere, which is built up by the device of witholding the object of the anguish until far into the sentence. This is accomplished through an accumulation of preparatory clauses: "c'est quand je vis," "levant les yeux," "dans la rue," which, by delaying the revelation, create a mounting expectancy. Only now do we learn that the narrator is in front of a lutemaker's shop, which establishes the bridge between inner and outer worlds: the memory of the wing brushing "les cordes d'un instrument," and the actual display of "vieux instruments pendus au mur." After the initial *rencontre* of the mental image and the external phenomenon of the key symbol — the poet's lyre — some of the accompanying symbolic images also find their phenomenological complement: palm and wings, mysteriously enveloped by shadows and paled with age. The motif of old age and a distant past — so predominant in the preceding prose poems, but especially in "Frisson d'Hiver" — is underlined with the "rue des antiquaires," "vendeur de vieux instruments pendus au mur," "palmes jaunes," and above all "Les ailes ... d'oiseaux anciens." Just as the "pendule de Saxe" was behind time and the "vieil almanach allemand" announced kings long since dead, our lute no longer sings, the palm leaves are no longer green, and the birds have long since died. And so the notion of "chute" is suggested again here, where every object is but the souvenir of a former state.

éprise d'elle-même et que sa volupté d'elle retombe délicieusement en mon âme."

Just as the narrator had been frightened upon discovering in his mirror reflection the image of a poet, so he now flees upon discovering beyond the glass the symbols of poetry. He is condemned to a vocation which sets him apart from the rest of mankind, condemned to mourn "l'inexplicable Pénultième." The final note of the poem certainly seems "inexplicable," and this is precisely how it appeared to contemporary critics. Gustave Kahn recalls that:

> La presse, toujours la même, avait accueilli d'un déferlement de rires la Pénultième. ... il y avait la Pénultième, cette fameuse Pénultième, dont on parlait il y a dix ou douze ans de la rive gauche à partout; la Pénultième était alors le nec plus ultra de l'incompréhensible, le Chimborazo de l'infranchissable, et le casse-tête chinois. [8]

And Mallarmé's close friend, Villiers de l'Isle-Adam, predicted that this prose poem would be even more incomprehensible for "le bourgeois" than the poet's verse. [9] We can now see, however, that "Le Démon de l'Analogie" not only takes the creative process as its theme, but is itself the artistic transformation of the creative process of poetry, a sort of Gidean "composition en abyme," where one finds transposed in a work of art the very subject of that work. [10] On this level, "Le Démon de l'Analogie" is a poem about

---

[8] Gustave Kahn, *Symbolistes et décadents* (Paris: Vannier, 1902), pp. 17 and 138.

[9] In a letter of 1867, quoted in *Correspondance* I, p. 260, Villiers writes to Mallarmé:

> Je viens de lire vos admirables poèmes en prose! je lirai samedi, c'est-à-dire demain soir, à neuf heures et demie, chez de Lisle, *Le Démon de l'Analogie* que j'étudie profondément. ... Jamais, on n'a vu ni entendu sa pareille et il faut absolument être au diapason du "violon démantibulé" de Louis Bertrand pour saisir la profondeur de votre idée et le talent excellent de la composition.

The reference to Bertrand is revealing, for the mysterious, somewhat anguished ambiance of our prose poem resembles, indeed, the general atmosphere of Bertrand's prose poems. We recall that Baudelaire praised these highly in his preface, "A Arsène Houssaye," to the *Spleen de Paris*. It might be due to the older poet's admiration that Mallarmé became interested in Bertrand, an interest he expresses, for example, in a letter of December 1865, to Victor Pavie, *Correspondance* I, p. 188.

[10] Although one tends to identify the "composition en abyme" usually with Gide's later work, and especially *Les Faux-Monnayeurs*, it should be

the creation of "le Démon de l'Analogie." The poem's particular tension, imaged in the taut string of the instrument, consists of the contrapuntal play of two antithetical themes: birth and death. We have discussed the former, the creative process, but the latter, which is paradoxically a part of it, remains to be explored. For, who or what dies in this birth process?

"La Pénutième," we saw, suggests a feminine presence, that of the "blanche créature" of "Plainte d'Automne," the white Maria, again evoked in our poem with such images as "aile," "plume," and "palme," images which are at the same time symbols for poetic inspiration, the writer's instrument, and man's — that is the poet's — triumph. Further, "antérieure" and "chute," again taking up the theme of "Plainte d'Automne," suggest both microcosmically and macrocosmically a blessed state now lost, and of which Maria was a part: the poet's childhood, and the lost unity of the universe. Maria not only belongs to, but represents, this childhood before the fall; and the fall for Mallarmé is that point where his own age of faith ceases, where he must choose, at the price of infinite anguish, the atheistic attitude. Whether the successive deaths of his mother, his sister, and finally his friend Harriet Smythe [11]

---

recalled that the young Gide belonged to Mallarmé's group, and that in his Symbolist *Traité du Narcisse* (also in *Le Voyage d'Urien*) of 1891, he was already fascinated with the play of reflections — as is evident, of course, in the very title of that piece. There is, aside from more serious correspondence, also this little "envoi" from the "Maître" to his young disciple:
> Attendu qu'elle y met du sien
> Vous feuillets de papier frigide
> Exaltez moi musicien
> Pour l'âme attentive de Gide (OC p. 151).

[11] For the influence of the death of his sister on Mallarmé's poetry, see Adile Ayda, *Le Drame Intérieur de Mallarmé* (Istanbul: Ed. de la Turquie Moderne, 1955). Charles Mauron's "psycho-critique" in *Introduction to the Psychoanalysis of Mallarmé* (Neuchatel: Griffon, 1950), is based on the Freudian principle that every action, although apparently meaningless [or "inexplicable"] has an unconscious significance. And so Mauron sees in "Penultimate," "the one before the last," the obsessive memory of the poet's mother, for the last one to die was the sister, Maria, and the one before, the mother. The maternal is, of course, constantly present in the poem, namely in the womb-shaped belly of the lute. This image, supporting the birth motif in my reading, is in Mauron linked to the other obsession. He does not discuss our prose poem except to point out that the obsessive image of the mother here appears under the form of the Penultimate. One could change the schema, of course, and say that the last one to die was

brought about the crisis is less important for this study than is the fact that without this paradoxical "fortunate fall" from faith to atheism, the poet could not have been born. To be born a poet, a self had to die, and we know how cruelly Mallarmé suffered the death agonies which set him free. [12]

This dying in order to be reborn, a voluntary death for the sake of gaining a new existence, is a literary theme and a spiritual experience as old as mythology. [13] Mallarmé's own participation in it is well described by Poulet in his essay on the poet, [14] which not only illuminates the experience of our poet-persona, but also points to his relationship with his dramatic counterpart, Igitur:

> ... la mort est un acte, une opération volontaire par laquelle on se donne une nouvelle existence et par laquelle on donne l'existence même au néant. La mort est le seul acte possible. Pressés que nous sommes entre un monde matériel vrai dont les combinaisons fortuites se produisent en nous sans nous, et un monde idéal faux dont le mensonge nous paralyse et nous ensorcelle, nous n'avons qu'un moyen de ne plus être livrés ni au néant ni au hasard. Ce moyen unique, cet acte unique, c'est la mort. La mort

---

Harriet, and the one before her, Maria. I base the presence of Maria on the internal evidence of some of these early prose poems, especially "Plainte d'Automne," where the theme of "chute" is fully developed. At the same time, the woman suggested is probably, as frequently in artistic transposition, a composite, and thus made up of all three, the mother, the sister, and the friend.

[12] *Correspondance* I, pp. 240-41, letter to Cazalis of 1867:
> Tout ce que, par contrecoup, mon être a souffert, pendant cette longue agonie, est inénarrable, mais, heureusement, je suis parfaitement mort ... ma lutte terrible avec ce vieux et méchant plumage, terrassé, heureusement, Dieu.

And in a letter of the same year, to Lefébure, *ibid.*, p. 249, Mallarmé again links the notions of birth and death:
> Toute naissance est une destruction, et toute vie d'un moment l'agonie dans laquelle on ressuscite ce qu'on a perdu, pour le voir, on l'ignorait avant.

[13] Mallarmé relates his participation in it in a letter to Aubanel in 1866, *ibid.*, p. 222:
> J'ai jeté les fondements d'un œuvre magnifique. ... Je suis mort, et ressuscité avec la clef de pierreries de ma dernière cassette spirituelle.

[14] Georges Poulet, *La Distance intérieure* (Paris: Plon, 1952), p. 325.

> volontaire. Par lui nous nous abolissons, mais par lui aussi nous nous fondons.

The persona's nostalgia for this lost past, which surges back touched by the wing of "le glorieux Souvenir," is also manifest in his literally walking toward it, "la rue des antiquaires instinctivement suivie." And so it is his own past which the poet mourns, "condamné à porter probablement le deuil de l'inexplicable Pénultième."

The important image of "la plume," here for the first time introduced in the prose poems, and which will later grow to heroic proportions in the "Coup de Dés," [15] suggests by association — "une toque de minuit" — another figure who will reappear in the *recueil,* that of Hamlet, "prince amer de l'écueil." The young Mallarmé more than once compared himself to [16]

> L'adolescent évanoui de nous aux commencements de la vie et qui hantera les esprits hauts ou pensifs par le deuil qu'il se plaît à porter... (OC p. 299).

And in the same essay, Mallarmé speaks of "Ophélie, vierge enfance objectivée du lamentable héritier royal. ... une image de soi qu'il y garde intacte autant qu'une Ophélie jamais noyée elle! prêt toujours à se ressaisir. Joyau intact sous le désastre." This establishes a close parallel with the hero of our poem, likewise in mourning, who, in singing the death of the Penult, or Maria, also laments the loss of his "vierge enfance objectivée."

---

[15] Robert Greer Cohn, *L'Œuvre de Mallarmé: Un Coup de Dés* (Paris: Les Lettres, 1951), p. 82: "La plume est donc un héros de Poème qui s'occupe constamment de soi."

[16] *Correspondance* I, p. 25, letter to Cazalis of 1862, the twenty-year old Mallarmé describes himself:

> Que vous serez désillusionné quand vous verrez cet individu maussade qui reste des journées entières la tête sur le marbre de la cheminée, sans penser: ridicule Hamlet qui ne peut se rendre compte de son affaissement.

One recalls, further, the identification of the poet-persona with Hamlet in the contemporary verse poem, "Le Pitre Châtié." Here the "Hamlet" was added later, but the association is there.

PAUVRE ENFANT PÂLE

"Pauvre Enfant Pâle," which appeared originally under the title "La Tête," was published under yet another name, "Fusain," in 1866, after which it reappeared only under its final heading. The first title, echoed in the last word of the piece, resembles in this respect the variant title of the preceding poem, where "La Pénultième" was likewise the title repeated in the last word of that composition. But Mallarmé then seems to have rejected in both cases this rather facile device of establishing circularity.[1] The second variant, "Fusain," suggests that this piece might be a preliminary expression of something yet to be developed, a sketch rather than a fully elaborated poem.[2]

The anecdote tells about a young street singer in a big city and the narrator's reflections about him. He foresees the future criminal in the child, and while initially feeling merely somewhat sympathetic toward the outcast, he gradually moves toward a sense of his own — and more so society's — guilt for this human fate. The poem's visual form with its division into eight paragraphs of similar length and a final one of a mere half line is striking. Each of the paragraphs is in the form of direct address, like a ritualistic supplication or a litany. Yet the vocabulary is not at all elevated, for almost all the words, except "soie incarnadine," are drawn from every-day language, and a term like "à tue-tête" is sheer colloquialism; a lofty word such as "seigneur" is used ironically, and "chan-

---

[1] In "Un Coup de Dés," on the contrary, the circular structure is profoundly inherent to the essence of the poem.

[2] "Fusain," moreover, suggests the sketches of Constantin Guys, Baudelaire's "peintre de la vie moderne," and our prose poem reads very much like a *tableau parisien*.

son" suggesting music and harmony is immediately undercut by "aiguë." The city-street setting, merely suggested in the three preceding pieces, is fully developed here with "toits," "volets," "étages," "rues," "pavés," "journaux," and "villes," finally culminating in a fusion of setting and theme with "crime reported in the papers."

The p-alliteration of the title, reverberating in the opening sentence where it is reinforced with "pourquoi" and "perd parmi," is so prominent throughout the piece to its very last sentence, that the haunting consonant is indicative, perhaps, of the gathering force of imminent disaster: crime and retribution. Robert Greer Cohn identifies "p" as a "male" consonant,[3] and the male and manlike stands in antithetical relationship to the notion of the child-like, thus creating a tension of Man and Child — guilt and innocence — which permeates the poem. "Pauvre" denotes the street singer's shabbiness and at the same time connotes the narrator's somewhat ambiguous attitude toward him: pity and sympathy on the one hand, and contempt on the other. "Pâle," recalling the complex of the faded and of decline developed in the preceding pieces, contrasts with childhood, rendering the "enfant" unchildlike, a paradox stressed by the repeated "petit homme." "Petit homme" evokes moreover the old paintings and sculptures of the "Madonna and the Christchild," with the "Infant Jesus" paradoxically appearing as a small full-grown man — Innocence and Wisdom — in the Virgin's arms. At the same time this image already vaguely foreshadows that of the Christ figure evoked later in the poem.

"Crier à tue-tête dans la rue ta chanson aiguë" onomatopoetically renders the shrillness of the child's singing and, at the same time, with the pun "à tue-tête" which is in harmony with the setting of "dans la rue" announces the decapitation theme. The song's "insolence" suggests both the contempt of the listener and the haughtiness of the singer; but his pride is undercut for his song "se perd parmi les chats," the only lords of this world. We are far from "le pur animal" of "Plainte d'Automne," and yet that closed world is present here by its very inaccessibility, both morally and also literally in space. There is a curious reversal in

---

[3] Cohn, *Toward the Poems*, p. 271.

"Pauvre Enfant Pâle" from both "Plainte d'Automne" and "Frisson d'Hiver," where we were on the inside with the persona — behind the windows — while now we are on the outside with the singer, looking up at those mysterious windows. The wretched song will never penetrate those shutters, whose very function is to shut out the city streets; and the poor child will never guess "de lourds rideaux de soie incarnadine" behind which we divine Venetian mirrors, and ancient clocks, and treasures, and dreams. A variant of this sentence reads: "derrière lesquels tu ne vois pas les lourds rideaux de soie rouge." The substitution of "ignores" removes the singer even farther from that closed world; in "les lourds rideaux de soie rouge" we recognize the "rideaux amortis" of "Frisson d'Hiver," "lourd" etymologically pointing to *luridus,* paled. This is reinforced by the substitution of "incarnadine," [4] a word so

---

[4] The unusual word, "incarnadine," which appears in no other prose poem, and whose closest relative in the *recueil* is the "incarnat" of "Plainte d'Automne," suggests the following association. As rare in English as in French, I know it only from one other usage, that in *Macbeth,* where it stresses the blood imagery so vividly figuring the "crime-punishment" theme throughout the play. Macbeth, right after the murder says:

> Whence is that knocking?
> How is't with me, when every noise appals me?
> What hands are here? Ha! they pluck out mine eyes.
> Will all great Neptune's ocean wash this blood
> Clean from my hands? No, this my hand will rather
> The multitudinous seas *incarnadine.*
> Making the green red.

Lady:
> My hands are of your color; but I shame
> To wear a heart so white.

Here the word is used as a verb in the sense of rendering something pink, or red. We don't know if Mallarmé had read *Macbeth* then, a play which he wrote about many years later, "La Fausse Entrée des sorcières dans Macbeth." But it is likely, for he had just spent some time in England, preparing himself for his profession of English professor. In this connection the "un crime n'est pas bien difficile à faire, va, il suffit d'avoir du courage après le désir," of our poem, is reminiscent of Lady Macbeth's:

> Art thou afeard
> To be the same in thine own act and valour
> As thou art in desire? Wouldst thou have that
> Which thou esteem'st the ornament of life,
> And live a coward in thine own esteem,
> Letting "I dare not" wait upon "I would,"
> Like the poor cat ith' adage?

much more luxurious than the original "rouge," yet meaning "faded red."

The beginning of the third paragraph, "Cependant tu chantes fatalement," whose first word underlines the unpoetic language of the piece, onomatopoetically renders the monotony of the song with the close repetition of the /ã/ sounds, while the sharp /s/ sounds of "assurance tenace" suggest the harshness of that unchild-like voice. He was "fated" to sing, which now answers the initial question, "pourquoi crier à tue-tête?"; moreover, "fatalement," reminiscent of the "fatidique" of the preceding poem, an evocation by association of the fates, again portends disaster.

Being neither child nor man, the singer is completely isolated not only from the world behind the windows but from that of the streets surrounding him, its children, "... sans baisser tes yeux méchants vers les autres enfants jouant sur le pavé," and its adults, "... qui s'en va seul par la vie." [5] He has not even the orphan's traditional "vieille" to beat him and make him forget his hunger. "La faim" sounds the first note of the hunger motif developed explicitly from here on, so that both orphanhood and hunger mingle in the gradual development of the Icarian theme of the poem and its principal symbol: the orphan-singer as a poet-figure. He sings unheard of for an uncomprehending audience, and no earthly food can allay his spiritual needs,[6] while his spiritual superiority makes him the child of no human parents. As an entertainer he reaches back to the Montreur of the first poem of the cycle.

The third paragraph, echoing the above "travaille pour soi" with a slight variation reveals a kind of *Leitmotif*: "seul," "pour soi," "pour toi," while "travailler" suggests a certain progression towards social acceptability from the initial "crier," to "chanter," and finally to the then repeated "travailler." Moreover the singer's posture, "debout" reinforced with "grand" and "sans abaisser," creates an ascending movement, so that he appears — "debout

---

[5] This isolation of a stranger among mankind recalls the Baudelaire prose poem, "L'Etranger," *Poèmes en Prose,* pp. 11-12.

[6] In a letter of the same year as the composition of our poem, Mallarmé writes to Cazalis, Mondor, *Correspondance* I, p. 118:

> Après tout, tu sais que la seule occupation d'un homme qui se respecte est à mes yeux de regarder l'azur en mourant de faim.

dans les rues" — as a single vertical line rising perpendicularly from the horizontal plane of the city streets and its humanity.

The singer's ambiguous nature is accentuated by his attire: faded clothes, cut like those of a man, that is not really man's clothing, but also not a child's. In the same sentence, "maigreur prématurée" echoes the hunger motif, while "trop grand à ton âge" again stresses the man-child tension and at the same time indicates the ascending movement, with a hint of its danger. "Tu chantes pour manger" again emphasizes hunger, and "avec acharnement," by its etymological associations, suggests a very physical desire while on the narrative level referring to the street-singer's toughness and also desperation. His eyes are not those of a child, but evil ones, and while those "yeux méchants" on the literal level describe the mean look of the young tough, they suggest that he has seen what others have not seen, that his eyes are no longer innocent, but guilty. Evil came into the world through the eating of forbidden fruit, and evil eyes have seen forbidden sights.

Now, almost half-way through the poem, with the anecdotical background established, the theme, only suggested and foreshadowed so far, is set forth: elevation, rupture and decapitation. As the "chanson" changes to "complainte" — a lament about some tragic event or legend — there is a vague intimation of a mythical past. "Si haute, si haute," on the literal level referring to the loud and shrill voice, recovers the upward movement suggested from the outset, the song rising up to the roofs, unable to penetrate the shutters above the street, with the child's posture, "debout," graphically delineating this upward direction, and "trop grand" suggesting its precariousness. "Monter" conveys not only ascension but also excess. And in this upward movement, voice and head seem to become one, for as the voice rises, the head goes up, up, straining to an almost unbearable tension, as the ascent, "si haute, si haute ... se lève ... monte," mounts to a peak, a culmination point, and then breaks, with the rupture suggested by "partir." This recalls the mounting tension and final tearing of the lyre's string of "Le Démon de l'Analogie," the rising of a song, and its death, symbolized by the broken instrument — or singer. In one cut the voice is shattered and the head severed — from the body, for which "tes petites épaules" is a synecdoche, perhaps suggestive of wings. The image of the head leaving the shoulders is a transposition, on the symbolic level, of mind leaving body, or spirit divorcing itself from matter; and the separation of spirit from matter implies for Mallarmé the basic struggle of "pensée" against "hasard."

The ultimate ascent of the voice, of song, isolates it completely from the world, and even from the singer, whose fulfillment is the very moment of his own death. This simultaneous disintegration of singer and song at the supreme moment is strikingly rendered in a late verse poem, "Petit Air II":

> Indomptablement a dû
> Comme mon espoir s'y lance
> Eclater là-haut perdu
> Avec furie et silence
>
> Voix étrangère au bosquet
> Ou par nul écho suivie,
> L'oiseau qu'on n'ouït jamais
> Une autre fois en la vie.
>
> Le hagard musicien,
> Cela dans le doute expire
> Si de mon sein pas du sien
> A jailli le sanglot pire
>
> Déchiré va-t-il entier
> Rester sur quelque sentier! (OC p. 66).

Here the traditional swan symbol, "l'oiseau qu'on n'on n'ouït jamais/Une autre fois en la vie," has been transformed into an entirely original image: "le hagard musicien," reminiscent of our street singer, gaunt and emaciated, with his head, "ta tête nue," already bared for the beheading. But the elevation-disintegration complex central to our prose poem — with its attendant notion of hubris-nemesis, associated from time immemorial with the poet singer — is not only reflected in Mallarmé's late verse, but also elsewhere in his prose, as for example in "La Musique et les Lettres":

> Mais, je vénère comment, par une supercherie, on projette, à quelque élévation défendue et de foudre! le conscient manque chez nous de ce qui là-haut éclate (OC p. 647).

The singer's rising voice becomes a constant symbol with Mallarmé for the transcendental nature of poetry. In "De Même," where he discusses the religious, transcendental, function of poetry, he says: "... car voici le miracle de chanter, on se projette haut comme va le cri" (OC p. 396).

The structure of this prose poem is that of a parabola: there is a mounting accumulation of imagery and, at the same time, the rising of the ascent, both culminating in the fourth paragraph of the eight, where the symbolic meaning explodes and bursts out of the imagery. In the four remaining sections, there is a falling off: the nature of the poem changes owing to a shift in point of view, from relatively detached description to a guilty and socially-conscious intervention by the narrative voice. And the prosaicness of this voice's commentary constitutes a deliberate deflation and trivialization of the lyrical élan, designed to follow the downturn of the parabola. Moreover, the second half of the piece consists of a mere elaboration of all the ingredients now posed: the anecdote and the ideas it symbolizes.

The fifth section conjectures on the omens, predicting the street singer's probable bad ending: his eventual infraction of the laws of a society from which he is an outcast. The theme of the pariah — who emerges as a poet figure — victimized and finally immolated by society, links this piece to a very early verse poem, "Aumône," whose several revisions reveal a gradual *rapprochement* of outcast and poet. The first version, "Haine du Pauvre," expresses unambiguous contempt for the beggar: "Tu comprends que le pauvre est le frère du chien;" in the version entitled "A un Mendiant" the tone becomes more sympathetic, and in "A un Pauvre," the change of the title itself is indicative. Finally, in "Aumône," the most revealing modification is the introduction of a "nous," spelling out the essential identity of poet and beggar. The final line is likewise changed from "Et surtout, ne va pas, drôle, acheter du pain!" to "Et surtout, ne va pas, *frère,* acheter du pain" [my italics]. In "Pauvre Enfant Pâle," "Un crime n'est pas bien difficile à faire" also suggests the narrator's empathy with the future criminal, and the second revision of this sentence reflected this orientation even more strongly: "... il suffit d'avoir du courage après le désir, et *nous* qui désirons" [my italics]. The final alteration might mean that Mallarmé found the penultimate version too direct and obvious, for the whole paragraph, even if ironic in tone, suggests — perhaps by that very irony — an involvement on the part of the narrator with the singer's fate.[7]

Another early verse poem, "Le Guignon" of 1862, explicitly links poet and beggar. Here the poets — pariahs like those in the Baudelairean models of the poem — are depicted as beggars of superhuman proportions, literally towering over the rest of humanity:

> Au-dessus du bétail ahuri des humains
> Bondissaient en clartés les sauvages crinières
> Des mendieurs d'azur dans nos chemins.

Like the street singer, they are starving on their quest:

> Ils voyageaient sans pain, sans bâtons et sans urnes
> Mordant au citron d'or de l'idéal amer.

They, too, are doomed to perish:

> La plupart râla dans les défilés nocturnes,
> . . . .
> Dérisoires martyrs de hasards tortueux (OC p. 28).

And there is even a veiled comparison of these outcasts with Christ: "Quand en face tous leur ont craché les dédains," rendering their death, again figured in a separation of head from body, a hanging, a sacrificial one. And the tragic finale is in this verse poem also undercut by a tone of irony, though very bitter, as well as by the low modern city setting: "Vont ridiculement se pendre au réverbère."

This city setting is in the following section of our poem seen from above, from those windows from which not a penny falls down into the wicker basket held in a hand "sans espoir." The hand seems already that of a corpse, foreboding the execution which is further suggested by the wicker basket evocative of those

---

[7] For a very similar identification of poet and street singer, see "La Muse Vénale," Baudelaire, *Fleurs,* p. 17.

in which guillotined heads were often caught. Moreover, "main pendue" as a synecdoche for "corps pendu" intimates that the hand, the instrument of our acts, is being punished. This scene recalls the final image of "Plainte d'Automne" with the barrel organ man playing under the windows, viewed — or rather heard — from above. But whereas his song "mit la gaité au cœur des faubourgs," our singer and his song go unheard in a city which refuses him its alms. And the victim's revenge is prophesied in the section's last word, "crime," here repeated for the second time.

The following paragraph again picks up the ascending movement of the fourth, head and voice again in unison, the former rising still while the voice is becoming more menacing. But now the ominousness of this singing is no longer merely apparent to the narrator, but to the head itself, which — "comme si d'avance elle savait"— seems to divine its fate. At the same time, the singer appears to become voice and head, for in this separation of head and body, it is in the former that consciousness and forebodings of misfortune reside. ". . . tu chantes d'un air," referring on the literal level to the way in which the boy sings, by association evokes melody, "tu chantes un air," and at the same time recalls the movement of head and voice high up into the *air,* that high point of the parabola, the "se lève en l'air" of the fourth part. In the last paragraph, the head is for the third time referred to by the pronoun, and the "elle te" juxtaposition with which it opens accentuates the notion of severance, the beheading. It is not the singer, "tu," who will bid farewell to the head, but the inverse, again emphasizing the growing identification of the singer with the head, which reflects the movement toward his spiritualization.

"Tu paieras" reintroduces the hubris-nemesis, or crime-punishment, theme, while "pour moi, pour ceux qui valent moins que moi" points to the sacrificial nature of the immolated victim's death. It is at this point that the narrator for the first time refers directly to himself. He is almost one with the others, sharing in their guilt, though he is less guilty than they. Later on, in the projected future, narrator and *foule* seem again to fuse with "*nous* te verrons dans les journaux." His ambiguous position is not resolved — not part of the city, he is perhaps still in that closed world, protected by those "lourds rideaux de soie incarnadine."

"Tu vins probablement au monde vers cela" — a barely veiled allusion to the divine mission of Christ who came into the world to expiate its sins — not only again presages the calamity but introduces the notion of destiny and vocation already suggested by the "tu chantes *fatalement*" of the second section. The "vers" stresses the forward movement, *toward* fulfillment, and its urgency is emphasized again with "et tu jeûnes dès maintenant." A variant of the phrase read: "et c'est pour cela que tu chantes dès maintenant," and the change is significant in that it brings back the hunger motif, now elaborated into "fasting." "Tu jeûnes," on the literal level referring to the street singer's starving existence, suggests a sacrificial abstinence in preparation for the final ordeal. And so the singer's sainthood is now disclosed, but it is then immediately undercut with "nous te verrons dans les journaux," a shocking dissonance produced by the sudden colliding of the narrative and the symbolic levels of meaning. The last line is the final invocation of the litany, where the "pauvre enfant pâle" has become a "pauvre petite tête," and the singer's apotheosis accomplished.

We have remarked that one of the poem's earlier titles, "Fusain," indicates that "Pauvre Enfant Pâle" might constitute a preliminary expression of something yet to be developed, a kind of sketch for another poem. This other poem is the "Cantique de Saint Jean," the third part of *Hérodiade,* published posthumously. Its date of composition is unknown, but Mondor says: "On peut penser que ce poème ne date pas de la dernière partie de la vie de Mallarmé" (OC p. 1446). The "Cantique" is a hymn by the Saint at the very moment of his beheading; [8] and, the Feast of Saint John corresponding with the summer solstice, Mallarmé here parallels the sun's trajectory with that traced by the severed head of John. The moment implied in "solstice," when the sun seems to stand still on the supreme point of the parabola, corresponds to the supreme moment of the Saint's death and spiritualization, his sanctification:

---

[8] Cohn, *Toward the Poems,* pp. 81:

> The hymn is sung by the Saint. It tells us of his decapitation. Whether it is sung before (in anticipation), during, or after (by his spectre) is not quite clear. Mallarmé seems to have envisaged various positions in the verse-drama for the piece.

> Le soleil que sa halte
> Surnaturelle exalte
> Aussitôt redescend
>   Incandescent
>
> Je sens comme aux vertèbres
> S'éployer des ténèbres
> Toutes dans un frisson
>   A l'unisson
>
> Et ma tête surgie
> Solitaire vigie
> Dans les vols triomphaux
>   De cette faux
>
> Comme rupture franche
> Plutôt refoule ou tranche
> Les anciens désaccords
>   Avec le corps
>
> Qu'elle de jeûnes ivre
> S'opiniâtre à suivre
> En quelque bond hagard
>   Son pur regard
>
> Là-haut où la froidure
> Eternelle n'endure
> Que vous le surpassiez
>   Tous ô glaciers
>
> Mais selon un baptême
> Illuminée au même
> Principe qui m'élut
>   Penche un salut (OC p. 49).

The parallels between this magnificent poem and our prose poem are obvious, on both the narrative and symbolic levels of meaning. Both poems' heroes, after a preparatory fasting,[9] realize their fulfillment at the moment of death by decapitation,[10] symbolizing

---

[9] Richard, *L'Univers*, p. 141:
> L'importance du thème du festin amoureux, c'est qu'il s'oppose au thème d'un contre-festin, ou plutôt d'une abstention alimentaire d'intention *spirituelle*. Comme la jouissance charnelle se dit en un repas, l'ascétisme se signifie par un jeûne; ... La faim est donc un thème de dégagement spirituel.

[10] Mauron, *Psychoanalysis*, pp. 41-42, links Saint John's beheading — a castration symbol and John's punishment for having beheld the naked

the divorce of spirit from matter. This is man's highest realization: the projection of thought into matter, order onto and against chance; and that both Saint and Singer stand for the Poet — Man par excellence for Mallarmé — is evident. Saint John is punished for having beheld Pure Beauty, Hérodiade; and in the prose poem we have pointed to the associations suggested by the singer's "yeux méchants." Just as the prose poem's structure delineates the shape of a parabola, the first stanza of the "Cantique" traces the form of the trajectory of the severed head, symbol of spirituality, on its ascent toward its "halte/Surnaturelle," though it is condemned to fall back to earth.

The solstice, like the poet's supreme moment of vision, is extratemporal, for when the sun reaches its highest point and "stands still," time stops. And the singer's threatened disintegration — as his song rises to higher and higher notes and, reaching a point beyond which it can no longer be heard, thus dies — is analogous with the ecstasy of vision where the limits of time and space are overcome and "pensée " is on the brink of the absolute, which is simultaneously the point of the mind's annihilation. Decapitation figures this danger — to lose one's mind, to become demented — of poetic vision, which threatened not only the young Mallarmé but other Symbolist poets, like Baudelaire, Nerval, Rimbaud and Lautréamont. This threat is many years later suggested in "Prose pour des Esseintes":

> Oh sache l'Esprit de litige
> A cette heure où nous nous taisons,
> Que de lis multiples la tige
> Grandissait trop pour nos raisons (OC p. 56).

Hérodiade — to that of "Pauvre Enfant Pâle," a punishment somehow linked with Maria (according to Mauron an early Hérodiade celebrated in "Plainte d'Automne"), likewise a castration symbol. The "leap" here lies in the fact that whereas the "Cantique" is the third part of *Hérodiade,* the two figures, Hérodiade and Saint John thus being thematically linked, no such link exists between the Maria of "Plainte d'Automne" and the hero of "Pauvre Enfant Pâle." Certainly, all poetry reflects the poet's psyche, but to connect the street singer's punishment, a transposition according to Mauron of the poet's guilt feelings, with Maria of the second prose poem seems farfetched; moreover, beheading as a castration symbol is fully acceptable, in both verse and prose poems, merely as an archetypal symbol.

Here the "grandissait trop pour nos raisons" echoes the "trop grand à ton âge" of our prose poem and the very first word of "Prose," "Hyperbole!," points to the hubris of the singer-poet and its danger.[11]

The threat of annihilation of the poet's mind links this prose poem, too, to *Igitur,* whose hero does, in fact, cross over into absolute thought, that Hegelian Absolute Notion which swallows up individual consciousness:

> Je n'aime pas ce bruit; cette perfection de ma certitude me gêne; tout est trop clair, la clarté montre le désir d'une évasion; tout est trop luisant, j'aimerais rentrer en mon Ombre incréée et antérieure, et dépouiller par la pensée le travestissement que m'a imposé la nécessité, d'habiter le cœur de cette race (que j'entends battre ici) seul reste d'ambiguïté.
> ...
> ... un personnage dont *la pensée* n'a pas conscience de lui-même, de ma dernière figure, *séparée de son personnage par une fraise arachnéenne* et qui ne se connaît pas ... (OC pp. 438 & 439) [my italics].[12]

The severing of individual consciousness and Absolute Thought is here also imaged by decapitation, and Igitur's "fraise arachnéenne" is intended to evoke Hamlet —[13] his twin brother in the Mallarméan mythology — as did already the "As-tu jamais eu un père?" of the prose poem.

---

[11] Cf. Cohn, *Toward the Poems,* p. 240:

> *Prose* later recounts to a sympathetic listener the story of how Mallarmé *really* attained a perfect vision and how his wiser, more patient self abandoned the attempt to capture that perfection which also threatened madness or the *néant.*

[12] For a lucid commentary of this passage of *Igitur,* see Gardner Davies, *Vers une explication rationnelle du Coup de Dés* (Paris: Corti, 1953), pp. 60-61.

[13] Cf. Richard, *L'Univers,* p. 227:

> Car Jean se possède idéalement lui-même dans la seconde exacte où la nuit annule en lui toute pensée, et grâce à cette annulation. L'acte qui supprime sa conscience est aussi celui qui allume en lui la plus haute et plus consciente lumière dont l'esprit humain soit sans doute capable ... Comme Saint Jean, le héros d'*Igitur* aura sa tête décollée, "séparée de son personnage par une fraise arachnéenne," mais cette fraise l'apparente aussi à la figure de Hamlet.

Our street singer, neither man nor child, like Hamlet "qui se débat sous le mal d'apparaître," (OC p. 299) is all becoming and still hesitating to be himself, to realize his essence; and it is in this that he reflects the growing pains of the young poet. Again, as in the preceding prose poem, becoming is a dying, and the death imagery of both pieces reflects the "coming into being" of the poet, threatened everywhere by a terrible birth into an existence of isolation from his fellowman, an existence which will find its ultimate fulfillment in death: "Tel qu'en lui-même enfin l'éternité le change."

The pale orphan is an outcast of society, like the poet,[14] be it Poe or Baudelaire, these two masters of the young Mallarmé who will many years later say:

> Pour moi, le cas d'un poëte, en cette société qui ne lui permet pas de vivre, c'est le cas d'un homme qui s'isole pour sculpter son propre tombeau (Oc p. 869).

Thus, the fifth poem of the cycle is again about the young poet; it is one of the last Baudelairean pieces, and as such masterfully demonstrates what Baudelaire expected of "modern" poetry:

> Qu'est-ce que l'art pur suivant la conception moderne? C'est créer une magie suggestive contenant à la fois l'objet et le sujet, le monde extérieur à l'artiste et l'artiste lui-même.[15]

"Pauvre Enfant Pâle" is also with "Le Phénomène Futur" one of the early examples of that poetry of suggestion in which the

---

[14] This strong consciousness of isolation from society on the part of the young poets who were Mallarmé's friends in those years is reflected in a letter of Villiers de l'Isle-Adam, written to Mallarmé in 1867, quoted in F. Jean-Aubry, *Une Amitié exemplaire: Villiers de l'Isle-Adam et Stéphane Mallarmé* (Paris: Mercure de France, 1942), p. 42:

> Chère âme tendre et charmante que vous êtes, mon cher Mallarmé, vous voilà malade! C'est juste, que faire ici, et quel serait notre prétexte de rester si nous n'étions pas percés, traqués volés, vilipendés, et saignants? ... Allons! mourons le plus tôt possible: c'est que nous avons de mieux à faire. ... Cependant ne mettons mon conseil à l'exécution que lorsqu'il n'y aura plus un seul, un seul capable d'échanger une idée avec nous.

[15] Baudelaire, *Poèmes en prose*, p. xxxvi.

symbolic meaning and the profounder theme remain hidden behind the literal story. For the theme of the poet singer, the Prometheus, Saint and Christ-like redeemer of mankind, is never stated but suggested throughout, in a poem whose vocabulary never rises above the "low-life" literal level.

LA PIPE

"La Pipe" is the last early prose poem of the collection and as such marks the end of a cycle within the *recueil,* that of the poems dealing with the emergence of the poet. He is now in possession of the traditional forms of his art and, with his master, can say: "Je sais l'art d'évoquer les minutes heureuses." [1] The piece — an evocation of the past where the *quotidien* becomes the marvelous — tells about the narrator's memories of a London winter which suddenly come back to him as he is about to settle down to work. And with that London winter return memories of Marie, the beloved, whom the little steamer carried back and forth across the Channel during that stormy season of their young romance.

"La Pipe," only known title, serves ostensibly as a mere pretext for the piece; on the narrative level, it is but the instrument which, like Proust's famous *madeleine,* releases the mechanism of involuntary memory to disclose a hidden mystery. However, whereas the *madeleine,* once "used" in this capacity, is then abandoned, the pipe is not. The persona prefers it to the frivolous cigarettes, and personifies it — "ma pipe... ma grave pipe" — in such a way that "it" seems to become a "she," "la fidèle amie," "cette délaissée," already foreshadowing part of the poem's anecdote. The pipe is thus the narrator's companion, and he reveals himself as a writer, a poet-persona. And so there is here perhaps a vague suggestion also of that other meaning of the word "pipe," that of a

---

[1] Mallarmé himself quotes these lines of Baudelaire's "Le Balcon" in a letter of 1862, written from London, Mondor, *Correspondance* I, p. 47:

Quel temps! Voici l'automne et l'hiver dans une même journée. L'automne. Ce matin des brouillards londoniens. ... "Je sais l'art d'évoquer les minutes heureuses."

musical instrument, and particularly the reeds of Pan by means of which the poet — like the Faun — evokes and perpetuates experience and dreams.

The first word, "hier," removes us into an immediate past serving as the stage for that more distant one — in both time and space — invited by the first two verbs of the poem: to find and to dream. In dreaming of "une longue soirée de travail," the poet-persona establishes a mood propitious for poetic creation, and finding his pipe — instrument of his inspiration — he will find the poem. The season particularly congenial to creative work is winter, and in this predilection the persona reflects the poet himself, for Mallarmé's references to winter as the season of art are numerous. In these early prose poems, "Frisson d'Hiver" showed how winter is the season of the poet's dreams. In a verse poem of the same year as these early prose pieces, "Renouveau," the persona condemns spring for having chased away winter, the poet's season:

> Le printemps maladif a chassé tristement
> L'hiver, saison de l'art serein, l'hiver lucide (Oc p. 34).

Many years later, in "Crayonné au Théâtre," Mallarmé says: "L'hiver est à la prose" (OC p. 340), and much later still, in one of the "réponses à des enquêtes," entitled "Sur le Printemps," we find :"... et l'hiver resterait la saison intellectuelle créatrice" (OC p. 882). Finally, the persona is not merely musing about winter work, but the very subject of the poem which he will write is a winter come back to him.

Though he now tosses his cigarettes, of unbecoming levity for a creative season, into the past of a summer, the summer itself is not discarded quite so lightly as the cigarettes and "les joies enfantines." For while barely touching it, the poet-persona, as though in spite of himself, ignites that summer, rendering it luminous with but a few impressionistic strokes of his pen. Illuminated by leaves "bleues de soleil" and white muslin evocative of billowy summer dresses worn by ladies in a garden setting, this summer resplendent with light calls to mind Claude Monet's many summer scenes. And as a favorite one, "Dans un Jardin," rises before the mind, we see there the flowing white muslin of the dresses and the sunlight quivering on the blue-green leaves: it is just this magic which the poet recaptures, before he can put away last summer.

After this brief, vivid illumination, the tone becomes almost humorous as the "grave pipe" is taken up by "un homme sérieux qui veut fumer longtemps sans se déranger, afin de mieux travailler." This "homme sérieux" is again the young poet viewing himself and who, still somewhat doubtful about his creative capacities, thus undercuts his self-portrait with irony. We recognize, moreover, the narrator of "Plainte d'Automne," who did not throw a penny to the barrel organ man in the street, "de peur de (se) déranger." The poet is once more listening intently to an inner voice and protecting it jealously from the slightest disturbance from without which might break its melody. [2]

But "fumer longtemps ... afin de mieux travailler" also links this prose poem to a sort of poetic tradition in the nineteenth century, which saw in tobacco, and especially the pipe, an inspirational instrument for the poet, and an opiate for life's ills for the unfortunate. This is largely due to the fact that many of the poets smoked opium and hashish, some to heighten their perceptual powers and thus create "paradis artificiels," others for the sake of "le dérèglement de tous les sens." Moreover the word "inspiration" itself etymologically points to the very act of smoking, and Mallarmé, so conscious of the etymological weight of words, many years later also played on this *âme*-breath-inspiration association in the verse poem "Toute l'âme résumée / Quand lente nous l'expirons" (OC p. 73). Not only is there a poem in "Les Fleurs du Mal" entitled "La Pipe," where Baudelaire in a whimsical mood makes the pipe the poem's narrator: "Je suis la pipe d'un auteur;" [3] but there is also a prose poem, much more serious in tone, by Alphonse Rabbe, named "La Pipe," in which that precursor of both Bertrand and Baudelaire celebrates in his pipe a narcotic which helps the

---

[2] Cf. *ibid.*, p. 181, letter to Aubanel of 1865:

> Je ne t'écris pas aujourd'hui, parce que toute distraction, même la plus charmante, m'est odieuse, et j'ai besoin de la plus silencieuse solitude de l'âme, et d'un *oubli* inconnu, pour entendre chanter en moi certaines notes mystérieuses.

[3] Baudelaire, *Fleurs,* pp. 73-74.

poet in transmuting "les chagrins du présent en passagères délices." [4]

For our poet-persona the pipe suddenly becomes the source of unexpected emotion and wonder, for the first inhalation of its smoke releases a train of associations which, taking the smoker completely by surprise, creates a privileged moment — where past becomes present and the remote the immediate — of which the poem is the objectification. The narrator, like Proust's at the instant of that particular physical stimulus, namely the sensation which recalls an identical one experienced in the past, is inexplicably entranced, and his good intentions — again ironically treated as "mes grands livres à faire" — sink into oblivion. Yet the tone is not at all bitter but gentle, creating a dramatic but very untragic irony, as we see those "big books to write" turn into this modest one-paragraph prose poem.

But as by-gone experience thus comes back magically, this London winter is not recreated but created now for this first time with the poem. Both time, "l'hiver dernier," and space, "tout

---

[4] Pierre Moreau in *La Tradition française du poème en prose avant Baudelaire* (Paris: Lettres Modernes, 1959), p. 29, quotes Rabbe's "La Pipe":

> Que cherchè-je moi-même au fond de ton petit fourneau, o ma pipe? Je cherche comme un alchimiste à transmuer les chagrins du présent en passagères délices. Je pompe ta vapeur à coups pressés, pour porter dans mon cerveau une heureuse confusion, un rapide délire préférable à la froide réflexion. Je cherche le doux oubli de ce qui est, le rêve de ce qui n'est pas et même de ce qui ne peut pas être.
>
> Tu me fais payer cher tes consolations faciles; le cerveau s'use et s'alanguit peut-être par le retour journalier de ces mouvements désordonnés. La pensée devient paresseuse et l'imagination se fait vagabonde, par l'habitude d'ébaucher en vacillant d'agréables fictions.
>
> Je périrai bientôt: tout ce qui compose mon être et le nom même dont on me nomme disparaîtra comme cette légère fumée ... Dans quelques jours, peut-être, à la place même où j'écris, on ne saura pas même si j'ai vécu ... Mais de ce corps si périssable s'exhalera-t-il quelque chose qui ne périsse pas et s'élève en haut? Réside-t-il en effet dans chaque homme une étincelle digne d'allumer le calumet des anges sur le parvis des cieux?
>
> O ma pipe! chasse, bannis ce désir ambitieux et funeste de l'inconnu, de l'impénétrable.

Clearly, this prose poem is much more in the tone of Baudelaire than of Mallarmé, and I do not know if Mallarmé even knew it; but in the genre of the prose poem, Rabbe is a precursor of Bertrand, in whom Mallarmé was interested in those years.

Londres," surge to the surface out of the poet's essence — a past which he has lived not only by, but within, himself: "tel que je le vécus en entier à moi seul."

From this point on, the piece abounds in vocabulary which is, especially for Mallarmé, extremely sense-oriented. It is not merely a taste which sets off involuntary memory here, for the taste of tobacco smoke is at the same time its smell, its feeling as it is inhaled and exhaled, and finally its appearance as it rises from the pipe; the tobacco "sentait," that is tasted like, smelled of, or felt like "une chambre sombre:" a Baudelairean synesthesia. The fogs have an odor all their own; the leather furniture is sprinkled with coal dust; the cat is scrawny and black; the maid's arms are red; and the coals falling from the iron bucket into the sheet-metal basket make their own particular noise; lastly, the mailman is perceived by his double knock on the door. And as the shabby furnished room in a strange city thus materializes, one notes that all of the adjectives describe ugliness: a dark room, a woman's red arms, dusty furniture, and a mangy cat. This ugliness continues outside the room as well, for through the windows, which let in the fog, we see a "square désert" with its sick trees, recalling "les rues vides" outside the windows of "Frisson d'Hiver," and the wan trees of both "Le Phénomène Futur" and "Plainte d'Automne." But there is a curious contrast here between the ugly reality recalled and the golden glow with which the poet envelopes it in the poem. For though the room is shabby and dark, as it is evoked here it has a kind of happiness about it, with its "grands feux!" and the expectancy of a new day. The black coal dust covering the old furniture, far from conveying the notion of neglect or dissolution, even participates in the ambiance of comfort provided by the bright morning fires which the robust maid watches over, just as the cat, though lean, seems content in all its shabbiness, rolled up on a dusty chair.[5]

---

[5] This poem, as most of these early prose pieces, is highly biographical. That the reality out of which this poem grew was far from happy is evident from Mallarmé's correspondence of this London winter; for example, Mondor, *Correspondance* I, p. 77, letter to Cazalis of 1863:

> Je suis seul, tout seul avec un chat noir. Et cela est affreux. Je vis replié sur moi-même et, quand je veux oublier, j'ai des remords.

Although the mailman's arrival with letters from France "(le) faisait vivre," one detects not the slightest note of sadness here, and one feels that these letters are at least as great a cause of joy as would be the actual visits of those left behind — as though the very distance between himself and his friends added to the charm of those friendships. [6] The abandoned "square" outside, and the little "steamer," both of which words help create a foreign ambiance, impart no uneasy strangeness; nor does the open sea, a sea familiar because "si souvent traversé cet hiver-là." But most of all, the characteristic London fogs, the foremost aspect of that winter come back to the narrator's mind — "d'abord les chers brouillards" — had nothing threatening as they crept under the casements. On the contrary, they, "qui emmitouflent nos cervelles et ont, là-bas, une odeur à eux," cozily muffled and bundled his mind. And so the lonely, cold and foggy London winter, as it is here summoned forth, suggests a paradoxical warmth and wellbeing, with the poet sheltered and protected both by the fires inside and the beloved fogs outside, and at the same time by his distance from the world left behind.

This notion of distance — one facet of the theme of the poet-persona's isolation running through all these prose poems — reflects Mallarmé's own strong sense of seperateness, which explains in part his repeatedly expressed love for those London fogs celebrated in this piece. [7] In a letter of that same London winter he says:

> Revoici le brouillard, sans lui j'aurais encore paressé aujourd'hui. Mais il est si beau, si gris, si jaune que je viens de rentrer avec Marie, jurant que jamais plus nous n'affronterions, par une brume pareille, la solitude de Hyde-Park. [8]

The last sentence refers to Marie Gerhard's frequent unhappy visits there. She will become "ma pauvre bien-aimée errante" of our poem.

[6] Cf. *ibid.*, p. 294, letter of 1869, to his best friend, Cazalis:

> ... c'est vraiment quand mes amis sont partis que je commence à être avec eux, avec leur souvenir voisin de mon Rêve, et que dérange un peu parfois leur apparition véritable — les tiennes surtout, inattendues et brèves.

[7] Cf. *Œuvres*, p. 636 and 825.
[8] Mondor, *Correspondance* I, p. 59.

Here the "brouillard" is linked to the park's "solitude," and though the beloved is at the poet's side now, one feels that he would have enjoyed the walk through the solitary park at least as much without her. Do not these fogs, in insinuating themselves between him and the world around him, isolate him even more by enclosing him in a haze, similar to that cloud of tobacco smoke which would surround him, many years later, when talking to his disciples on those famous mardis? [9] Finally, the celebration of the fogs which, like tobacco smoke, put a distance between himself and the world, perhaps already presages a style — yet to be born — which will isolate not only the poet, but the poetry itself, from most of mankind. The magic atmosphere, moreover, while thus enclosing the poet, at the same time envelops the big city surrounding him, hiding its ugliness and blurring its sharp outlines under a mysterious veil, [10] whose fine translucent globules refract the sun's cruel light into a softly luminous haze — like the resplendent ambiance of the Impressionists, which the poet allusively evoked in the poem's opening lines. [11]

Now that the narrator has left the room and the square for the open sea, yet another image unfolds before the inner eye, "j'ai revu... j'ai vu." Once again shivering on the steamer's bridge, "mouillé de bruine et noirci de fumée," the persona beholds the misery surrounding him without partaking in it, for he appears enveloped still by the warmth and glowing ambiance created in the poem. It is only at this point that the companion of that Lon-

---

[9] The many references to these fascinating evenings at the rue de Rome are too numerous to mention all; most of them tell of the china bowl of tobacco for host and guests, and the cigarette or pipe in the master's hand, smoke filling the modest room as incense a chapel. Cf. Arthur Symons, *The Symbolist Movement in Literature* (New York: Dutton, 1958), p. 64.

Mondor in *Vie de Mallarmé* (Paris: Gallimard, 1941), pp. 794-95, emphasizes the feeling of distance emanating from Mallarmé:

> Cet homme paraissait immensément éloigné, isolé de tout contact par le magnétisme d'un génie secret, par l'insaisissable réticence qui penchait sa tête en arrière.

[10] Mondor, *Correspondance* I, p. 92, letter to Cazalis of 1863:

> Je hais Londres quand il n'y a pas de brouillards; dans ses brumes c'est une ville incomparable.

[11] For discussions of Mallarmé's predilection for English fogs, cf. Richard, *L'Univers*, p. 496; and Poulet, *Distance*, pp. 311-12.

don winter is introduced; her presence not even suggested until now, she appears here suddenly as almost an attribute of the poet, "ma pauvre bien-aimée errante." And though the remainder of the one-paragraph poem is devoted to her, its unity is in no way broken, for the beloved's presence is as unobtrusive here as it was in "Frisson d'Hiver." Moreover, the detailed description of phenomena characterizing the piece is continued with that of her poor, worn traveling costume. The poet seems to love her because of those faded garments, the outer manifestation of her essence, for in her "longue robe terne couleur de la poussière des routes," she appears the very incarnation of "la grâce des choses fanées"; at the same time this "bien-aimée errante" brings with her the mystery of the far-away, reminiscent of the china clock "venue de Saxe par les longues diligences d'autrefois," and the outdated German almanac, both loved for their fragile, time-worn charm. And as we recognize the "sœur au regard de jadis" of that other winter poem, the "calme enfant" — as silent here as she was there — with her poverty as lovingly depicted as that of the shabby London room, her distress seems not shared by the poet-persona who fondly beholds, but never holds, her. [12]

Only once does the young poet-persona in the description of the beloved mention part of her body, "ses épaules froides" shivering under the damp coat. And this cold body is again vaguely reminiscent of Maria, silent and cold in her coffin, which is probably the secret of the poet's love for that woman who never quite seems to come alive, in love or even in motherhood. For is she not the same who will become the innocent, maidenly mother of "Don du Poëme," written one year after our prose poem?

> O la berceuse, avec ta fille et l'innocence
> De vos pieds froids accueille une horrible naissance:
> Et ta voix rappelant viole et clavecin,
> Avec le doigt fané presseras-tu le sein
> Par qui coule en blancheur sibylline la femme
> Pour les lèvres que l'air du vierge azur affame? (OC p. 40).

---

[12] That some of Marie Gerhard's charm for the young Mallarmé was her very poverty and the sadness inherent in her humble condition is revealed by the correspondence. Cf. Mondor, *Correspondance* I, p. 45.

And as this is the last prose poem celebrating the young poet's love for the virginal woman who with every silent appearance seems to resurrect the companion of his childhood — thus bridging at once the distance to the past and to the beyond — it is also the last piece to sing "la grâce des choses fanées;" and the poem's final words, "adieu pour toujours," aside from their literal meaning on the narrative level, certainly suggest this. A markedly different ideal of beauty will be celebrated in the mature prose poems, where the woman sung will have the vibrant splendor of "Le Phénomène Futur," as dazzling as the poetry dreamed of, and her attire will be of the greatest elegance. [13]

Having depicted the beloved's dress, the persona now gives so minute a description of her hat that, again, it must be the visible sign of her hidden nature. It is "sans plume et presque sans rubans," wilted from the sea air, the very sea air which the poet loves and will celebrate a year later in "Brise Marine," where it summons him on his solitary venture — already foreshadowing "Un Coup de Dés" — a venture for which he must forsake everyone: woman and child, and even his masters. Similarly, this prose poem is doubly a farewell: it is not only the last in the *recueil* reflecting the persona's nostalgia for the innocence of childhood — embodied in the two chaste Maries — but it is at the same time the last where the Baudelairean influence is apparent. Finally, "La Pipe" is the last prose poem written in the language inherited from tradition.

The last sentence with the "terrible mouchoir qu'on agite en se disant adieu pour toujours" — echoed later in the "adieu suprême des mouchoirs" of "Brise Marine" — would end our poem on a hopelessly sentimental note were it not for the use of the impersonal pronoun and the present tense and present participle of the verbs in the relative clause. These devices convert a personal

---

[13] Mallarmé's interest in feminine elegance, which is reflected in the second part of the prose-poem cycle, is also evident from his short-lived but incomparable ladies journal, LA DERNIÈRE MODE. Moreover, one cannot help recalling the contrast between the poet's humble wife and the dazzling beauty and elegance of Méry Laurent, who entered the life of the poet's later years and directly influenced one of the later prose poems.

experience into a general one, [14] known to all lovers, and contribute to establishing that aesthetic distance which we have felt to permeate the poem. Though the letters Mallarmé wrote at almost the same time about the underlying experience are most emotional, [15] the poem is not, for while *Erlebnisdichtung,* it is not the expression of emotions, but their transposition into poetry.

For these reasons, in concluding a reading of the early prose poems comprising the first half of the *recueil,* I cannot agree with those critics [16] who, in their admiration for Mallarmé's mature

---

[14] A brilliant modern critic, Serge Doubrovsky, *Pourquoi la nouvelle critique* (Paris: Mercure de France, 1966), p. 206, sees in this universalizing the essence of literature:

> ... les textes-moyens ne font que nous parler d'*un* homme; les textes-fins, à travers un homme, nous parlent de *l'*homme. Ce passage de l'article indéfini à l'article défini, c'est, dira-t-on, peu de chose; mais c'est toute la littérature.

[15] In 1862, Mallarmé writes to Cazalis, Mondor, *Correspondance* I, p. 41:

> De toutes les amertumes humaines, celle qui naît du départ, cette mort momentanée, est la plus affreuse.

ibid., p. 70, again to Cazalis:

> Mon frère, je voulais t'écrire sur le bateau, mais je pleurais. Hier, non plus, je ne le pouvais pas. Oh figure-toi, c'est affreux, quand on s'aime, de se quitter pour la vie. A une heure du matin, par une bruine sombre, je l'ai menée à la gare, et, quand la porte s'est ouverte, elle a glissé de mes bras à moitié morte.

ibid., p. 82, to the same:

> Nous étions convenus que nous aurions beaucoup de courage; et en effet, nous nous sommes longtemps embrassés et regardés sur le bateau sans pouvoir pleurer tellement nous étions fous de douleur. Longtemps, nous avons agité nos mouchoirs et, quand je n'ai plus vu le sien, j'ai sangloté à travers les rues.

[16] For example, Suzanne Bernard, *Le Poème en prose,* p. 258:

> ... alors que plus tard le moindre incident de la vie courante lui sera un prétexte pour remonter, par le miracle d'un style savant condensé et métaphorique, jusqu'à l'essence des choses, on trouve ici l'élément biographique utilisé de façon directe, presque naïve: on reconnaît sans peine la maison de Tournon et sa "pendule de Saxe, qui retarde et sonne treize heures parmi ses fleurs et ses dieux" dans *Causerie d'hiver*; Penton Square dans *L'Orgue de Barbarie*; et, dans *La Pipe,* la maison de Londres, les "arbres malades du square désert," et Marie Gerhard secouant, du steamer, "le terrible mouchoir qu'on agite en se disant adieu pour toujours." Il n'y a dans *La Pipe* aucun effort de "composition" artistique; le style est uni jusqu'au prosaïsme, la seule recherche étant celle d'un certain "réalisme" moderniste.

style, underestimate the power of this early poetry, although the poet himself selected it for inclusion in *Divagations* shortly before his death. The fact that one might easily recognize the experience underlying a poem makes it no less a poem, the whole question being what the artist makes of this experience. It is precisely in examining the correspondence which has revealed this experience that one learns to appreciate its transposition in even these early pieces. Finally, Mallarmé frequently insisted on the importance of the role of "souvenir" in poetic creation, as in the very first line of his "art poétique," the late "Prose pour des Esseintes":

> Hyperbole! de ma mémoire
> Triomphalement ne sais-tu
> Te lever, aujourd'hui grimoire
> Dans un livre de fer vêtu; (OC p. 55)

and the Faun says:

> O nymphes, regonflons des SOUVENIRS divers. (OC p. 51)

UN SPECTACLE INTERROMPU

The seventh piece of the "Anecdotes ou Poèmes" marks a significant moment in the cycle, for it belongs no longer to the early prose poems and not yet to the late ones. While the six preceding poems were all of 1864, and the six following ones of 1885 or after, "Un Spectacle Interrompu," published in 1875, occupies an intermediate position. It is safe to assume that it was written near its publication date, for stylistically it is as different from the early poems as it is from the late ones.

Almost all commentators on Mallarmé's poetry agree that a decisive stylistic change took place shortly after 1870;[1] and this change is as striking in his prose as it is in his verse. Mallarmé is beginning to form a new language of art, where he no longer distinguishes in the traditional way between a language of verse and one of prose, but between *écriture* and *parole:*

> L'écrit, envol tacite d'abstraction, reprend ses droits en face de la chute des sons nus; tous deux, Musique et lui, intimant une préalable disjonction, celle de la parole, certainement par effroi de fournir au bavardage (OC p. 385).

Ecriture constitutes for Mallarmé a closed system of artistic expression which would have to be mastered like the fundamentals of any other art — as those, for example, of music — for an intelligent appreciation. And this incipient metamorphosis of language into style — of contingency and *hasard* into necessity — is already presaged in the very youthful "Hérésies Artistiques: L'Art pour Tous" of 1862, in which the then twenty-year old poet says:

---

[1] Cf. Scherer, *L'Expression*, pp. 225-26.

> Toute chose sacrée et qui veut demeurer sacrée s'enveloppe de mystère. Les religions se retranchent à l'abri d'arcanes dévoilés au seul prédestiné: l'art a les siens.
> La musique nous offre un exemple. Ouvrons à la légère Mozart, Beethoven ou Wagner, jetons sur la première page de leur œuvre un œil indifférent, nous sommes pris d'un religieux étonnement à la vue de ces processions macabres de signes sévères, chastes, inconnus. Et nous refermons le missel vierge d'aucune pensée profanatrice.
> J'ai souvent demandé pourquoi ce caractère nécessaire a été refusé à un seul art, au plus grand. Celui-là est sans mystère contre les curiosités hypocrites, sans terreur contre les impiétés, ou sous le sourire et la grimace de l'ignorant et de l'ennemi.
> Je parle de la poésie (OC p. 257).

After 1870, both verse and prose reflect the increasingly complex system of analogies, the structural principle of this poetic universe, which in ordering simplifies the world:

> Tout l'acte disponible, à jamais et seulement, reste de saisir les rapports, entre temps, rares ou multipliés; d'après quelque état intérieur et que l'on veuille à son gré étendre, simplifier le monde (OC p. 647).

Paradoxically, this "simplifying," which makes a cosmos out of chaos by reducing the world to the word, results, in the prose work, in a most difficult syntax. The Mallarméan sentence, though always rigorously correct, will become as intricate as the analogies it expresses. Does the poet change his style, then, to better express his ideas? "L'Art pour Tous" — prophetic like "Le Phénomène Futur" — forebodes a new hermetic form years before Mallarmé encounters some of the ideas the new form is to convey; yet it is only after decisive ideological developments that the new style appears. Form and function, then, are inextricably linked: for the poet a new world vision is a new language; the latter cannot come into being without the former.

In the preceding chapters we saw that the crisis of Tournon, that spiritual descent and return transposed in *Igitur,* already overshadowed some of the early prose poems. *Igitur* was written in 1869 at Avignon, where the poet read it to his friends, Villiers de l'Isle-Adam and Catulle Mendès, who had eagerly looked forward to this reading. But these friends and fellow-poets did not understand it. [2] This is perhaps why the dramatic (and for the poet cathartic) *Igitur,* that key to the Mallarméan ideology, was never finished but has come down to us in the fragmentary form of 1869. Is this "failure" somehow connected with the drastic change in the poet's style so shortly after? [3] Shortly after, around 1870, decisive changes took place in Mallarmé's life, not the least significant of which was his long desired move to Paris. And as Mallarmé begins to realize himself, some of the fears and anguish reflected in several of the early prose poems make room for a tone of confidence, a new tone which permeates "Un Spectacle Interrompu."

That poem is not only written in the new style, but is, in fact, about the distinction between the language of art and that of communication, between writing and journalism, the poem's anecdote being the vehicle for its demonstration. [4] For in this piece the privileged vision of the artist is set apart from the common vision, and "mon regard de poëte" is contrasted with that of the "reporters," a contrast which Mallarmé elsewhere expresses by a striking analogy:

> Narrer, enseigner, même décrire, cela va et encore qu'à chacun suffirait peut-être pour échanger la pensée humaine, de prendre ou de mettre dans la main d'autrui en silence une piece de monnaie, l'employ élémentaire du discours dessert l'universel *reportage* dont, la littérature exceptée, participe tout entre les genres d'écrits contemporains (OC p. 368).

The poem is, moreover, the first longer piece of the *recueil,* and it no longer deals with the private world of the narrator. Its

---

[2] This disastrous reading of *Igitur* is related in Mondor, *Vie,* pp. 229-302.
[3] Cf. Paxton, *The Development,* p. 50.
[4] Mauclair, *Princes,* p. 112, recalls Mallarmé confiding to him:

> Que de fois, j'ai résolu de me mettre à écrire les livres que je portais dans mon cerveau, en me contentant d'une forme française habituelle, d'un à peu près éloquent et expressif, avec des rythmes et une syntaxe d'usage courant, en me jurant à moi-même de secouer le joug; et puis, au moment de commencer, je sentais que je ne pouvais pas, que l'on n'a pas le droit de mesuser ainsi de la langue écrite — et je recommençais à étudier ce qu'elle exige.

very title recalls "Le Phénomène Futur," but while in that poem the showman's tent was but vaguely evoked, here the theatrical event is, as the narrator terms it, "anecdotal," that is it has all the trappings of a particular factual occurrence. Further, whereas in "Le Phénomène Futur" the essence of the poetic vision seemed dressed up and placed into the fairground setting, in this poem the theatrical event appears to have given birth to the vision, and to the reflections aroused by it. The persona relates his attendance at a performance, and while describing the act, he gives us his own interpretation of the event, which to the rest of the audience is a mere animal act ending in a rather dangerous climax, as a bear comes too close to a human acrobat. The vocabulary of the piece is of the domain of the theatre; it is, moreover, one of contrasts — poet-reporter, ideal-factual, reality-dream, little theatre-"Prodigality," genius-beast, and heaviness-silvery nudity, darkness-brilliance — for contrast is inherent in the very essence of the theatre: the show of *appearance* which both reflects and corrects *reality*.

"Spectacle" leaves the exact nature of the performance vague, and on the narrative level Mallarmé never clarifies precisely whether we have to do with a puppet show, a marionette-play, a ballet, a circus act, or a simple pantomime; yet he evokes the atmosphere so vividly that one never doubts the factuality of the event. Etymologically "spectacle" points to its Roman origin and the games which included confrontations of man and animal in the arena; and an "animal act" is precisely that part of the show which constitutes our anecdote.

The first sentence, in evoking the classical exhortations over a dying civilization in the manner of the Ciceronian *O tempora! O mores!* or its bombastic Rousseauistic echoes, is a somewhat ironic derogatory commentary on modern civilization. This hortatory opening reintroduces the "tableau parisien" setting familiar from "Pauvre Enfant Pâle" and deplores the absence of poetry in an age of decline, reminiscent of the desolate atmosphere of "Le Phénomène Futur." One of the most powerful products of modern civilization, "le journal" in which *"reporters* par la foule dressés" report the commonplace, is contrasted with an imaginary journal of "rêveurs." "Rêve" [5] juxtaposed with "artifice que la réalité" results in a paradoxical inversion where "les mirages d'un fait," that is reality, become illusory, implying by contrast that dream is true. And whereas the reporters "divulge" for "l'intellect moyen," the poet-persona will write "en vue de moi seul." Both poet and reporters will treat the same "anecdote," but while the latter only see and write about the factual, the poet will transpose it into the ideal. In an article about a fellow poet, Banville, Mallarmé will later say:

> La divine transposition, pour l'accomplissement de quoi existe l'homme, va du fait à l'idéal (OC p. 522).

But does reality, by the very fact of "fixing" the average mind in a common way of viewing it, not rest on some universal understanding, an idea(l)? The poet proposes to discover, then, whether a chance event might not be tamed as it were, that is reduced to meaning and order. And so, while establishing the contrast between actualities expressed by every-day language and their ideal transposition into artistic language, [6] the persona in reporting an anecdote "sous le jour propre au rêve" gives us a sample of what the imaginary journal would contain. [7] Thus the early, still somewhat

---

[5] "Rêve" is one of the most frequent terms in Mallarmé's poetic dictionary, and it is so multivalent, that its meaning tends to vary according to its use. While it often is the first principle of poetry, and sometimes the process of poetic creation itself, it can at other times also be the enemy of poetry. Walter Naumann in *Der Sprachgebrauch Mallarmés* (Marburg: Hermann Bauer, 1936), pp. 196-98, furnishes an index for the usage of "rêve" in Mallarmé's poetry and prose, outlining the most frequent meanings the word carries. Nowhere, however, does Mallarmé refer to "rêve" in the sense of the Surrealists, and the exploitation of night dream for "écriture automatique."

[6] To the charge of obscurity in this artistic prose, Mallarmé answers, again contrasting his language with that of the newspapers, as follows:

> Je préfère, devant l'agression, retorquer que des contemporains ne savent pas lire—
> Sinon dans le journal; il dépense, certes, l'avantage de n'interrompre le chœur de préoccupations (OC p. 386).

[7] A sample of the imaginary journal itself is, of course, LA DERNIÈRE MODE, in which not only fashions, but theatrical and other "events" of interest to the readers, are "reported," but certainly "sous le jour propre au rêve," and at the same time in the new prose style. The fact that LA

Baudelairean, prose poem has evolved into a new form, namely this paradoxical *reportage* of the ideal in which the Mallarméan prose poem will fully come into its own, and where the chance events of every-day life will be transmuted by poetic vision — objectified in a new prose style.

The second paragraph presents the anecdote proper, the *exemplum,* while the last one, set off from the rest of the poem by double spacing, gives its moral. "Le petit théâtre des PRODIGALITÉS" has an air of factuality about it, probably because the poet is creating an anecdote for us;[8] for the ironic contrast of "little theatre" and its grandiose name suggests to me a Mallarméan invention, as might also be the show itself, the "féerie classique La Bête et le Génie," echoing the well-known folk tale "La Belle et la Bête."[9] In our act, "added to" the main attraction, the theme of beast and genius will be mimed by acrobat and bear, "Atta

---

DERNIÈRE MODE was so shortlived testifies to modern civilization's inability "de procurer les jouissances attribuables à cet état!"

[8] Bernard, *Le Poème en Prose,* p. 293:

> Lors d'un spectacle, un ours s'était soudain redressé contre le clown qui le faisait manœuvrer, et l'avait étreint dangereusement, jusqu'au moment où l'appât d'un quartier de viande lui avait fait lacher prise: telle est, en style de "reporter" cette "anecdote" que je n'ai trouvée rapportée nulle part dans les journaux de l'époque, pas plus que je n'ai trouvé la mention d'un théâtre des "Prodigalités."

And Charles Beaumont Wicks, *The Parisian Stage,* II, III, IV, 1815-1875 (Univ. of Alabama Press, University: 1961 and 1967), mentions neither "La Bête et le Génie," nor lists "Le Théâtre des Prodigalités" in the thorough index. The act itself, "added to the main attraction," would not be expected to appear. There is listed, however, in the index of Part III, 1831-1850, a "Théâtre Sans Prétention," a somewhat ironic counterpart to that of our poem. "La Belle et la Bête" is listed in the same volume as a "féerie-vaudeville," by Simonnin, and performed at the Théâtre de M. Compte, December 24, 1850.

[9] Juan Eduardo Ciriot, *A Dictionary of Symbols* (New York: Philosophical Library, 1962); Jean Chevalier, *Dictionnaire des Symboles* (Paris: Laffont, 1969); Gertrude Jobes, *Dictionary of Mythology and Folklore Symbols* (New York: Scarecrow Press, 1962); Stith-Thompson, *Motif-Index of Folk-literature* (Bloomington: Univ. of Indiana Press, 1958); Funk & Wagnalls, *Dictionary of Folklore, Mythology and Legend* (New York: Wilfred Funk, 1949); Bolte & Polivka, *Anmerkungen zu Grimms Kinder und Hausmärchen* (Hildesheim: G. Olms, 1963) fail to come up with a reference to "La Bête et le Génie."

Troll"[10] or "Martin," the proverbial "ours retenu et dressé dans les ménageries." "Féerie" leaves the type of performance as vague as did the "spectacle" of the title; but "féerie" with "génie" echoing the Arabic "jinniy" suggests vaguely the "conte oriental," the ambiance of the Arabian Nights, also evoked with the stage settings. Most of the imagery describing the act itself seems, as in a dream, to shift somewhat. At times it suggests a marionette theatre, but that could not accommodate "le vivant cousin d'Atta Troll ou de Martin," who nevertheless later will be "ému au leger vent," rather strange for a heavy bear. Clearly, this is not the copying of reality, but an impressionistic painting of a scene whose vagueness in no way reduces its vividness.

The persona's isolation from the other spectators, la foule, is evident in "la stalle vacante à mes côtés"; and "une absence d'ami" is not only typically Mallarméan in its nominalization and its suggestion of presence through absence, but it causes the notion of "absence" to predominate over the other term, as "le vide de signification" in "Le Démon de l'Analogie" underlined the notion of emptiness. With "stalle," not the most common word for a theatre seat, and which can also refer to a church bench, there is here a very vague hint already of the theatre-church association which will be developed later in the poem. The persona's isolation is again stressed by the "goût général à esquiver ce naïf spectacle," which, by his very presence, he seems not to share. That the performance is only "naïve" to the naïve who fail to realize its deeper significance — for "ce spectacle naïf" hides "un des drames de l'histoire astrale" — is ironically implied.

---

[10] "Atta Troll" is of German origin; it is the title of a poem by Heinrich Heine, about which J. G. Robertson, *A History of German Literature* (Edinburgh and London: Blackwood & Sons, 1959), p. 424, says:

> ... but in 1843 [Heinrich Heine] published in the *Zeitung für die elegante Welt* [a title curiously resembling that of LA DERNIÈRE MODE] the finest of his longer poems, *Atta Troll, ein Sommernachtstraum*. Atta Troll is a dancing-bear in the Pyrenean village of Cauterets, but the bear's adventures — he escapes from his keeper and takes refuge in the famous Vale of Roncevaux, where he is ultimately shot — provide only the framework for an attack on the tendentious poetry which was spreading over Germany.

It is interesting to note that Heine, like Mallarmé, tells his "bear story" to talk about poetry.

"Que se passait-il devant moi?" Part of the meandering sentence which answers that question reflects the narrator's attempt to orient himself to the action on the stage (or is it, with its pedestals "en architecture de Bagdad," a circus arena?) as he turns his inner eye from his reflections toward the outside where the show begins. Throughout the piece we will follow this movement from the "inside" to the "outside" and back, in the sense that the outer events lead to inner meditations, climaxing with the complete internalizing of the "spectacle" into the poet's vision which totally transforms it. And it is this perpetual oscillation which renders the prose of the poem so vibrant and impressionistic, as bright flashes of instantaneous images and abstract musings mutually beget and destroy one another. "Pâleurs évasives de mousseline se réfugiant..." evokes Degas' dancers, bright limbs and ruffles which appear as a brilliant flare of movement caught suspended in space. That they are dancers is never stated, but suggested [11] by their attributes: brilliant lightness and graceful smiles and open arms reaching down from their pedestals toward, and contrasting with, "la lourdeur triste de l'ours," which, with its dark and heavy sounds, onomatopoetically paints what it designates. These airy "sylphides" are the only dancers in these prose poems, but their brief evocation is unforgettable and reminds us that the ballet was one of Mallarmé's favorite art forms. [12] Only now is the "hero" of the

---

[11] This tendency to "suggest" rather than "name" will become stronger as Mallarmé's style matures; he proposes it as one of the most important characteristics of modern poetry in his "Crise de Vers":

> Décadente, Mystique, les Ecoles se déclarent ou étiquetées en hâte par notre presse d'information, adoptent, comme rencontre, le point d'un Idéalisme qui (pareillement aux fugues, aux sonates) refuse les matériaux naturels et, comme brutale, une pensée exacte les ordonnant; pour ne garder de rien que la suggestion. Instituer une relation entre les images exacte, et que s'en détache un tiers aspect fusible et clair présente à la divination ... Abolie, la prétention, esthétiquement une erreur, quoiqu'elle régît les chefs-d'œuvre, d'inclure au papier subtil du volume autre chose que par exemple l'horreur de la forêt, ou le tonnerre muet épars au feuillage; non le bois intrinsèque et dense des arbres (OC pp. 365-66).

[12] The significance of the dancer for the poet lies in the fact that she also writes, and creates a kind of visual metaphor:

> ... la danseuse *n'est pas une femme qui danse,* pour ces motifs juxtaposés qu'elle *n'est pas une femme* mais une métaphore résumant un des aspects élémentaires de notre forme, glaive,

act introduced, "de ces sylphides évocateur et leur gardien, un clown," with "clown" somewhat undercutting the "héros." His "haute nudité d'argent," the tightly fitting leotards and the white rice powder makeup under the bright lights, contrasts with the squat heaviness of the bear. And the "high-walking" acrobat banters his humble fellow-performer, living reminder of the primordial raw material of animal existence, with a show of man's superiority. But in all his white splendor, the clown is by definition a grotesque figure who, having the dancer's agility but none of his grace, can at best put on a ludicrous show, a caricature of genius.

As the narrator now returns to his reflections, he seems, while welcoming the absence of friends, to identify momentarily with the anonymous crowd, "jouir comme la foule du mythe inclus dans toute banalité, quel repos." But this is an illusory association, for he cannot enjoy the show like those who see and enjoy merely "toute banalité." He alone is conscious of the "mythe inclus" as the performance, both "ordinaire" and "splendide," becomes part of his perpetual quest for "imaginations" or "symboles," a poetic quest in which the little theatre is transformed into the bright and fleeting images of an impressionistically vibrant scene, and its simple action raised to symbolic stature. The following sentence which traces every turn of the persona's thought and vision rhythmically reflects this experience. Its opening clause, verbless and luxuriously *précieux,* is suddenly and brusquely interrupted from the "outside," with the sharp, short syllables: "l'accident le plus neuf! suscita mon attention." A wave of applause had suddenly stopped short, a burst of noise turned to instant silence, and the "cesser net" imitates the abruptness of the break, "brisé par quoi?" This interrupted applause, "décerné selon l'enthousiasme," has been dehumanized somehow, for it is not people who applaud performers, but enthusiasm applauds an "illustration du privilège authentique de l'Homme." The degree of abstraction here sharply separates the poet's experience from that of the audience for whom only the visual and concrete performance is accessible. Paradoxically,

---

coupe, fleur, etc., et *qu'elle ne danse pas,* suggérant, par le prodige de raccourcis ou d'élans, avec une écriture corporelle ce qu'il faudrait des paragraphes en prose dialoguée autant que descriptive, pour exprimer, dans la rédaction: poëme dégagé de tout appareil du scribe (OC p. 304).

as the actual scene disappears in the poetic vision, the image of the applause, "un fracas de gloire à l'apogée, inhabile à se répandre," becomes concrete like a tangible element arrested in dense turbulence at its highest point, "à l'apogée," straining, but being unable, to flow off, to spread out again. In this brilliant inversion, the visual scene before us is abstracted so that we can no longer see it at all, while the abstract, but to the theatre so essential, enthusiasm of the audience is concretized to the point of becoming both visual and almost tactile, a powerful element menacing with latent force.

But back to the stage action — for "il fallait être tout yeux" — where the "pantin" performs one of the traditional *lazzi*. "Pantin," a puppet or marionette, figuratively designates one "qui gesticule sans motif et ridiculement," thus fitting our hero, whose gesture, "une paume crispée dans l'air," strikingly resembles that of the "maître" of the "Coup de Dés" — that clenched fist up in the air before final shipwreck. [13] With his *lazzi,* the fist now opening wide as though catching something in flight, the "ingénieux" had won the crowd's approbation; but the trick, a figure of the ease with which everyone grasps an idea, is richly ironic, for the crowd, on the contrary, sees merely appearance while failing to grasp the idea which it hides.

The bear, "ému au leger vent" like a marionette, now rises with a live animal's supple movement, "rythmiquement et doucement," as he examines the trick, the hero's "exploit." And the heavy bear claw coming to rest on the ribbons of the clown's costume, rather than shoulder, makes for an even stronger contrast in this rapprochement of the bestial and the artificial. But the narrator who contemplates the spectacle with ironic distance, as he muses on "de conséquences graves pour l'honneur de la race," does not share the audience's mounting excitement. "Honneur" is but another ironic use of a heroic term in harmony with "héros" and "exploit." This ironic tone is completely absent, however, from

---

[13] This "geste du pantin, une paume crispée dans l'air" reveals an underlying association, at that time still unconscious, connecting the grotesque show of "le Génie" with "l'Homme" *par excellence,* the Master Poet, who in the "Coup de Dés" is seen "la main / crispée / par-delà l'inutile tête" (OC p. 464).

the idealized description of the animal, gentle and good, and aspiring after genius. The persona alone sees "un homme inférieur" concealed under the bear gradually rising "debout sur l'écartement de deux jambes de poil." One paw on the acrobat's shoulder, the other on his arm, the heavy beast appears to be reaching up toward the slender human form to embrace, not to harm, his "frère brillant et surnaturel." But this union of the fundamental double aspect of man, bestiality and genius, with the former both threatening, and at the same time desiring to be saved or sublimated by, the latter, is a "secret rapprochement," hidden from the audience who merely see the bear's dangerous proximity to the clown. And so the poet-persona in describing the outer event gradually internalizes it, fusing outer phenomena and inner vision, the banal spectacle with the "mythe inclus." [14]

As the hero performs his act, he raises his head, "chef affreux," probably both horrible and horrified, his "bouche folle de vague," his mouth open and grotesquely painted by the clown's make-up, in order to stare after a paper and gold fly which is absent. The sentence is as tricky as the act it describes, for the prop after which the clown stares is called into existence only by the suggestiveness of his play; and the ambiguous "fil visible," again vaguely suggestive of a marionette play, stresses the actor's mechanical performance of the *lazzi*. "Spectacle clair" of the following sentence refers both to the brightly lit stage and the clear meaning of the act: the bear fails to grasp the play of genius. But for the persona the play transcends its little stage — "tréteau," théâtre de charlatan — and while for the audience the moment seems to last forever because of its danger, for the poet it takes on the dimension of art — *ars longa*.... As his vision now entirely separates itself from theirs, "sans que m'offusquât l'attitude probablement fatale prise par le mime dépositaire de notre orgueil," not only is the clown's play again ironically undercut, but he is called a mime. And since in a pantomime the actors by definition may only use gesture to express themselves, we have a paradoxical inversion here where discourse, "interdit au rejeton des sites arctiques" under

---

[14] For the symbolic significance of "génie," cf. Chevalier, *Dictionnaire*, pp. 383-84.

natural but not artistic laws, is accorded to the animal while human genius must remain silent. At the same time the bear is identified as a polar bear, introducing the association with "the most conspicuous of the northern constellations, *Ursa Major*," that is the Great Bear, which will be the final constellation of the "Coup de Dés," and which in our poem foreshadows "un des drames de l'histoire astrale" into which the pantomime will be transformed in the poetic vision.

The bear's imaginary monologue is an appeal to human charity, to explain to him this splendid theatrical atmosphere in which man has taught him, the beast, to move. But it is not an atmosphere of splendor alone, but also one of dust, and splendor and dust befit not merely the stage with its glaring lights and dusty sets. They describe modern civilization as it might appear to an outsider such as the bear and, paradoxically, the poet, the one aspiring after, the other transcending it. "Splendeur... poussière... et voix"[15] characterize "toute grande ville," and we recall that "la poussière du temps" had also marked that late, death-bound civilization of "Le Phénomène Futur." The bear, addressing his "aîné subtil," claims that his request, both pressing and just, should and could be granted by him whose fear he believes but feigned — is the clown's every gesture not theatrical make-believe? For this brother in his "haute nudité d'argent" is "élancé aux régions de la sagesse" only because he, the beast who still wears the attire of the caves of a primitive age, has reimmersed his latent strength in pre-historic darkness to set the other free. And so a secret bond unites man and beast, the bear suggestive of the Jungian "terrible parent" archetype, that is a figure for a demonic anima whose "force latente" threatens to be destructive when it is repressed. And it is this dark brother who is now seeking reconciliation, sealing the

---

[15] This "atmosphère de splendeur, de poussière et de voix" is strikingly similar to that of Baudelaire's "Le Vieux Saltimbanque," *Poèmes en Prose*, p. 72:

> Les hercules, fiers de l'énormité de leurs membres, sans front et sans crâne, comme les orangs-outangs, se prélassaient majestueusement sous les maillots lavés la veille pour la circonstance. Les danseuses, belles comme les fées ou des princesses, sautaient et cabriolaient sous le feu des lanternes qui remplissaient leurs jupes d'étincelles.
> Tout n'était que lumière, poussière, cris.

pact of their brotherhood "devant la multitude siégeant à cette fin." This transforms the theatre audience into an assembly or tribunal of witnesses, both audience and stage action thus being absorbed into and fused with the ideal vision.[16]

Not only the stage action and the spectators, but the modest dimensions of the little theatre itself are now magically expanded as the breathless attention of the excited audience becomes "l'absence d'aucun souffle unie à l'espace." "Quel lieu absolu" evokes cosmic spaces, absolute time and place, which creates a setting of eternity and the infinite, where the evolution of a race is but moment and constellations not remote — presaging "des circonstances éternelles" of that final drama of the "Coup de Dés." For our "spectacle" has become a cosmic drama, "un des drames de l'histoire astrale," with the theatre audience fading away now ("la foule s'effaçait toute") to become the ritual communicants and unconscious but indispensable witnesses of their "situation spirituelle" of which the stage has become the emblem. "L'emblème" is, like the symbol, the visible sign of an idea; however, it is not traditional, but the poet's own, a symbol peculiar to the Mallarméan poetic universe. In this universe, the theatre in its ideal form is ritualistic and the inheritor of the spiritual function of the dying Church, thus becoming a kind of new Church itself.[17] In "Crayonné au Théâtre" Mallarmé says:

---

[16] This vision, with a kind of vague comprehension on the part of the idealized bear, of the process of evolution or by extension the Hugolian idea of the gradual upward movement of all forms of life toward spiritualization on the Great Chain of Being, recalls that in the early "Plainte d'Automne" the narrator's cat had become his "compagnon mystique, un esprit."

[17] Haskell M. Block, *Mallarmé and the Symbolist Drama* (Detroit: Wayne State Univ. Press, 1963), pp. 85-86:

> In his highly personal reformulation of the drama, Mallarmé is not concerned with the details of the "explication de l'homme," but rather with the spiritual attitudes and values that the new theater will express: the primacy of mystery, dream, and imaginative vision, projected beyond any particular time or circumstances. The magic and mystery of the theater reside within its very substance, as an evocation of the absolute, embracing the destiny of all humanity. In this sense, Mallarmé's ritual drama is the means of the propagation of a new religion, a secularization of the liturgy and rites of ancient dramatic performances.
>
> This vision of a ceremonial theater is in fact a configuration of elements derived from a variety of sources: Greek drama, the

> Notre seule magnificence, la scène, à qui le concours d'arts divers scellés par la poésie attribue selon moi quelque caractère religieux ou officiel, si l'un de ces mots a un sens, je constate que le siècle finissant n'en a cure, ainsi comprise (OC p. 313).

And late in his life in one of the responses to Jules Huret the poet explicitly reaffirms:

> Je crois que la Littérature, reprise à sa source qui est l'Art et la Science, nous fournira un Théâtre, dont les représentations seront le vrai culte moderne (OC p. 875).

In the little theatre's ideal metamorphosis the gas light, which has replaced the church tapers of yore, plays its part in the rite as "dispensateur moderne de l'extase," and "extase," as a mystical term, well describes the narrator's situation among the audience.[18] The theatre's traditional chandelier, which in our "drame astrale" setting figures like a giant constellation "dans les hauteurs de la salle," plays, moreover, an important role in Mallarmé's conception of the theatre even outside our prose poems, as a reflector of both stage action and the multiple consciousness of the spectators, that is the communicants in the ceremony:

> ... le lustre, dans la salle, représentât, par ses multiples facettes, une lucidité chez le public, relativement à ce qu'on vient faire (OC p. 388).

But at this culminating moment, the summit and apex of elevation and expectancy, there occurs an absolute break. And as "le charme se rompit," the rupture is visually indicated in the poem by double spacing: the vision disappears, and we no longer see the event "sous le jour propre au rêve." Nothing could more vividly image the crassness of the natural order which now replaces magic and dream than the piece of flesh, that "loque saignant[e]," "un

---

medieval liturgical drama, Shakespeare, Wagner, Banville and the tradition of poetic drama, and the Catholic Mass. Mallarmé saw the theater of both the past and the future as a temple, wherein actor and spectator participate in a sacred rite.

[18] The gas light, one of the newest products of modern civilization, held a special fascination for Mallarmé. Cf. Richard, *L'Univers*, p. 502.

morceau de chair, nu, brutal," thrown on the scene which is no longer a "lieu absolu," but a humble stage with dusty sets and the customary, but usually hidden, gory feedings of the beasts after an animal act.[19] The theatre's magic, "le rayonnement théâtral," which in the poetic vision had endowed the bear with a higher aspiration and, above all, with speech, has vanished as the beast with muffled tread seems to carry "Silence" away with him. The contrast of the ideal and the real is further stressed by the suggestion that the animal, no longer aspiring after human, that is supernatural, wisdom and splendor, would now have to degrade man, "*notre image*," to the level of crudest matter, to shreds of torn flesh, to enjoy him. Once more the theatre's bright lights are evoked as the uncomprehending and spellbound audience watches the bloody feast, rows of shiny opera glasses both reflecting, and glaringly staring at, the action.

The circular form of the poem now comes to a close with the lowering of "la toile et son journal de tarifs et de lieux communs," which echoes the "journal," "reporters," and "caractère commun" of the opening paragraph. For this curtain with its advertisements and price schedules moves us back into that modern civilization in which the poet-persona is a stranger. And as he steps outside "comme tout le monde," with the crowd but not of it, he has the answer to his original question: if "la réalité" and "les mirages d'un fait" hide the ideal and "un aspect nécessaire," it is not evident to *la foule,* for the vision of the ideal is not shared, but his alone. But the now mature poet, in his solitude and isolation from his fellow man, is nevertheless serene, for he knows that his "façon de voir" is not only superior, but alone true. And thus Mallarmé chose the closing of this prose poem which inaugurates a new style and form to proclaim, with a rather uncharacteristic directness, his faith in his privileged poetic vision.

In "Un Spectacle Interrompu," the only prose poem where the poet-persona is a spectator in a theatre and not, as frequently, a

---

[19] The image of the raw, bloody shred of flesh contrasting with the ideal astral vision recalls Rimbaud's prose poem, "Barbare," *Œuvres,* p. 292, with its similar juxtaposition of arctic purity and the food of animal instincts, bloody meat:

> Oh! Le pavillon en viande saignante sur la soie des mers et des fleurs arctiques; (elles n'existent pas).

performer himself, several important Mallarméan themes, then, converge. One of the most obvious, developed poetically, that is by suggestion, is that of the theatre itself. And we have seen how in this ritual theatre of spiritual regeneration a crucial kinship is established between the performance — or more widely a work of art — and the beholder, who becomes a participant. In the interaction of the ideal beholder and performance a dialectical relationship comes into being bringing about an interplay of three planes, where an object, in our case "le spectacle," is perceived by a subject, the poet-persona, the intercourse of the two giving birth to a new object.[20] This synthesis, here the potential liberation and sublimation of the animal — the spiritualization of the bestial by art — at the same time modifies the poet-beholder in raising him from creature to creator. Our "new object" is, moreover, also the definition of the Mallarméan prose poem, of which "Un Spectacle Interrompu" is the demonstration: *reportage* of the ideal.

Central to these ideas is the notion of both the power and the isolation of poetic vision — an isolation reflected in, and protected by, the new hermetic style — developed throughout this prose poem whose main theme is *poesis*.

---

[20] This dynamic relationship, the "dialectics" between *Kunstwerk und Betrachter,* a work of art and its beholder, is the subject of Steland's *Dialektische Gedanken,* where he concentrates on Mallarmé's essays on the ballet.

RÉMINISCENCE

"Réminiscence," dating from 1888, is the first late piece of the *recueil*. Though it originated from "L'Orphelin" of 1867, it is not so much a modification of that version as it is an entirely new prose poem, which is why Mallarmé placed it in the second group of the cycle. A reading of the two pieces reveals not a mere progression from the early to the late style, but instead two different works. [1] Hence, rather than examining variants, we shall refer to the early sketch of our poem only as it helps our appreciation of the mature work.

The change of the title itself [2] indicates the poem's transformation, for "L'Orphelin" was one of the young poet's obsessive themes, which pervades his adolescent lyric poetry, is suggested in the early prose poems "Plainte d'Automne" and "Le Démon de l'Analogie," and is finally fully developed in "Pauvre Enfant Pâle." "Réminiscence," however, shows by the very definition of the title-word that the mature Mallarmé is no longer obsessed by the experience which produced that early theme but that, rather than being haunted by it, he has it now at his command, to recall it at will, to paint it in the light, the colors, and above all the style of a mature artistic imagination. From the theme's slave, he has become its master, to possess and control it artistically, that is with cool aesthetic distance. "Réminiscence" moreover suggests by association the apprehension

---

[1] For a full text of "L'Orphelin," see OC pp. 1559-60. Paxton, *The Development*, pp. 18-19, offers a minute listing of the variants.

[2] The poem's title had undergone successive changes from "L'Orphelin" to "Le Petit Saltimbanque" to "Le Môme Sagace" before its final form. The intermediate titles, however, were not published but only mentioned in Mallarmé's correspondence. Cf. OC p. 1560.

of perfect Forms in the sense of the Platonic Idea, the poem being about the archetypal idea of the Orphan in this poetic universe, or what Mallarmé would call its "notion pure" the Idea itself rather than its particular manifestation:

> Je dis une fleur! et, hors de l'oubli où ma voix relègue aucun contour, en tant que quelque chose d'autre que les calices sus, musicalement se lève, idée même et suave, l'absente de tous bouquets (OC p. 368).

The poem's anecdote recounts the meeting of the orphan with the children of a circus come to town. The lonely child feels instinctively drawn toward the vagabonds, and the mature narrator in reminiscing about this experience wonders whether this early affinity might not have presaged already his own artistic vocation.

"Orphelin j'errais en noir et l'œil vacant de famille" introduces at once the narrative subject, a first-person narrator, the Hamlet-Igitur theme, and an example of the extraordinary stylistic virtuosity which characterizes the poem. The first word is reminiscent of the opening of "Pauvre Enfant Pâle," with which the original version is almost contemporary. But while that poem's narrator identified himself with the "pauvre enfant" only indirectly, here he "was" the orphan himself. Yet, the temporal distance and, above all, the one created stylistically are such that from the outset the orphan and the first-person narrator constitute two clearly distinguished voices, with the poetic one almost completely absorbing that of the child. This opening phrase, by its high compression — and, in inverse relationship to it, its infinitely extended suggestiveness — creates the key image of the poem, and also presages Mallarmé's very latest manner, that of the "Coup de Dés," as in that poem's Preface: "Tout se passe, par raccourci, en hypothèse; on évite le récit" (OC p. 455). For in a sense this opening line is, or contains, the whole poem; and in compressing a vast theme thus into its essential image, the poet creates here the high tension of some of his late verse, as the pregnant phrase and each of its terms strain with potential expansion. But in the prose poem we now pass to the elaboration of the theme, "le récit."

In the anecdote, we see a child dressed in black, who recalls "une personne condamnée à porter probablement le deuil de l'inexplicable Pénultième," wandering somewhat aimlessly, for he is not yet a singer like the "pale child" but still without a mission. His most striking aspect is his eyes, mirrors of his soul reflecting an outer, and expressing an inner, state: the loneliness, isolation, and separateness of one searching for those to whom he belongs.[3] The second part of the sentence provides the setting of the piece, the festive tents of a fairground among the trees[4] outside the city, recalling "Le Phénomène Futur" and "Le Pitre Châtié." In "Le Pitre Châtié" the poet-persona, who was a showman in "Le Phénomène Futur," is a circus clown, "le mauvais Hamlet," indicating an underlying association of Poet, Showman or Clown, Hamlet, and Orphan, all of which converge in "Réminiscence." But while this association is still spelled out in "L'Orphelin" ("... déjà, enfant avec tristesse pressentant le Poëte, j'errais vêtu de noir, les yeux baissés du ciel et cherchant ma famille sur la terre,") it is merely suggested here. Only the orphan's fascination with the gypsies is affirmed, and expressed not in a child's terms, but in the poet's: "J'aimais le parfum des vagabonds"; and it is the narrator who then intimates that the orphan perhaps already felt a spiritual kinship with the itinerant entertainers, "vagabonds," where he echoes "j'errais" once more, somehow stressing this affinity. "Vers eux à oublier mes camarades" — where the preposition, as in its use in "tu vins ... au monde vers cela" of "Pauvre Enfant Pâle," conveys a strong sense of anticipation — is immensely condensed by the suppression of the finite verb, extending the suggestiveness of not only this final clause but of the whole sentence. Like the somber Hamlet, leaving behind his courtiers to seek out the wandering players come to festive Elsinore, our black-clothed child, who contrasts with the colorful fairgrounds surrounding him, forgets his

---

[3] Clearly, this image and theme reflect Mallarmé's early loss of his mother (which, as we have seen, influenced several of the early prose poems) and also the neglect he experienced through his father's remarriage shortly thereafter. That these facts contributed to form the poetic vocation itself cannot be questioned. Kurt Wais, *Mallarmé*, p. 48, goes so far as to see a direct causal relationship here: "Mit dem jähen Bewusstsein des Kleinen, elternlos zu sein, began jene Störung im inneren Wachstum, ohne die es den dichterischen Funken nicht gäbe."

[4] In the "L'Orphelin" version these trees, in their sickliness, "les arbres dont le vent cassait le bois mort," were most reminiscent of the trees whitened by the dust of time of "Le Phénomène Futur."

own comrades, his own kind among whom he is a stranger, to devote his attention to the strangers come to town. Thus the Hamlet association, though not stated, is most powerfully called to mind in this opening sentence.

The word "fête," which implies the entire atmosphere that the show people bring with them, introduces a vocabulary cluster of religious imagery and language set side by side with the "low" and colloquial language, the slang even, of the gypsy children. This religious language is that of the persona's reflections on the nature of the theatre, whose sacred and ritual character was developed in the preceding prose poem, and which is now expressed by "chœurs," "drame," "heure sainte," the mention of the poet of the Divine Comedy, "prier," "chaste," "repas supérieur," and the celebration of "blancheur" in "neiges des cimes, lys, ailes." At the same time, this sentence introduces the action proper, but only after what seems like an interminable absolute phrase, an elaborate adverbial stage and mood setting.[5] It is that quiet hour before the show begins, the momentary calm before the multifarious agitation of the colorful scene, and for Mallarmé this moment of *suspens,* in its rich potentiality, held a particular fascination. In our poem it has a manifold significance, for while it refers on the literal level to the moment of expectancy before the performance, it also suggests an analogous point in both the persona's and the Poet's — that is Man's — becoming. It is Hamlet's stage of indecision which is yet already pregnant with the Act, the present of potency preceding the future of actualization of the self. In his "Hamlet" essay, which is almost contemporary with "Réminiscence," Mallarmé says:

> Son solitaire drame! et qui, parfois, tant ce promeneur d'un labyrinthe de trouble et de griefs en prolonge les circuits avec le suspens d'un acte inachevé, semble le spectacle même pourquoi existent la rampe ainsi que l'espace doré quasi moral qu'elle defend, ... (OC p. 300).

---

[5] This device is similar to what Leo Spitzer in *Stilstudien* (München, Huber, 1961), p. 125, calls *"Inszenierende" Adverbialbestimmungen,* which he feels are characteristic of "newer French literature"; he does not mention Mallarmé, however, in the chapter he devotes to the subject.

"Chœurs" not only suggests the chorus of Greek drama, but also the *enfants de chœur* who participate in the Christian ritual of the Mass, and the "brise ancienne des chœurs" of "L'Orphelin" was still more explicit in bringing out these associations. The "déchirure" of either show tent or theatre curtain has about it a mysteriousness, heightened by the very vagueness of the phrase, of things hidden from the uninitiated, on the literal level the secret preparations for the show. "Tirade" suggests the long declamatory monologues of classical theatre, reinforced with "le drame," while "loin," referring on the literal level to spatial distance, also evokes a temporal and an artistic one. In this way, by the merest suggestion, the humble fairground stage reaches back through the ages to classical drama, from which it is as far removed temporally as it is artistically. We have here, then, not merely an ironic juxtaposition of the "low comedy" characteristic of the *théâtre de foire* with elevated ritual drama, but an intimation of their secret kinship. And while "quinquets," phonetically echoing "quinconce" above, and recalling "la suie ignoble des quinquets" of "Le Pitre Châtié," marks this theatre with a touch of modernity, "l'heure sainte," with its flavor of the canonical hours is, again, richly evocative of the past.

The "action" of the orphan-hero is more correctly a mere wish to act: "je souhaitais de parler"; and the child he feels instinctively drawn to is himself a little outsider, "un môme trop vacillant pour figurer parmi sa race." "Môme" suggesting "mômerie," that is a masquerade, underlines the show atmosphere of the poem. And this urchin appears like a spiritual brother to the orphan by the similarity of his condition, for "vacillant," aside from literally describing the little one as too shaky on his legs to work with his acrobat family, suggests figuratively the undecidedness inherent in the moment before finding one's vocation. Moreover, just as the orphan is marked by his somber costume, so this lonely child is wearing a rather peculiar attire, that strange Dantesque night-cap, a long, pointed cowl that seems to come from another age. This allusion to the Middle Ages was in "L'Orphelin" reinforced with "des toiles ... paintes par le maître qui, peut-être, à cet instant, croyait seul au moyen âge." But the mere allusion to the medieval poet which, by association, evokes the original *théâtres de foire* and also medieval religious drama, is infinitely richer, for the name

Dante summons forth the eternal celebration of human destiny in Poetry and an age of faith.

The juxtaposition of the trivial and the sublime, of the recalled childhood experience and its poetic elaboration, reaches its culmination in the line "qui rentrait en soi, sous l'aspect d'une tartine de fromage mou, déjà la neige des cimes, le lys ou autre blancheur constitutive d'ailes au-dedans." For the rather unaesthetic slice of bread covered with soft cheese on which the little gypsy is munching paradoxically releases in the poet an explosion of imagery celebrating whiteness. The cheese has become "l'aspect," that is the mere external appearance, the sacramental species, under the form of which the little Dante already takes possession of what in "L'Orphelin" was called "toutes les blancheurs sacrées des poëtes." The sacredness to poets of this absolute whiteness — which will evolve into Mallarmé's absolute *Néant* — is merely suggested here with "blancheur constitutive d'ailes au-dedans," "aile" again being symbolic for poetic creative power, as it was in "Le Démon de l'Analogie." There is here, then, a mysterious, almost sacramental, conversion of "nourritures terrestres" in the crassest sense to spiritual food. And the cold "neige des cimes," "le lys," this absolute purity, recalls that other orphan, the virginal Hérodiade, motherless and abandoned by her father, and suspended in that solitary young moment of expectancy before fulfillment:

> J'attends une chose inconnue
> Ou peut-être, ignorant le mystère et vos cris,
> Jetez-vous les sanglots suprêmes et meurtris
> D'une enfance sentant parmi les rêveries
> Se séparer enfin ses froides pierreries. (OC p. 48)

The rapprochement of the orphan and the little Dante, who innocently carries a still secret artistic mission within him, never quite comes about, for the orphan does not speak, and "je l'eusse prié de m'admettre à son repas supérieur" — doubly ironic in its stilted phrasing with the pluperfect subjunctive and the formal verb "prier" — expresses merely the unfulfilled wish. Again "repas supérieur" for bread and cheese is suggestive of a ritual meal, where the communicant under the species of earthly food partakes of divine substance, and to which the orphan would have "prayed to be admitted," had not a dazzling older boy, seemingly surging out of nowhere, interposed himself.

The past participle "partagé," followed by "vite," stresses the swiftness of that "ainé fameux" — echoing the "ainé subtil" which designated the acrobat in "Un Spectacle Interrompu" — who has already obtained what the orphan never even succeeded in asking for. "Contre une proche toile en train des tours de force et banalités alliables au jour" vaguely suggests a backdrop of canvas tents, fitting setting to the young acrobat's nimble tricks, though it is not quite clear here whether the "tours de force" emanate from the tents or are the boy's, while in "L'Orphelin" the scene was so precisely drawn that it left much less to our imagination: "la baraque voisine dans laquelle on allait donner les tours de force." Not merely his easy *lazzi,* but his nakedness in "sa prestesse de maillot," where the performer's agility seems to become part of his costume and that a part of him, recalls again the clown-acrobat of the preceding poem in "sa haute nudité d'argent." And this nude form of the dancer-acrobat-clown, barely disguised under the tightly fitting leotards, always fascinated Mallarmé, perhaps as an attribute of the dancer's freedom, as is his very mobility.

For this other one, contrasting with and admired by the orphan, appears sovereignly free, both of body and of speech, and his easy freedom immediately apparent in his uninhibited eating of the little one's piece of bread, effected so fast that we did not even see it, continues to manifest itself in his tricks and talk. Into this static silent scene it is he who introduces action, movement and speech, all the words concerning him, "jaillir," "vite," "tours," "prestesse," "pirouetter," designating motion. But a peculiar tension is created by a certain weakening of verbal expression through the use of the narrative infinitive, present and past participles, or even nominalization: "partagé," "jailli," "de pirouetter," "de triompher en elevant," and "de mordre." This stylistic device not only creates tension, but also, by keeping in check the very motion whose quickness and ease the verbs describe, somehow catches and fixes this motion in the act, freezing it into an instantaneous impressionistic *tableau.*

The acrobat contrasts with the other two children not only because of his physical superiority; but his speech, a happy torrent of slang — which swallows up the orphan's only line, a melancholy "je n'en ai pas" — underlines by contrast the theme of orphanage in stressing his own strong sense of belonging. For he is securely attached not only to the whole tribe of homeless performers, those gypsies forever wandering on the fringe of society, but particularly to his own father and mother and thus doubly to "sa race." His "c'est farce, un père" (much richer than the "c'est amusant un père" of "L'Orphelin") befits the chatter about his life, which is show life. Among his kind, art and life are inseparable so that while not in the show, but still waiting for it to begin, he puts on a show, already resembling his father who is so thoroughly an artist that even when he is ill he performs his "grimaces aussi belles." Since the father's feat is to make faces, he is a clown and, therefore, the expression "que bouda la soupe" to indicate that he could not eat is especially amusing here, for it literally means that "the soup made faces" at him. Whether the older clown got the ringmaster's "claques et coups de pied" because he was sick, or whether it was the other way around, is not quite clear. Nor do we know whether those slaps and kicks reveal some of circus life behind the scenes, or whether they were part of the "act," which suggests again how inextricably art and life are interwoven among the show people. And it is possibly their unreserved commitment to their art which makes the gypsies so attractive to the Poet, like them an outsider to society.

The young acrobat's triumphant "élevant... la jambe avec aisance glorieuse," in contrasting with the "coups de pied" received by the older clown, suggests at once the strength and beauty of youth and its fugitive nature, and vaguely intimates the theme of Baudelaire's prose poem, "Le Vieux Saltimbanque." [6] And "il

---

[6] Baudelaire, *Poèmes en Prose*, 71-75. Here the poet-persona contrasts the carefree activity of the younger showpeople with the misery of the old "saltimbanque," with whom he then openly identifies:

> Je viens de voir l'image du vieil homme de lettres qui a survécu à la génération dont il fut le brillant amuseur; du vieux poète sans amis, ... dégradé par sa misère et par l'ingratitude publique, et dans la baraque de qui le monde oublieux ne veut plus entrer!" (p. 74)

Although this theme is suggested in our prose poem, it is not nearly as fully developed as it will be in "La Déclaration Foraine," where the persona will put on a "charity performance" for the old clown.

nous épate, papa," expresses not so much the child's admiration for his father as for his father's showmanship. After a quick bite into the smaller one's piece of bread — the "régal chaste" echoing the earlier "repas supérieur" and doubly ironic when juxtaposed with "mordre" — he now begins to display his mother's talents, whose greatness is attested by public acclamation. The orphan's motherlessness, "peut-être que tu es seul?," is passed over quickly by the youth, who now disappears as suddenly as he had appeared, for "la parade s'exaltait." "La parade s'exaltait" is much more suggestive than "sa parade venait de commencer" of "L'Orphelin," because it not only indicates the long-awaited beginning of the show, but it evokes all the excitement and heightened intensity of the moment. This mood, along with the acrobat's last words, "des parents sont des gens drôles, qui font rire," contrasts with the orphan's "moi, je soupirais" and his sudden sadness at not having parents, pointing back to the beginning of the poem, where it was expressed only in his eyes. The last sentence of "L'Orphelin," in its more sentimental but also more explicit manner, "moi, je m'en allais tout seul, songeant que c'était bien triste que je n'eusse pas comme lui des parents," stresses more than the orphan's simple regret at lacking parents: he does not have parents "comme lui," like the little showman. For our orphan, wandering toward the gypsies, is already vaguely looking for the familty of Poets, symbolized by these wandering entertainers.

And just as the little orphan is doubly burdened — by his past and also already by his future — so the poem itself in recalling the past prepares the future, thus occupying within the *recueil* as decisive a moment as the one artistically fixed within the piece. The poem on the narrative level recalls a moment in the persona's youth, but it is also an image of that moment when Man confronts his destiny alone, those threatening worlds both within and without, a moment which for Mallarmé was embodied in the modern myth of Hamlet.[7] And this figure, the incarnation of that moment sus-

---

[7] René Taupin in "The Myth of Hamlet in France in Mallarmé's Generation," *Modern Language Quarterly*, XIV (1953), 432-47, discusses *Hamlet*'s significance in the nineteenth century, and the transformation of the myth from Romanticism to Laforgue. And Charles Chassé in "Le Thème de Hamlet chez Mallarmé," *Revue des Sciences Humaines*, 77-78 (1955),

pended between the alternatives of action or refusal, acceptance or suicice (in Mallarmé's universe symbolized by the twin figures of the white Hérodiade and the somber Igitur) encountered in almost all the early prose poems, is here recalled for the last time. But "Réminiscence," in suggesting the association of poet and *saltimbanque*, that is poet and performer, and thus reaching back to the first poem of the cycle, also foreshadows the following poem, "La Déclaration Foraine," where the poet performs, mounts the fairground stage himself to entertain *la foule*, with poetry. [8]

157-69, outlines how Mallarmé, influenced by theatre and painting, appropriated and subsequenly transformed the figure of Hamlet, which pervades his poetry from such early verse pieces as "Le Guignon" [original version] and "Le Pitre Châtié" through *Igitur* and "Un Coup de Dés."

[8] Wallace Fowlie, *Mallarmé* (Chicago: Univ. of Chicago Press, 1962), pp. 243-44, discusses "Réminiscence" pointing to its relationship with *Hamlet*, whose significance for the poet he explains as follows:

> Hamlet has to play many parts in his tragedy: the jilted lover, the friend of the two courtiers, the king's nephew, the avenging son, the son of his mother. Only briefly in his soliloquies does he manifest the part he didn't invent: the griefstricken son unable to execute the revenge and whose mind wavers under the tragic burden. To continue living he needs a theatre, a play in which to test himself and the world he knows. To live one's own part is not sufficient for Hamlet and for the poet. A scene has to be constructed by them in which their destiny may be re-enacted theatrically. In his ordinary life a man, in his lack of knowledge and imperfect vision, is unable to comprehend his own fatality. Only by projecting his life into an art form, a Shakespeare tragedy or a Mallarmé poem, is he able to discover some reasonableness in the mystery that is his (p. 244).

LA DÉCLARATION FORAINE

"La Déclaration Foraine," stylistically the most difficult prose poem of the *recueil*, is, with the exception of "Conflit," possibly one of the latest in both composition and conception. For there are no earlier versions known, and the piece, published for the first time in 1887, appears practically unchanged in *Divagations*.[1] The stylistic virtuosity of the poem renders its explication extremely complicated; even each word of the title carries multiple meanings. "Déclaration" here means both "déclaration publique" and "aveu d'amour"; and while "foraine" immediately evokes the *foire* setting of "Le Phénomène Futur" and "Réminiscence," it also means "foreign, strange,"[2] each discrete signification being of equal importance in the context of our poem.

The anecdote is about the sunset carriage ride of the narrator and a lady friend out into the suburbs where they pass by a fair. The lady wants to visit it, and they stroll through the crowd. When they come to an empty stand, she suddenly decides to mount the stage, and as a crowd of onlookers begins to gather, the poet-

---

[1] The only variant, from the poem's appearance in *Pages*, five years before *Divagations*, is an insignificant one of punctuation (OC p. 1553).

[2] While the adjective "forain" carries today principally the meaning "traveling, itinerant, or strolling," Littré lists as its first definition "qui est dehors, étranger," and as its second one "qui n'est pas du lieu"; then he makes the following point: "bien que forain signifie qui est étranger, et non qui est de la foire, par confusion de sens, comme si, dans marchand forain, forain voulait dire qui est de la foire, théâtre forain, petit théâtre dressé à la foire." As so often, Mallarmé here certainly plays with multiple meanings, the "foreign," that is the English sonnet, which he takes care to indicate in a footnote, and the "fairground" performance, so important in this poetic universe.

persona entertains them by reciting a poem celebrating the beautiful woman on the stage.

The first word of the poem, set off from the rest of the sentence by an exclamation mark, sets the mood of the first-person narrator and of the opening scene, as well as establishing a tension by contrast with the title and the whole world of the poem indicated by it. "Le Silence," resonant in "songes," "bercement," and "assoupissant," is a condition for which Mallarmé has a predilection,[8] a state of being denoting absence — not merely of noise, but of agitation, and passion even, a state almost of the absence of existence — out of which alone, paradoxically, the essence of things, which is poetry, is born.

And now the scene unfolds, with the narrator riding in a coach in the company of a lady who will recognize her portrait in this poem, in which she is a figure, however, for "toute femme." She is "dreamily" stretched by his side — with "ainsi que songes" intimating the woman's two-fold presence, the real one and that in the poet's mental world of dreams — lulled by the gentle motion of the carriage, whose wheels appese the interjection of the flowers bending under them. So silent seems this dreamy ride that the flowers' weak resistance even is calmed; but, "interjection" by association implying passion, these flowers are a beautiful manifestation of a hidden sexuality and so resemble the "femme" with which they alliterate, hence vaguely suggesting erotic passion and thus a tension hidden under the surface calm. This calmness would be broken were the narrator to compliment his lady aloud on her costume, all the mystery of which constitutes a gift to him who lives or dreams this privileged moment. And her elegance, "quelque interrogatrice toilette," is in harmony with her face, her smile and its dimple. For they establish a perfect equilibrium, a balance, of nearness and familiarity on the one hand, and of distance and reserve on the other. Just as the dress is both provocative and protective, so the dimple evokes the physical charms of the woman's

---

[8] We recall the silence pervading "Plainte d'Automne" and "Frisson d'Hiver;" and we will find the notion of silence richly developed in the late prose poems, "Le Nénuphar Blanc," "La Gloire," and, above all, "Conflit."

face, while "sourire spirituel" suggests the disembodiment of the physical expression of her laughter. [4]

But the harmony is now abruptly broken as reality erupts and interrupts the ideal moment, the direct brevity of "ainsi ne consent la réalité" emphasizing the break. And in the remainder of the long sentence, the dying moment's bliss is contrasted with reality's crass vulgarity in which it is mercilessly swallowed up. The sunbeam "felt" luxuriously on the landau's varnish is an emanation of brightness, warmth and sumptuous magnificence, but dying there like the dream itself and the sun which it reflects. [5] For there was "trop de tacite félicité," and so the poet-persona's favorite hour is now submerged in a violent outcry, "avec orage" menacing with all its figurative connotations of revolt, war, danger, and passion — the threat of multitudes, already foreshadowing some of the poem's later moments — and contrasting with "Le Silence!" And "dans tous les sens à la fois et sans motif" underlines the atmosphere of disorder and confusion, the wild profusion of matter with its "rire strident" which now replaces the "spirituel sourire" of a beautifully mysterious and silent face. This grating "rire strident ordinaire des choses" with their "cuivrerie triomphale" is reminiscent of "les objets neufs avec leur hardiesse criarde" of "Frisson d'Hiver"; but while the silent companion of that early piece shared the poet's feelings and soul, this poem's lady does not.

---

[4] To interpret the smile as belonging to the narrator, which is syntactically possible and is the reading of one of Mallarmé's German translators, Carl Fischer, *Stéphane Mallarmé Sämtliche Gedichte Französisch mit Deutscher Übersetzung* (Heidelberg: Lambert Schneider Verlag, 1957), p. 233, seems to me less appropriate. Moreover, nowhere does the persona of these prose poems describe his own person; on the contrary, though assuming various "roles," he becomes progressively more anonymous, above all in the second part of the cycle.

[5] The celebration of reflected sunlight, which prepares already for the sonnet within our prose poem, is reminiscent of Mallarmé's verse poetry, especially the almost contemporary love sonnet "M'introduire dans ton histoire," and "Tout orgueil fume-t-il du soir," of exactly the same year, but particularly "Victorieusement fui le suicide beau," which celebrates the sunlight's death and subsequent resurrection in the beloved's hair and is, thus, thematically similar to the sonnet in our poem. The image of the reflected evening sun is, of course, part of the major theme of the solar drama, brilliantly discussed in Davies, *Le Drame solaire*.

"La cacophonie à l'ouïe de quiconque" onomatopoetically renders the discord it signifies, and which remains shrilly present to the narrator, "un instant écarté, plutôt qu'il ne s'y fond, auprès de son idée," that is to whoever fails to abandon himself fully to the ideal, and thus remains haunted by existence.[6] "Un instant ... auprès de son idée" was the brief perfect moment of silence with its intimation of absence, now drowned in the tumultuous uproar of existence round about.

And it is toward this noisy commotion that "l'enfant voiturée dans mes distractions" — suggesting both the real woman and the ideal one of the poet's rêveries and thus juxtaposing inner and outer, essential and existential, realms — feels drawn and draws him: the fairground and "fête," under whose spell he, too, will fall. "J'obéis" introduces the tone of chivalry and courtly love, which will be predominant throughout the poem, and which was already vaguely suggested at the opening with the gallant note of secrecy which at once acknowledged and masked the identity of the Lady celebrated. This motif of *fin amour* will be supported by a vocabulary cluster of terms like "gonfalon," "tambour," "exploit," "altesse," "Madame," "péril," "honneur" and "héros."

But the narrator needs to orient himself in the very disorder, and his "besoin d'explication" is one "plausible" for a poet's mind, a "figurative" one, which he then immediately symbolizes in a beautiful image: the lighting up of the lamps of the fairground in the evening dusk, in which his mind discovers — or creates — an order of garlands and attributes, purposefully arranged wreaths and emblems, that is a design. And so we recognize once again the poet and his "recherche assoupie d'imaginations ou de symboles" of the little theatre of "Un Spectacle Interrompu." For this need to create meaning, only compensation for the shock experienced by the harsh clash of dream and reality, touches in passing Mallarmé's basic theme of the defeat of *hasard* by the poetic mind; and the lamps coming to life in the falling evening recall the multitude of stars in the night sky, which become meaningful as constel-

---

[6] This passage recalls *Igitur,* where, as the hero almost fully "melts into" the realm of pure ideal essence, one after another "les choses" disappear about him, including his own existential manifestation, his mirror image.

lations. Our poem, then, is a demonstration again of the creation of order, the ideal which is poetry, out of chance circumstances.

As the narrator now definitely gives up "solitude," mentioned here for a last time, and throws himself with a mockingly chivalric show of daring, "même avec bravoure," into the violent confusion "naguères fui dans une gracieuse compagnie," she, in keeping with the rules of *fin amour*, accepts his service without surprise, a *belle dame sans merci* ready for adventure and relying on her knight with her "bras ingénu." "Ingénu," originally a feudal term, points back to the youthful beauty of the "enfant voiturée" above. They enter the fairground, their eyes on the rows of stands, and walk down its center aisle, to both sides of which the occasion's confusion, echoing noisily everywhere, is spread out. And so this setting, already evoked several times in these prose poems, is most richly developed here, as a miniature medieval world in which the crowd for a time limits its universe, and of which our aristocratic couple will briefly and magically become a part. The whole section is not merely about an aristocratic attitude amidst the masses, whose amusements appear to it like "assauts d'un médiocre dévergondage," but it reflects this attitude in a highly *précieux* style. For example, the rather cumbersome long adverb, "subséquemment," which is at the same time a term of jurisprudence, juxtaposed with a military term, "aux assauts," is not merely *précieux*, but strongly flavored with irony. And ironically, too, the surrounding vulgarity does divert the couple's "stagnation," again a highly precious latinism to indicate merely that they had stopped walking. The dying sunset by its etymological association, *creperus*, suggests an uncertain state of transition, moreover, not merely of the sky, but within the poem, where we pass now from the introduction to the action proper, whose occasion is the "humain spectacle, poignant," while the sunset's "nue incendiaire" foreshadows the "déclaration foraine" itself. The touching human spectacle is touching because of the very absence of the human: an apparently empty, miserable shanty, "renié," abandoned, even by a multicolored facade or boldly-lettered inscription like those which adorn other stands and once did this one. Its former gaiety is evoked by its present absence.

And now, as with the little theatre of "Un Spectacle Interrompu," which was transformed into the absolute stage of a cosmic drama, this poor shack is endowed by the poet with an aura of sanctity, contrasting sharply with its actual shabbiness. In fact, the whole paragraph has that peculiar tension created by the repeated juxtaposition of trivial and sublime imagery, couched in a tone of transparent irony which barely veils the tragic, and which recalls "Réminiscence." Thus, the "matelas décousu" hiding the lowly stage, or marking it, parodies not only heavy velvet theatre curtains, but "les voiles dans tous les temps et les temples," where "dans tous les temps" evokes the mythological past of the race, with "temples" intimating churches, the temples of antiquity, even the Temple of Jerusalem and its costly Veil hiding the Holy of Holies, perhaps vaguely suggested here by "l'arcane." For the absent showman had hung his dismantled mattres cover here "pour improviser l'arcane;" and while "arcane" thus confers on the sideshow the spirituality of a ritual performance, "improviser" once more foreshadows "la déclaration foraine," to be, in fact, "improvised" by the poet performer. The show tents, then, are the holy places of the fairground universe.

But now, in contrast to the sublimity inherent in the ideal stage, some of the real human misery indicated by that poor mattress shred is suggested: the hungry nights — visited not by marvelous dreams but only the nothingness of hunger-inspired nightmares — spent on it by its starving owner. And, as in "Pauvre Enfant Pâle," this miserable performer's hunger is also sublimated to a devotional abstinence by "jeûne," in harmony with the ambiance created above. The mystery of the "fête" had transformed the uninspired one, so that he had made of his bitter nights' companion his "gonfalon d'espoirs en liesse," the sign of his readiness for daring feats. For the daily misery seems excluded from the fraternal and festive [7] magic of the fairground which bans both loneliness, "des souliers nombreux y piétinant," and hunger, its atmosphere being such that it arouses "aux profondeurs des vêtements... [le] dur sou" to

---

[7] I have not been able to find "frérial" in Littré, nor in such dictionaries as Larousse and Robert, or the bilingual Heath; and though its meaning is obviously "brotherly" from *frère*, it strongly suggests "férial," not only phonetically, but particularly in our context.

emerge, thus causing the inanimate, even, to come to life. Therefore, "lui, aussi" had come "de tout dénué sauf de la notion qu'il y avait lieu pour être un des élus," which ironically plays with the Doctrine of Salvation by Faith, not works. He had yielded to the fair's calling in order to, if not sell, at least show; and the "mais quoi" now reminds us that "he" is not there at all but absent, for he had only been put on the scene because of this very absence, which left the poet-persona free to create him. "Très prosaïquement" undercuts the preceding speculations with the simple conjecture that perhaps the absence of a trained rat prevents the show from going on, this brief evocation of the most humble kind of animal act mocking "l'arcane" above. Or did this imaginary "mendiant" count on a display of his own physique to flatter popular taste, "l'athlétique vigueur de ses muscles" ironically juxtaposing the sorry figure of the starveling with the youthful beauty and strength of athletes. But the irony barely hides the tragic surging particularly out of the final part of the sentence, which on the narrative level offers a possible explanation for the absence of the trained rat, perhaps caused "comme cela résulte souvent de la mise en demeure de l'homme par les circonstances générales." And "mise en demeure" here plays both with its meaning as a legal term and its figurative one; however the humorous intimation that this particular show business may have fallen prey to bankruptcy almost disappears behind the presence of the most basically tragic of themes, which Mallarmé expresses with stark directness in his essay on "Hamlet":

> ... car il n'est point d'autre sujet, sachez bien: l'antagonisme de rêve chez l'homme avec les fatalités à son existence départies par le malheur (OC p. 300).

The meditations about the chimerical owner of the shanty are now interrupted by an imperative "Battez la caisse," proposed by the very real companion. "Madame," formerly the title reserved "aux seules femmes des chevaliers," is in harmony with the chivalric motif, which is reinforced with "seule tu sais Qui," echoing "une qui voit clair ici" of the opening and its gallant secrecy, while "en altesse" indicates her fitting haughtiness and sums up, with a fine hint of irony, the portrait of a courtly lady. As she points to the old drum, there rises from it its equally old owner, perhaps the guardian of the forsaken stage, who now uncrosses his idle arms to indicate to them that there will be no show, with "théâtre" here for the first time actually named in the piece. "Sans prestige," on the narrative level designating the lowliness of the little stage, etymologically — *praestigium* — suggests that this theatre is no longer capable of creating the illusion of sorcery and magic and, thus, has lost its vital powers, like the speechless old showman and the silent drum, his companion. Yet his life-long fellowship, perhaps, with this "instrument de rumeur et d'appel," which again ironically evokes the world of knightly adventure and also vaguely the masses' threatening discontent, make the old one beat his drum, "[le] séduisit à son vacant dessein," her as yet unrevealed scheme.

In the following clause we encounter an example of a Mallarméan analogy as brilliant as the precious gem which is one of its terms. The method of "raccourci" leaves the narrator's questions to his companion unstated, to be merely suggested by "le manque de réponse," which creates "l'énigme." And the poet then likens the lady's enigmatic silence to the jeweled pin at her throat, because like her jewelry her silence is an adornment, closing her mysterious lips and hiding her thoughts the way the sparkling pin closes her blouse and veils her body.

But she is already engulfed by the crowd whom the drum has attracted, "engouffrée" vaguely hinting at the danger of the moment whose mock military ambiance is suggested with "halte" and the beating of the drum. "Ma surprise de pitre coi" is in character with the narrator's role of his lady's servant and fool and recalls "Le Pitre Chatié;" but our nonplussed clown's speechlessness is broken as he automatically assumes his part of *montreur,* with the *boniment* "invariable et obscur d'abord pour moi-même" and deafened by the drum's noise, beginning to pour out of him mysteriously, as he, too, has now fallen under the fair's magic spell and from spectator turned performer.

And so, in keeping with the tenets of chivalry, our aristocratic couple gives a charity performance for the poor old man. "Le nimbe en paillasson dans le remerciement joignant deux paumes séniles vidé," in its vagueness, is highly suggestive, for the totally original image of "straw halo" for hat, in which the poet-persona has collected the alms which he now empties into the old man's cupped hands, suggests at the same time the image of the old man as a medieval saint, wearing his hat like a halo and his two "paumes séniles" joined in a gesture of prayer for alms received. "Le nimbe en paillasson" would thus be the subject of "dans le remerciement joignant deux paumes séniles." [8] And although this reading would leave the past participle, "vidé," somehow floating, I have the feeling that both images, that of the persona's collecting the receipts in the hat and then pouring them into the old man's hands, as well as that of the old man wearing his hat which makes him look like a haloed saint praying, are somehow compressed into one elliptical and richly evocative phrase. The collection completed, the narrator now waves in knightly fashion "les couleurs," probably the ribbons of the hat, as a signal from afar for the crowd that the show is to begin. And the "je me coiffai" here parodies the donning of the helmet before action: "prêt à fendre la masse debout en le secret de ce qu'avait su faire avec ce lieu sans rêve l'initiative d'une contemporaine de nos soirs," the stylistic elegance of this final clause both distancing and elevating the friend and companion to an apparition on its stage.

Her *entrée en scène,* set off from the rest of the poem, with "émergeait" vaguely suggesting a rising out of water, recalls the Birth of Venus image of "Le Phénomène Futur," with the *foule,* "cent têtes," figuring as the sea from which the apparition rises and into which it will later again disappear.

The comparison of the sudden bright beam of light striking the figure on the stage with the lucidity of an idea striking the narrator, both illuminations flashing forth simultaneously and "électriquement," links inner and outer events. And the resulting "calculation," that the woman without anything but her *elegant* presence — rather than without anything but her *mere* presence — amply repays the crowd for the alms exacted from it, recalls the opening of the poem where, even in the narrator's private world which

---

[8] This and similar willfully created ambiguities contribute to that "technique of strangeness," to which James L. Kugel has devoted a book, *The Techniques of Strangeness in Symbolist Poetry* (New Haven and London: Yale Univ. Press, 1971), in which he characterizes Mallarmé's particular technique as "Grammatical Chaos," and then discusses, however, only "Soupir" as an example of it.

was symbolized by the landau, the companion's beauty was celebrated in her dress as much as in her features. This balance between the artificial and the natural in her beauty is elegantly rendered with: "elle, selon que la mode, une fantaisie ou l'humeur du ciel circonstanciaient sa beauté." Not only does this celebration of elegance recall the Baudelairean inheritance with its cult of the artificial, but it perfectly fits the courtly ambiance of our poem, which, in turn, reflects that Mallarméan *préciosité* and delicate refinement which produced LA DERNIÈRE MODE and, above all, the very style of "La Déclaration Foraine."

Again, some of the essential ingredients of theatre, "danse ou chant," are evoked by their absence, but the dangerous presence of the audience, "cohue," dictates the narrator's course of action, inducing him to that other knightly duty of the defense of ladies in peril. For her "exhibition" seems indeed too "subtile" for the general comprehension of the throng who appear to be losing interest; and the only power in the world which the poet-persona feels he can resort to now is the absolute one of Metaphor, significantly capitalized, and surely a synecdoche for poetry, identifying the narrator of this prose poem explicitly as a poet. "Dégoiser" not merely ironically undercuts the tone established but, above all, the magnificent poem which will be "spouted forth" until a certain enlightenment on their faces indicates that they, the crowd, believe that they are getting their money's worth. "Leur sécurité" is a synecdoche for *la foule,* who will by the "évidence impliquée en la parole," that is by the sonnet, be induced to "exchange their cheap coin for superior presumptions," an allusion to the alchemical operation of changing base metal into gold, the gold being that revealed by the poet who will celebrate the lady's hair as a golden flame.

Before he begins, the poet-persona glances one last time at the apparition, all of whose loveliness appears to be concentrated in her hair. The hair seems, therefore, not merely a synecdoche for, but the symbol of, that woman who represents both dramatically in this little theatre and figuratively — "la vivante allégorie" — in the poem feminine beauty. And this burning hair, "une chevelure où fume puis éclaire," resembles that of "Le Phénomène Futur" which was "une extase d'or." But, curiously, the hair is in our vision so inextricably linked to the carefully described hat which complements it — of pale-colored crepe and decorated with flowers — that they seem to melt into one, igniting into a golden crown of flowery magnificence, recalling the "casque guerrier d'impératrice enfant/Dont... il tomberait des roses" of the sonnet "Victorieusement fui le suicide beau." The "fastes de jardins," moreover, while designating the flowers on the hat, again with "jardins" stresses the artificial. Further, the poet-persona takes care to indicate that this lovely hat matches both dress and shoes, a dress animated by the woman wearing it, "statuesque." And the foot, a traditionally erotic image, is then immediately associated not with the woman's body, but with her costume, "comme le reste hortensia," and its pale color of the hydrangea blossom. The whole paragraph would, without modification almost, perfectly fit the "Fashions" section of any of the issues of LA DERNIÈRE MODE.

And now the poet-persona improvises his "déclaration foraine" which has become one of Mallarmé's most famous sonnets, "La Chevelure vol d'une flamme."

In the verse poem converge some of the major motifs and themes of the prose poem of which it is a part: the burning hair of the woman melting into the sunset of the dying day, the beloved's ambiguity, and the humble poet-hero's celebration of Beauty before the doubting crowd. As the persona beholds his companion on the stage, he imagines her long, flame-colored hair — which we know is pinned up under the luxurious hat — unfolded in surrender to the passion it inspires, a passion which dies at the point of its fulfillment; "a l'extrême/Occident de désirs" superimposes both the notions of the "extreme death of desire" and of the sun's flaming death in the western sky. The death motif is reinforced with the "mourir" of the following line where the hair, pinned up high, is likened to a diadem expiring in the oncoming darkness of the night. We must imagine the little shanty without artificial lighting, and the erstwhile flaming up of the hair due to its having been struck by the last glowing of the sunset. The image of the diadem is then transformed into that of a crown, "le front couronné" evoking a princess, the courtly lady of our prose poem. Her crowned brow is the hair's "ancien foyer," as well as the origin of the flame, its hearth. The second quatrain continues the juxtaposition of the golden hair and sky and fire — "or," "vive nue," "feu" — but now the woman's inward fire is reflected in her eyes which, like those of the Phénomène Futur, are precious gems. And those eyes — traditionally mirrors of the soul — express our lady's temperament, that attitude of mocking haughtiness and at the same time of an almost child-like ingenuousness. The last quatrain introduces the poet-persona, "héros tendre," who feels that he cannot do justice to the Beauty he celebrates and thus "defames" her. The "nudité" is not that of the lover, but of the poet, whose new-born poem, itself "nu de peur" as it is thus exposed to the public also exposes him. The apparition on the stage — who does not need theatre's customary accessories to charm her audience — needs no jewelry nor rings on her fingers to enhance her beauty. Her natural ornament, "simplifying woman with glory," is her flaming hair. With it she accomplishes the feat of "sowing with ruby," that is scattering its red-golden sparks over the doubt, that of the poet-persona about his Muse's enigmatic ways as well as that of the uncomprehending crowd in the little theatre — figuring the reader of this poetry — like an almost divine, "tutélaire," and "joyous torch." [9]

The poem, in which the poet has "fixed" both the intensity and the evanescence of beauty and of the passion it inspires in the image of the flame which, like the sun itself, rises, mounts to a climax, and then dies, and which was foreshadowed in the prose poem's opening with the expiring sunset, falls into the dead silence of an uncomprehending crowd, much like that described — predicted — in "Le Phénomène Futur:" "... indifférents, car ils n'auront pas eu la force de comprendre." Nothing could better

---

[9] This sonnet was for the first time published in the body of our prose poem, but subsequently placed by the poet into his volume of verse poetry, the Deman edition of the *Poésies* (1899), prepared by him; and it appears in the *Pléiade* edition (OC. p. 53) also at the place which Mallarmé had assigned it in *Poésies*. It has been thoroughly explicated many times, sometimes with reference to its original context. Cf. e.g., Charles Chadwick, *Mallarmé sa pensée dans sa poésie* (Paris: Corti, 1962), pp. 101-104; Chassé, *Les Clefs*, who has a whole chapter on "Les Poèmes sur la Chevelure," pp. 190-200; Cohn, *Toward the Poems*, pp. 147-152; Davies, *Le Drame solaire*, pp. 165-191; Fowlie, *Mallarmé*, pp. 39-42; Noulet, *L'Œuvre*, pp. 194-200; Richard, *L'Univers*, pp. 347-349; Thibaudet, *La Poésie*, p. 196; Wais, *Mallarmé*, pp. 598-99; A. R. Chisholm, *Mallarmé's "Grand Œuvre"* (Univ. of Manchester Press; London: 1962), pp. 19-21.

convey the absence of their reaction than the poet's own white silence, before he pursues the anecdote — as though the magnificent poem had never taken place — "RIEN de la mémorable crise ... N'AURA EU LIEU ... QUE LE LIEU" (OC p. 474-75). The indifferent *foule* from which the Poet rises — like his Muse from the "cent têtes" — and into which he returns, is, indeed, suggestive of the elemental sea whence the solitary Maître almost casts his "Coup de Dés."

The lady celebrated has not understood her poem either, but, then, she had at this point lost her individual identity; for, like the dancer who "*n'est pas une femme* qui danse, pour ces motifs juxtaposés qu'elle *n'est pas une femme,* mais une métaphore" (OC p. 304), she had, in fact, become "la vivante allégorie," and this designation in its seeming contradiction indicates the woman's transformation and suggests the tension between life and art. The woman served so gallantly — "mon aide à la taille afin d'en assoupir l'élan gentiment à terre" — herself in turn serves the poet as an occasion of poetry, as his Muse. For "courtly love" was never a way of life, but a way of art, and the *Minnesänger* not a lover but a singer.

The lady, again in mock-chivalric tone, "resigns her faction," and the narrator's phrase, "faute ... de faconde ultérieure," after his recitation of the "déclaration," is bitterly ironic, reflecting the isolation of the poet who now resorts to prose to put himself on the audience' level of understanding, "de plain-pied avec l'entendement des visiteurs." But as he tries to convince them by flattery that they have had a complete show (expressing his previous calculation, that the lady's elegance amply replaces the theatre's customary accessories) what keeps the crowd in the temporary "suspens de marque appréciative" long enough for our couple to disappear among them is not, ironically, what he is saying, but their very incomprehension of his words. For "ce naturel s'accommode de l'allusion parfaite que fournit la toilette toujours à l'un des motifs primordiaux de la femme, et suffit, ainsi que votre sympathique approbation m'en convainc" though prose, is that of a prose *poet*. And as the poet-persona cuts short their dangerous surprise with "une affectation de retour à l'authenticité du spectacle," "affectation," which on the narrative level refers to a method, a "faux-semblant," at the same time describes the manner, a "manière qui s'éloigne du naturel," which is one way to characterize this style. [10]

As our couple, submerged now in the crowd, is led with it to the exit "sur une vacance d'arbres et de nuit," there is, as if until the eyes get accustomed to the dark, a momentary ambiguity of vision. Is it "une vacance d'arbres," an absence of trees? But then we recognize the trees of the fairground in the dark, and that festively white-gloved "enfantin tourlourou" — recalling the "gant blanc des tourlourous" of "Petit Air Guerrier" — hanging back. And does not his humorously suggested dreaming of unstiffening those new gloves "à l'estimation d'une jarretière hautaine" intimate but another reaction to the Beauty displayed inside? [11]

The conclusion of the piece is, like a fable's moral which teaches its lesson, about what the poem demonstrated: the creation of a poem, from its conception to its delivery and reception into the world. Yet this conclusion is an integral part of the whole structure, presented as a dialogue between the hero and heroine, the Poet and his Muse, now alone again as they were in the beginning, and thus closing the circle. The lady, both celebrated and rescued by her poet, characteristically "consents" to thanking him for this double service, while drinking in the night air, "une bouffée droit à elle d'une constellation ou des feuilles," to regain her habitual coolness of voice befitting the distant smile we know. She had, of course, never lost her serenity, for Beauty is self-confident.

---

[10] This smiling and gentle self-irony, whether intended or not in this particular case, is frequent, especially in the poet's late work.

[11] Thibaudet, *La Poésie*, p. 70, identifies the soldier boy, who wants to touch the vision, i.e., the poetry, with "la critique:"

> Et le malentendu entre Mallarmé et la critique n'est-il pas ici symbolisé? Le public en général, la critique en particulier, tiennent à pouvoir toucher le mollet de la Muse. C'est même cela souvent que l'on entend par ce mot: comprendre. Sentir les trophes du *Lac* effleurer comme des rames une eau musicale n'est rien, si l'on n'a résolu des palpitants problèmes sur Madame Charles, et dégourdi, comme les gants blancs du bleu, des doigts tachés d'encre à l'estimation de sa jarretière.

It is true that every critic who has had anything to say about "La Déclaration Foraine" has felt called upon to discuss Mallarmé and Méry Laurent. Thibaudet might thus well be correct in seeing the little soldier as a symbol for "biographical criticism."

Her "j'ai dans l'esprit le souvenir de choses qui ne s'oublient" is enigmatic — as are her ways — for does it refer to her own display or its celebration by the poet-persona? He, at any rate, accepts it as a compliment which he politely diminishes, reducing his magnificent creation to a mere convention, "rien que lieu commun," which suggests the rhetorical "lieux oratoires." She accepts it so, but indicates that, perhaps, without the occasion the poem would not have been born; and was she herself not doubly that, in being the one celebrated by it, and in having produced the need to utter it, that is "une impatience de gens" and the resulting "coup de poing brutal à l'estomac?" And what could better express this brutal, but practical and efficient, midwifery of the public? The poet admits it, and "la rêverie," the new poem, "qui s'ignore et se lance nue de peur, en travers du public," at the moment of its birth, this fearful naked creation — like "l'enfant d'une nuit d'Idumée" of "Don du Poème" which was almost too fragile to live through the night of its birth — also exposes its creator, "Une nudité de héros tendre," the poet-hero. And he now not only explains the strange and literally foreign features of his creation, which he takes care to point out to us in a footnote, but also that, just as he had needed *la foule,* so did she, his companion. For would she have so clearly appreciated the refinements of his "boniment" without its repercussion from the many?

Under the jesting irony of the narrative level, however, is hidden again the serious business of poetry. For neither had the poem been received by "la compréhension multiple" nor is it certain that it had "charmed" the lady's mind. And what could better indicate the indifference of that "contemporaine" than her final "peut-être!" as the persona soliloquizes on another aspect of his craft: the need of a work of art to create its audience. After the poem is born, it has to live in the world, but this life, we know, may well begin only after the poet's death.

And so "La Déclaration Foraine," again about the poet's unique preoccupation, his art, also ends on a note of solitude, as did some of the early pieces, but especially "Un Spectacle Interrompu" and "Réminiscence." Yet, "La Déclaration Foraine," demonstrating in its anecdote and restating in its conclusion, also manifests the solitary artist's paradoxical need of "the others," *la foule,* without which, like the "Montreur" of "Le Phénomène Futur," he would cease to exist. It is perhaps for this reason that Mallarmé chose to place that earlier piece — which, as I have mentioned, was not the earliest composed — at the head of the cycle, where it appears like a still vague premonition of the destiny unfolded here, both of and by the mature poet.

The paradoxical tension of the artist's need of both solitude and the multitude is reflected in his exigency of both silence and utterance, a silence which is, as we saw, almost like an absence of existence, which the poet needs to create its essence. Is it not the very meaninglessness of the world as it exists which sets the artist on his search for meaning and ideal order? Not only did our poet-persona need the fairground's haphazard array of lamps lighting up in the night in order to discover there "guirlandes et attributs," but the Poet needs the night to see the stars, and these to discover — or create — Constellations.

And as the poet needs both the absence of the world and its presence to conceive his Declaration, this declaration, even if it is a soliloquy, is a declaration to someone; the soliloquizing Hamlet needs the stage of the world, *theatrum mundi,* both to speak and to be heard, in order to find himself. Thus, aside from the traditional kinship of the Orpheus-singer with the entertainer, the troubadour with the harlequin, some of the secret affinity of Poet and Showman lies in this: they both need *la foule* as a proof of their existence, as the solitary Igitur needs his mirror image. [12] In this sense, "the others" perform a most vital function in the creative act for the poet, who, in turn, performs for them. And as the ideal poet-priest's performance is a mystery — "improviser ici l'arcane" — both to and for those who participate in the ritual, so the crowd in our poem, though not understanding that it beheld Pure Beauty, beheld it, however, only because the poet celebrated it before and

---

[12] Richard, *L'Univers,* p. 346:
> Le même besoin qui l'amenait à se faire le poète du miroir, le pousse donc maintenant à rechercher l'épreuve d'un "éclat multiple." ... Privée d'attestation divine, la pensée tendra, et surtout à partir des années 1880-1885, à trouver une consécration dans l'appel de cette nouvelle "divinité éparse," la foule.

for — and as we now know with — them.[13] But in order to celebrate the Ideal, the poet sacrifices his own existence by transmuting it into art, which becomes the theme of "Le Nénuphar Blanc," and which was rendered in "La Déclaration Foraine" by a courtly poet-persona for whom a beautiful woman, "la flamme," was not an occasion of love, but of poetry.

---

[13] Block, *Symbolist Drama,* pp. 78-79:

> Though intimate, Mallarmé's poetic recitation was envisaged as a public ceremony and a means of revealing spiritual truths to the masses. This aspiration seems to go back at least as far as Mallarmé's participation in the Théâtre de Valvins: "Un de ses vœux," reports Margueritte, "était que le poète, en des salles immenses, devant des foules attentives, prononçât les phrases lapidaires de l'enseignement esthétique, d'où tout découlait. Seul, le poète sachant, affirmait-il, révéler la beauté, source de vertu parfaite, aux masses."

LE NÉNUPHAR BLANC

"Le Nénuphar Blanc" is by far the best known of Mallarmé's prose poems; composed and published in 1895, it remained practically unchanged in its successive publications.[1] One of the poem's great attractions lies, undoubtedly, in its perfect marriage of thought and expression, so that, though of the "late" style, its difficulties seem to dissolve as we submit to the gentle flow of its opening passages.

The title, which introduces the major symbolic image of the poem, discloses both its setting of a water world and one of its principal themes, that of absence, symbolized as so often in Mallarmé by his favorite color, the white of pure negation or nonexistence.[2] And though this whiteness is that of a flower, it is of one not rooted in the earth, but a floating, shimmering blossom which appears like matter refined and sublimated into pure form — the Ideal — by Nature herself.

The anecdote tells of a summer day which the poet-persona spends in his little boat on the Seine. Having lost himself in his rowing, he realizes, as the boat comes to a stop in a clump of reeds, that he has run aground near the property of a friend's

---

[1] The principal variant is the orthographic one of the title, originally "Nénufar," which applies, of course, also to that word's appearance in the body of the poem. Both spellings are lexical, but the final one is more common, while the first points to the word's arabic origin, "nînûfar." The other variants from the poem's publication in *Pages,* such as the omission of commas and conjunctions, are minor.

[2] This pure white absence recalls Mallarmé's obsession with the white virgin page prior to the birth of poetry, which manifests itself both in his verse and prose, as well as in his correspondence.

friend, a lady to whom he was supposed to introduce himself. But instead of meeting her, he avoids the real encounter in order to create the poetic image of the woman idealized in "Le Nénuphar Blanc."

The opening sentence introduces a first-person narrator and suggests a former gradual slipping away of his consciousness, with the verb reaching back to an anterior time, between which and the present moment there was only absence in his mind. For with his eyes unseeing and, like an embryo's, turned inward "sur l'entier oubli" of his journey, he had lost himself in a rhythm, the rowing motion of his body and the gliding of his boat on the water. And from this drowsiness his awareness now emerges, as from a Lethean oblivion, to be born into time, that of a mid-summer day.[3] "Comme le rire de l'heure coulait alentour" not merely describes the harmony of the One with the All — consciousness of time, and time flowing into space — but with its gentle vowels and softly alliterating r's and l's renders the blissful fluidity of this water-environment which carries the drowsy dreamer. This orchestration continues throughout the paragraph, with "frôle," "fila" and "yole" suggesting the continuity of the boat's gliding and the flowing of the water, while "l'étincellement stable d'initiales" onomatopoetically imitates its breaking up into sparkling, glittering globules, the translucent fragments of space and time in suspense.

The rower had been so unaware of his rowing as he partook of the summer morning's apparent immobility and idleness [4]— "tant

---

[3] For the maternal aspect of water, see Gaston Bachelard, *L'eau et les rêves* (Paris: Corti, 1942), pp. 177-78:

> Des quatre éléments, il n'y a que l'eau qui puisse bercer. C'est elle l'élément berçant. C'est un trait de plus de son caractère féminin: elle berce comme une mère. ... L'eau nous porte. L'eau nous berce. L'eau nous endort. L'eau nous rend notre mère.

[4] "Le Nénuphar Blanc" reflects Mallarmé's summers at his vacation retreat, Valvins, which also serves as the setting of "Conflit." His love for the Seine, which he enjoyed at Valvins with his little boat, "idling away" time without losing it, is expressed in his "biographical letter" to Verlaine, *Correspondance* II, p. 304:

> J'honore la rivière, qui laisse s'engouffrer dans son eau des journées entières sans qu'on ait l'impression de les avoir perdues, ni une ombre de remords. Simple promeneur en yoles d'acajou, mais voilier avec furie, très-fier de sa flotille.

d'immobilité paressait" — that he had not noticed the boat's slowing to a halt. But the bright and insistent scintillation of the initials on the oars, pulled in inadvertently, awakens him to his identity in the world. And this birth into existence vaguely echos the opening of "La Déclaration Foraine," where its narrator awakened from "Le Silence!" into the world of "les choses." But while it was harsh and shocking there, forcing the poet-persona out of his solitude, it is gentle here, for he remains alone. The "initiales sur les avirons," the occasion of the narrator's return into the world surrounding him, are richly symbolic. For "initiales," etymologically from *in ire,* suggest the hero's entering the mysterious territory of his adventure while at the same time they constitute a veiled erotic allusion. "Avirons," from "virer," a verb important later on in the poem, reminds us that the seemingly drifting boat — its drifting symbolizing the mind's subconscious wanderings — is not wind-driven, but directed by the rower who, now awakened, will not leave its course to chance. Though the little boat had almost floated into a chance encounter — symbolized by its entanglement in the reeds — its pilot wakes up in time still to direct it.

"Qu'arrivait-il, où étais-je?" He tries to orient himself on the threshold between inner and outer worlds, "arrivait" etymologically again alluding to the nautical venture. "Pour voir clair en l'aventure" — "voir clair" by contrast recalling his "yeux au-dedans fixés" above — the narrator has to cross that gap of absence and reach to his "départ tôt." And "tôt," from *tostus* — "brulé par assimilation de la rapidité de la flamme" — leads directly into "ce juillet de flamme," an impression of the moment's atmosphere which, not only by its image, but also phonetically as well as by the visual arrangement of the letters, suggests light quivering in heat vibrations. "L'intervalle vif," the river flowing among its vegetation, reinforces that impression, "vif" referring both to the water's flow and the sun's play on its surface. The triple alliteration of the v's, "l'intervalle vif ... végétations," conveys an agitation of flickering light, with the plants' secret energy, *vegetatio,* hidden under their sun-drenched sleep.

The traditional early departure for "l'aventure" suggests the chivalric quest, underlined with "*en quête* de floraisons d'eau." And since this quest is nautical, the traditional forest is transformed "en fluvial bosquet," a water forest. "Un dessein de reconnaître l'emplacement occupé par la propriété de l'amie d'une amie, à qui je devais improviser un bonjour" reveals, moreover, that the quest is not merely for flowers and that the boat had, paradoxically, drifted toward the dreaming rower's intended destination. The originally military "reconnaître" picks up the chivalric motif, reinforced with "l'emplacement occupé"; and this vocabulary of conquest has the erotic undertones appropriate not only to the subconscious voyage, but also to the courtly love theme, which appears in this poem as it did in the preceding one. "Amie" is also a term of *fin amour,* and the distance implied, moreover, with "l'amie d'une amie" fits the world of *Minne,* as does the identification of a courted lady by her property, which constituted, in fact, a medieval lady's identity.

In his absence of mind the narrator had become one with the "distrait ruisseau" on which he was driven along, his oarstrokes, merging with surrounding nature's fundamental rhythm, "chasing" the boat along the lawns — or, impressionistically, the landscapes along the boat — inevitably and without stopping before any. And this "même impartial coup de rame" which breaks the landscapes' mirror reflections with the regularity and impassibility of day following day, season upon season, and year upon year, recalls the gaslight of "Un Spectacle Interrompu," humming inexorably "avec l'impartialité d'une chose élémentaire." But amidst nature's relentless indifference, "je venais échouer" vaguely suggests the "naufrage" ever haunting the poetic sea voyage from "Brise Marine" to the "Coup de Dés." And the obstacle in the water, "quelque touffe de roseaux," is doubly the journey's "terme mystérieux." For as the narrator on the literal level reaches the limits of the sought-after "propriété de l'amie d'une amie," on a more obscure and hidden level of consciousness "touffe de roseaux" is associated with a Faun's erotic dreams — of having "divisé la touffe échevelée" of forest and water-dwelling nymphs espied in their "sommeils touffus." Mysterious obstacles, moreover, characterize the traditional quest voyage through the magic forest.

The river, both symbol and thoroughfare of the journey, becomes at the destination a proudly displayed pond, its "nonchaloir" underlining the stagnant water etymologically implied by "étang," which connotes, however, no dullness, for its ripples suggest the potentiality "des hésitations à partir qu'a une source." And this potentiality, this promise of unrealized possibilities, throws its charm over the whole adventure. "Source," echoing "ma course" above, evokes the notion of first origins associated with water, [5] and modulated in the birth motif — of the hero's consciousness — in the opening passages of the poem.

The narrator now discovers that the obstacle of greenery on the water "masquait l'arche unique d'un pont," and bridges are a traditional quest obstacle, whose mystery (where do they lead, are they to be crossed?) the hero must solve. [6] Ours reveals itself as part of the unknown lady's estate, which the rower is approaching. Significantly, however, he does not arrive at either entrance of the bridge, but at right angles to it, seeing the curve of its single arch spanning the water. It is "prolongé, à terre, d'ici et de là, par une haie clôturant des pelouses," the little bridge's balanced symmetry rendered by "d'ici et de là," with its two short syllables to either side of their conjunction. This passage, moreover, displays a significant image cluster, dominating the whole poem, namely that of enclosure, introduced already with the boat, and then the pond, now reinforced with "une haie clôturant," whose insistence is almost redundant, a hedge by definition being a *clôture* protecting and limiting a territory. This imagery will become more and more predominant, culminating finally in the swan's egg — whose shell will remain unbroken — and the closed "nénuphar" itself. The unknown one's park surrounding her is, again, by definition an

---

[5] Mircea Eliade, *The Sacred and the Profane* (New York: Harcourt, Brace and World, 1959), p. 130, in his chapter on "Structure of Aquatic Symbolism" discusses the notion of first origins associated with water, and which is one of the motifs developed in "Le Nénuphar Blanc:"

> The waters symbolize the universal sum of virtualities; they are *fons et origo,* "spring and origin," the reservoir of all the possibilities of existence; they precede every form and support every creation. ... immersion in water signifies regression to the preformal, reincorporation into the undifferentiated mode of preexistence.

We recall that the "Phénomène Futur," symbol of Mallarmé's poetry, was marked by "le sel de la mer première."

[6] One of the best-known examples that comes to mind is Lancelot's "Pont de l'Epée" in *Le Chevalier à la Charette.*

enclosure which at the same time stresses the imposition of the artificial upon the natural, already vaguely suggested above with "le ruban d'aucune herbe" and "pelouses."

As the narrator now moves from the description of the outer world to the reflections aroused by it — the world of his imagination which permits him to cross those enclosures — the very passage reflects a tension between the apparent and the hidden, reality and dream. For though its tone is banal and trite, "un joli voisinage, pendant la saison," and though it approaches the woman in the most distant manner, "la nature d'une personne qui ... ne pouvant être que conforme à mon goût," it suggests the closest intimacy. Is the persona not in fact, mentally, entering her "retraite aussi humidement impénétrable," revealing her innermost privacy to an unseen beholder? The erotic suggestiveness of the sentence, as well as that of the "paysage" itself, surges strongly through the surface of its apparent nonchalance, like the very ripples on the pond. And it is this intense eroticism, not only veiled by *préciosité* of language and attitude, but sublimated into an aesthetic spirituality, which constitutes the tension of this poem, culminating finally in the "rapt de mon idéale fleur."

The woman alone with her mirror, "elle avait fait de ce cristal son miroir intérieur," evokes Hérodiade before hers, solitary also and separated from the world by "l'eau morne" and of whom a glance had cost the beholder's life, while "l'indiscrétion éclatante des après-midi" recalls the Faun, already evoked above. And not only has the natural river become part of an artificial park, but the pond and "la buée d'argent glaçant des saules" have become part of their owner, the willows' silvery mist the approaching lady's "limpid glance," and the surface of the pond, enclosed by bushes and greenery, the reflection of its solitary beholder's psyche, thus doubly "intérieur." "Glaçant" and "cristal," etymologically suggesting cold and ice, intimate an absence or refusal of passion, Hérodiade's virginity. The poet-persona did, indeed, evoke her "lustrale," which in suggesting the purification of baptismal waters not only sublimates the absent heroine of the poem but vaguely recalls the birth motif of its opening.

In the following paragraph we see the narrator in a posture of one leaning forward to see without wanting to be seen, which foreshadows his stance in the opening of "L'Ecclésiastique." [7] He is "courbé ... comme sous le silence spacieux de ce que s'annonçait l'étrangère," under the spell of "spacious silence," of absence which is pregnant with expectancy. And then he smilingly associates this submissive-looking pose with the potential enslavement imposed by "une possibilité féminine," which under its apparently distant tone again hides suggestions of intimacy, both the notions of "esclavage" and distance befitting the courtly motif. Haunted by his "démon," the poet-persona now creates another one of those sparkling and surprising analogies, by comparing the potential bondage to the lady who inspires him to the straps attaching the rower's feet to his boat, the instrument of his enchantment which had drifted into the magic garden. And since in this universe the sea voyage is a figure for the poetic quest, the poet's magic instrument, which while being part of him at the same time casts its spell on him, is his poetry.

But then a barely audible noise — and in this magic world noise is softened and diminished almost into silence, as with the initial "bruit inerte" — makes the musing hero wonder whether "l'habitant du bord" is approaching. Is she merely haunting his mind, or really coming to the water's edge "inespérément"? The sentence indicates not only a fusion, a confusion almost, of inner and outer worlds, but implies a preference for that of the imagination, for "inespérément," though literally meaning "unexpectedly," already vaguely suggests the narrator's hope that the mysterious one remain hidden.

And as we follow the narrator in his mental divagations, where he seems to pause, meditate, then pause again, we notice now how

---

[7] Richard, *L'Univers*, in his chapter "Les Rêveries Amoureuses" devotes many pages to "le regard," but the motif is there isolated from its contexts. He generalizes, as follows, on p. 95:

> ... l'amant pourra user d'un instrument fort efficace: son regard. Qu'est-ce en effet que celui-ci, sinon une transparence intime, capable de traverser, sans la toucher ni la briser, la transparence d'un dehors? Il se jette au delà, mais il n'entame rien; merveilleuse arme d'hyperbole, outil dangereux d'indiscrétion... Rien de plus monotone, en un sens, que la dramaturgie mallarméenne du désir: parfaitement illustratrice de l'attitude érotique baptisée par d'aucuns "complexe d'Acteon," elle reproduit çà et là, avec assez de variantes, le même geste essentiel, celui du vol oculaire.

almost every sentence, some long some short, becomes a separate paragraph. And this significant typographical arrangement is more striking even in the original *Divagations,* where the spaces between paragraphs are wider. The poet here literally utilizes empty space — absence and silence — poetically, the spacing between the sentences isolating his ideas and images as by a halo, so that the white of the paper itself makes the "Nénuphar" poem even whiter. [8]

But why did the walking stop?

It stopped in time, like the hero's boat, for the foot — gracefully displayed in "La Déclaration Foraine" in its silken shoe — has a more subtle and elusive power if unrevealed. It is the rhythm only of the unseen feet, "qui vont, viennent, conduisent," which charms and leads the dreamer's mind where the absent lady, her mere shadow, wishes. And as she is enclosed in the misty elegance of batiste and lace, reminiscent of LA DERNIÈRE MODE, so are these secret feet by a skirt flowing to and on the ground. "Circonvenir" stresses at once the notions of enclosure and approach, while "affluant" and "dans une flottaison," echoing "floraisons d'eau" above, are in harmony with the water ambiance. The elegant woman's walk appears like a rhythmically moving ship, [9] and the vision of flowing whiteness already suggests the water lily itself, which — though the steps' "initiative" vaguely intimates commencements of adventure, reinforced with "s'ouvre" — we know will remain closed. The concluding analogy is that of a gliding vessel's prow throwing a misty train of foam behind its path with the flowing white lace folds thrown back "en traîne" by the walking feet's "double flèche savante," the veiled allusion to Cupid stressing their erotic attraction.

---

[8] Mallarmé discusses his utilization of the silence of the white page in one of his "Réponses à des Enquêtes," while talking about Poe:

> L'armature intellectuelle du poème se dissimule et tient — a lieu — dans l'espace qui isole les strophes et parmi le blanc du papier: significatif silence qu'il n'est pas moins beau de composer, que les vers (OC p. 872).

[9] "Le Beau Navire," Baudelaire, *Fleurs,* pp. 57-58, comes to mind, and especially the following stanza:

> Quand tu vas balayant l'air de ta jupe large,
> Tu fais l'effet d'un beau vaisseau qui prend le large,
>   Chargé de toile, et va roulant
> Suivant un rythme doux, et paresseux, et lent.

In the manneristic "connaît-elle un motif à sa station, elle-même la promeneuse?" a tension is created by the juxtaposition of "motif" and "station," counterbalancing the notions of movement and its absence, as later in the sentence with the contrast of "mentale somnolence" and "lucidité," while "la promeneuse" continues a modulation begun with "l'amie d'une amie," "l'inconnue," "l'étrangère," "l'habitante du bord," and "la chère ombre," leading up to and preparing for "La Méditative ou la Hautaine, la Farouche, la Gaie." [10] To find out why she stopped walking would destroy "le mystère" by questioning, which, in the tradition of romance, breaks the magic spell. And the narrator's raising his head beyond the reeds which hide him would not merely expose him, but also force him out of the magical drowsiness which permeates the moment; for just as in the outer world the reeds hide his head, so in the inner one that "mentale somnolence" hides his lucidity. "Trop haut la tête," moreover, suggests the punishment of decapitation for having beheld the forbidden, which recalls the *hubris* theme of "Pauvre Enfant Pâle" as well as again linking the Nénuphar lady to Hérodiade.

While shunning the real one, the poet-persona approaches the lady in and of his imagination with the courteous and courtly "Madame," warning her that the revelation of her features' "précision" would break the spell of the mere suggestion of her presence, that mysterious vagueness of "chose installée ici par le bruissement d'une venue." And the "charme instinctif d'en dessous" of not only the absent one, but the moment itself, intimates a hidden melody — "charme" pointing to *carmen* — and the poet's hiding in the reeds, potential instruments of song. The whole pas-

---

[10] Thibaudet, *La Pensée*, p. 328, is particularly charmed with this sentence:

> On suit avec un plaisir curieux, chez Mallarmé, la virtuosité des coupes syntaxiques. Dans le *Nénuphar Blanc*, arrêtant sa barque sur la rive d'un parc, un bruit le fait douter si l'habitante du bord ne s'approche pas de l'eau: "Connaît-elle un motif à sa station, elle-même la promeneuse." Les trois membres de la phrase, dont les deux virgules marquent les articulations, se présentent dans l'ordre inverse de l'usage français qui exigerait "La promeneuse elle-même connaît-elle un motif à sa station?" 3-2-1 remplace 1-2-3. Ne dirait-on pas que cet ordre inverse des trois membres, comme la tête, le buste et les jambes se mireraient réverbérés sous l'eau, suspend la vision du rameur?

sage is highly evocative of the Faun's aestival and sylvan world with the pulsation of its desires modulated into melody. But the "plus authentiquement nouée, avec une boucle en diamant, des ceintures" not only recalls the Faun, but also again Hérodiade, those opposite poles in this poetic universe. For the allusion to the chastity belt, "authentiquement nouée" but vainly, as it does not defend "her" charms against the explorer, directly recalls the Faun's dream of the nymphs:

> Moi, de ma rumeur fier, je vais parler longtemps
> Des déesses; et par d'idolâtres peintures,
> A leur ombre enlever encore des ceintures (OC p. 51)

And the "boucle en diamant" become useless intimates the melting of hard purity [11] and Hérodiade's nubility: "... une enfance sentant parmi ses rêveries / Se séparer enfin ses froides pierreries." But while the Faun, like the punished Pitre, had almost forsaken Art for Eros — "Tâche donc, instrument des fuites, ô maligne / Syrinx, de refleurir aux lacs où tu m'attends!" — our whole poem constitutes desire's sublimation. And for the sake of that ideal transposition into "le délice empreint de généralité" which not only permits but demands the exclusion of the particular and the contingent, and which had transformed the companion of "La Déclaration Foraine" into "toute femme," the poet must protect the threshold of his universe from the intrusion of reality and chance:

> A quoi bon la merveille de transposer un fait de nature en sa presque disparition vibratoire selon le jeu de la parole, cependant, si ce n'est pour qu'en émane, sans la gêne d'un proche ou concret rappel, la notion pure (OC p. 857).

Thus he will not introduce himself to the lady, though the excuse of chance would justify his "tenue de maraudeur aquatique"; for in

---

[11] Elsewhere in Mallarmé's poetry, the melting of the diamond is a symbol for orgasm, as in "Sonnet," almost contemporary with the "Nénuphar:"

> Dame
>   sans trop d'ardeur à la fois enflammant
> La rose qui cruelle ou déchirée et lasse
> Même du blanc habit de pourpre le délace
> Pour ouïr dans sa chair pleurer le diamant

refusing the encounter he has conquered chance, avoiding the contingent doubly, the unforeseen and what it implies etymologically, *tangere*. At the same time, the ironic designation of his costume alludes again to the everywhere suggested goal of the nautical quest: the abduction of the nymphs.

In "séparés, on est ensemble," we again recognize the narrator of the earlier prose poems, who enjoyed the charms of love and friendship in distance and absence more than in nearness and presence. The short phrase again has that tension brought about by the juxtaposition of opposites, the impersonal pronoun stressing the notion of distance, which is then, however, immediately juxtaposed with the suggestion of the greatest intimacy: "je m'immisce à de sa confuse intimité." Both the noun "intimité" itself and the verb connote closeness while also pointing to resistance on her part.[12]

"Ce suspens sur l'eau où mon songe attarde l'indécise" echoes the above "le silence spacieux de ce que s'annonçait l'étrangère," both empty moments of absence pregnant with virtuality. The moment's uncertainty hovers over the water like the lady's hesitation, a state of suspense in which the poet's musing keeps and delays the undecided one who is thus, in turn, under his spell. And just as the "ceinture avec une boucle en diamant" could not defend her against the poet's dreams, so here those dreams authorize more intimacy than any real visits, "visite" suggesting its etymological origin, *videre*. The blissful absence of "discours oiseux," which reflects Mallarmé's distrust of "la parole,"[13] befits the silence of this dream world, the "intuitif accord" of the conversation held "pour n'être pas entendu" recalling the unheard harmonies of Saint Cecilia, "Musicienne du silence." And "le sable entier qui s'est tu" not only suggests absolute silence, but the stopping of the sand in an hourglass, time "standing still" for the privileged moment.

---

[12] The whole phrase recalls the almost contemporary sonnet "M'introduire dans ton histoire." Cf. Cohn, *Toward the Poems*, pp. 223-28, where in analyzing the sonnet, he points to its kinship with not only other verse poetry, but also with our prose poem.

[13] The futility of "la parole" is one of the motifs of our last prose poem, "Conflit," and is discussed in the related essay, "Confrontation:"

> ... le meilleur qui se passe entre deux gens, toujours, leur échappe, en tant qu'interlocuteurs (OC p. 411).

"La pause se mesure au temps de ma détermination" — of which a variant read "sa détermination," the change suggesting the poet-persona's control of the moment — with "temps" marks the end of the ecstasy, as we are also gradually approaching the end of the poem; for "que faire" reintroduces preoccupation, concern with the here and now, while the moment out of time was marked not by "doing," but pure "being," that *être* which always borders on the *néant*.

"Résumer" marks the beginning of the conclusion, where the poem's tensions, though not resolved, are brought into the consonance of one symbolic image, while on the narrative level the persona decides to depart. A last glance at "la vierge absence éparse en cette solitude," a virgin absence which is ideal presence, he will leave as secretly as he had arrived by chance, taking along as a souvenir of this unrealized experience "l'un de ces magiques nénuphars clos," the symbol of its idealization. The closed water lily is, moreover, a figure for our poem itself, which, like the blossom, is closed, enfolding "a nothing made of dreams." We are at the heart of Mallarmé's life-long preoccupation with the transmutation of nothingness, "le Rien qui est la vérité," into poetry, and which for him constitutes the essence of fiction.[14] The water lily's "creuse blancheur" recalls the mandola's "creux néant musicien," virgin wombs both, empty and yet paradoxically pregnant with the possibility of birth — of poetry and, therefore, the poet.

He will row away quietly, careful not to break "l'illusion," like the calm water surface, by the strokes of his oars, lest the foamy trail of his departure, similar to "les plis rejetés en traîne" by the lady's walk, might after all reveal his secret presence to her. "Aux pieds survenus" once more evokes the charm of these hidden feet celebrated above. In the simile of "la bulle visible de l'écume enroulée" and "[le] rapt de mon idéale fleur" — the juxtaposition of "rapt" and "idéale fleur" bringing to a culmination, as I have said, the poem's tension of the erotic and its sublimation — "bulle" and "nénuphar" are likened as fragile enclosures of nothingness, while "écume" once more vaguely suggests the agitation of passion.

---

[14] Cf. Mondor, *Correspondance* I, p. 208, the letter to Cazalis which sets forth Mallarmé's discovery of "le Rien qui est la vérité," and the plan of his *œuvre*.

Should she, however, have come to the shore, it is now too late for him to ever know her features which will, thus, remain "indicible," and which may be those of a lady Meditative, Haughty, Wild, Cruel, or Gay, sheer possibilities of which not any one — because merely virtual — excludes any of the others. And this wealth of unrealized possibilities constitutes precisely "le délice empreint de généralité qui permet et ordonne d'exclure tous visages." "Car j'accomplis selon les règles la manœuvre" emphasizes control, on the narrative level that of the boat by the rower, but at the same time also the artistic control of the poem, whose form is that of a spiral. It is circular in that the persona now departs exactly from where he had arrived for "l'aventure," but just as in the opening the chance nature of that arrival was elaborately modulated, so in the poem's closing the notion of purpose is stressed, that is "a higher level." "Manœuvre" reinforced with "selon les règles," brings to mind, moreover, "la manœuvre avec l'âge oubliée" of the "Coup de Dés," where the loss of control becomes shipwreck, that "naufrage" which was suggested in our poem's beginning with "je venais échouer."

The narrator's "me dégageai, virai," which shows him on the narrative level finally freeing his boat from the reeds and turning it around, with "me dégageai" again suggests the artistic refusal of "engagement" in a life which is sacrificed in order to become the matter of art, thus once more pointing to the theme of our poem: the transposition of reality into ideality. This is also the theme of much of Mallarmé's verse poetry, [15] and especially of the sonnet chosen by him to close his *Poésies,* a poem written two years after ours, "Mes bouquins refermés sur le nom de Paphos," in which the poet renounces the "real" for the "ideal" fruits, not without evoking, however, as he has in the "Nénuphar," all their savor:

> Ma faim qui d'aucuns fruits ici ne se régale
> Trouve en leur docte manque une saveur égale:
> Qu'un éclate de chair humain et parfumant!
>
> Le pied sur quelque guivre où notre amour tisonne
> Je pense plus longtemps peut-être éperdument
> A l'autre, au sein brulé d'une antique amazone. (OC p. 76)

---

[15] For example, "Le Pitre Châtié," "Quelle soie aux baumes de temps," "M'introduire dans ton histoire," "Dame sans trop d'ardeur," and others.

But even "Le Nénuphar Blanc," Mallarmé's "whitest" poem — any poem for that matter — involves, or engages, the poet in the contingent, namely that of language itself, where he continues, in creating the intricate structures of his style, to combat chance. For the total abolishment of "hasard," pure absence, would (as the image of the bubble suggests in our poem) not be any poem, but the empty page of the poet's silence:

> ... le hasard vaincu mot par mot, indéfectiblement le blanc revient, tout à l'heure gratuit, certain maintenant, pour conclure que rien au-delà et authentiquer le silence — (OC p. 387).

And the "noble swan's egg from which flight will never spring" symbolizes that absolute silence. For from this white virtuality the singer-poet would never be born, as his song — "le vol," Mallarmé's constant symbol for poetic *envol* — would never break the fragile shell, "qui ne se gonfle d'autre chose sinon de la vacance de soi."[16] And the poem closes with this modulation of exquisite absence and emptiness of self, from which the dreamer had awakened into a summer morning, and which the ideal woman — "toute dame" — likes to pursue in those privileged intervals, those absences, "dans les allées de son parc, arrêtée parfois et longtemps, comme au bord d'une source à franchir ou de quelque pièce d'eau." As it gently fades away now — this magic world which we leave silently with the poet — some of its loveliness, like the park, the moment of rest, the spring, and finally the water itself, are echoed once more softly, like the waves on the disappearing pond.

---

[16] Royère, *Mallarmé,* p. 44, in discussing Mallarmé's fervent quest for purity says:

> Quiconque sent que le dire n'est qu'un à-peu-près se réfugie dans le silence. Ce silence actif est le foyer de l'émotion haute; il devient une ivresse mentale et, pour Mallarmé, une espèce d'incantation en retour... C'est au silence qu'aboutit la quête du poème pour le poème. Il réside dans "la vacance exquise de soi" ... A l'égard du poète c'est un non-être; c'est cependant un absolu.

L'ECCLÉSIASTIQUE

"L'Ecclésiastique," published for the first time in 1886, has only one variant, that of the title which in one of its subsequent publications was "Actualité. Printemps au Bois de Boulogne." This heading, with "actualité" and the reference to the Paris setting, pointed to that "modernité" underlined in the poem's conclusion and identifies it, moreover, rather explicitly as *reportage* of an anecdote "comme elle frappa mon regard de poëte." However, it is not merely this variant title which, in recalling the definition of the prose poem developed in "Un Spectacle Interrompu," recalls that piece. For the opening of "L'Ecclésiastique" itself reveals a striking similarity to that of the earlier poem, the poet-persona in both cases deploring the rarity of the kind of writing exemplified in each by his own composition.

The anecdote of our prose poem relates how the narrator, strolling in the Bois de Boulogne on a spring day, had observed an ecclesiastic "responding" to the season, and how he steals away unseen to elaborate in his imagination the strange scene just witnessed.

The definitive title would appear to have no connection with the opening sentence, were it not for its suggested contrast with the very first word. For the term "ecclésiastique" not only evokes, in designating a priest, a black figure, but by its Greek character suggests the great age of many centuries, while "printemps," evocative of fresh and bright greens, brings with it the notions of newness and youth. The sentence would read like a simple, factual statement, except for the touch of *préciosité* in the plural "les printemps"; and its coda-like ending, "chez les animaux," makes one wonder what that could possibly have to do with priests. Thus the surprising contrast underlying the whole poem is introduced in its beginning, as is its characteristic style. This style of ironic detachment, in fact, alone makes possible our prose poem, of the secretly observed priest behaving in rather unpriestly fashion. "Les printemps," moreover, situates "L'Ecclésiastique," the only one of these prose poems (almost every one is placed in one of the seasons) in the poet's "bad season." [1]

For spring is not the season of art, but of nature, "poussant l'organisme à des actes" implying the creatures' passive subjection to its forces. And in this evocation of *Physis,* that primordial force pulsating through and animating matter, "actes" suggests a curious contrast with its inherent opposition to passivity; but it is precisely this paradox which renders the "acte" witnessed so bizarre. In view of the title, "actes" also recalls its function as an ecclesiastical term, the passage already revealing the poem's alternate use of vocabulary drawn from the domain of "termes de physique" on the one hand and that of theology on the other, which accentuates the theme of the somewhat mock-heroic defeat of spirit by matter. Further, certain expressions belonging to one of these two spheres will sometimes suggest the other by the merest hint, as for example "histoire naturelle." This phrase, while perfectly unequivocal within the context of its sentence, brings to mind "histoire sainte" in the wider and mildly burlesque one of the whole poem which is, after all, about the acts of a priest!

The narrator who in the first sentence noted the existence of treatises on the strange behavior of animals induced by spring, in the second sentence regrets that there are no such treatises on the season's effects on "individuals made for spirituality." The tagged-on phrase which ends the first sentence — "chez les animaux" — is a veiled but unmistakable reference to the animals' mating season, and paralleled exactly and ironically by the closing phrase of the second sentence: "individus faits pour la spiritualité." Both

---

[1] In these prose poems, this dislike for spring was brought out clearly in "Plainte d'Automne," where it was part of the young poet's infatuation with decadence. It is further reflected in the verse poetry, as for example in "Renouveau," and in the correspondence, where Mallarmé at times literally seems to hide from the season behind his window, as for example in a letter to Cazalis of 1866, *Mondor, Correspondance,* I, p. 208. Cf. also *ibid.,* p. 213, and Mauron, *Introduction,* p. 76.

the poet's theme and his ironic approach become apparent with this opening parallel, and the two sentences likewise juxtapose a zoological-botanical term with one of metaphysics. The smoothly alliterating "plus plausible" reinforces the ironic tone by its etymological association of "worthy of applause," not without also pointing to the virtuosity of the very poem which accomplishes that collecting of "certaines des altérations qu'apporte l'instant climatérique dans les allures . . ." "Altérations," again etymologically a term from natural science, in ordinary usage denotes a change for the worse, and further "se dit aussi des dérangements de la santé," befitting the use of medical terminology later in the poem. "Climatérique," in our narrative context referring to "les printemps," by association suggests the climacteric year at which decadence begins and so with "l'altération" points to deterioration. [2] But the adjective also signifies, again according to Littré, a "période de la vie humaine qui présente un caractère dangereux," a notion picked up later with such terms as "diabolique" and "énergumène," all pointing, with gentle mockery, to the dangerous abdication of reason.

Then the very general opening of the poem is linked to its specific anecdote, by touching upon spring's effect on the narrator himself, though it first mentions, however, the season of his preference. "Mal quitté par l'ironie de l'hiver" expresses its ambiguous hold on him, which only now has begun to wane. For, like "l'azur," it can be beneficent, as "saison de l'art serein, l'hiver lucide," and as the season of the poet's dreams as in "Frisson d'Hiver," but also a torture, a cruel season and "white agony" for the poet plagued by sterility: "Quand du stérile hiver a resplendi l'ennui." And it is spring, then, which frees him from this "état équivoque" by "un naturalisme absolu ou naïf, capable de poursuivre une jouissance dans la différentiation de plusieurs brins d'herbes," which hints at a kind of reconciliation with the unloved time of the year. "L'Ecclésistique" constitutes, in fact, a victory over the enemy season, a season which even in "Bucolique," of

---

[2] Littré takes pains to note that "il ne faut pas, comme font quelques-uns, faire dériver ce mot de climat, ni dire influence climatérique pour influence de climat," which recalls Mallarmé's deliberate playing with both correct and incorrect uses of "foraine" in that other prose poem.

the 1890's, is still called "le vénéneux printemps" (OC p. 401). But our sentence really is more about the poet-persona's contact with nature than with spring, and suggests his role vis-a-vis nature as that of a beholder, which is in sharp contrast, of course, with the ecclesiastic's attitude. This relationship with nature, which becomes progressively more important in the poet's mature work, prepares for Mallarmé's notion of Nature as a Spectacle, which is fully developed elsewhere in the late prose, but above all in the last two prose poems, where the Poet becomes both a beholder of, and a participant in, a rite on nature's stage. And it may be such reflections — not "de profit à la foule" until they are objectified in art — which draw the persona "sous quelques ombrages environnant d'hier la ville." The beautiful and richly elaborate phrase, which in its very style reflects the poet's transformation of the outer sylvan setting, at the same time indicates the general movement of the prose poems out of the confines of rooms, houses, and finally the city itself, into the open natural setting, the suburbs, Valvins, the Bois de Boulogne, and the forest of Fontainebleau.

And so, in the Bois de Boulogne, in his customary isolation so propitious to poetic creation, the poet-persona finds its unexpected occasion, "un exemple saisissable et frappant," the *exemplum* of "springtime inspirations" on an individual made for spirituality. The evocation of sylvan mysteries, vaguely suggestive of the celebration of secret pagan rites, is duly undercut with "presque banal," while "j'exhiberai" recalls the poet's role of *montreur*.

The anecdote proper begins with the second and final paragraph, whose first sentence introduces its hero. It is a highly impressionistic rendition of the narrator's encounter with a phenomenon, in which visual impressions, rendered in the order of their surprising appearance, precede the explanation of their cause. [8] The first impression, "sombre agitation basse," is "obscure" not merely because of

---

[8] This sentence is very similar in its "impressionistic" technique to the justly famous Proustian one, painting the beginning of a summer rain in Combray. Proust, *A la Recherche* I, pp. 101-2:

> Un petit coup au carreau, comme si quelque chose l'avait heurté, suivi d'une ample chute légère comme de grains de sable qu'on eut laissés tomber d'une fenêtre au-dessus, puis la chute s'entendant, se réglant, adoptant un rythme devenant fluide, sonore, musicale, innombrable, universelle: c'était la pluie.

the priest's black gown, but because the image is at first indistinct through the "mille interstices d'arbustes bons à ne rien cacher," the beholder thus not understanding, at this point, what he is looking at. "Basse" because whatever it is, it is on the ground, but with the suggestion of "vil, méprisable, honteux," which reinforces that same undertone produced by "cacher." And "interstices," is aside from its meaning on the narrative level both a "terme de physique" and also a "terme de l'Eglise," as the latter referring to the period of time between the reception of holy orders, which points ahead to the "gambades du séminaire." The vague commotion comes gradually into focus, and a three-cornered hat, now its wearer, down to his silver-buckled shoes, a priest! appears; "battements supérieurs" ironically refers both literally and figuratively to man's highest part, his head, that seat of reason, on the ground now, like the rest. With "des souliers affermis," that is not merely "fastened," but "strengthened" and "made firm" with silver buckles, their wearer's feet have lost their ground! And only now is the poem's title both echoed and explained: an ecclesiastic, "à l'écart de témoins" like the poet, "répondait aux sollicitations du gazon," where he finds, however, a different kind of enjoyment than that derived from "la différentiation de plusieurs brins d'herbes." [4]

The narrator steals away unobserved, as he does in the preceding piece, and again as in "Le Nénuphar Blanc" secretly bearing away material for a poem. For in "L'Ecclésiastique" also, the vision painted in the larger part of the poem is not the observed one, but the one created by the poet-persona's imagination. Far from acting scandalized, or embarrassing the other by seizing a pebble from the road, or merely acknowledging his presence to him by a "sourire même d'intelligence," he avoids the real encounter. But there is, at the same time, a suggested one; for does not that smile, evoked by its absence, and juxtaposed with the other's "rougeur

---

[4] The difference must be stressed, for some critics, as for example, Franz Rauhut, *Das Französische Prosagedicht* (Hamburg: Friederichson, de Gruyter, & Co., m. b. H., 1929), p. 84, in his sole commentary on our poem says:
> ... das in übermütigster Laune verfasste Stück *L'Ecclésiastique* symbolisiert in der Gestalt eines Geistlichen, den Frühlingsgefühle zu wenig würdevollen Kapriolen verleiten, wiederum den geistlichen Menschen, den Dichter.

sur le visage à deux mains voilé," in fact unmask "le pauvre homme"? Thus penetrating those protecting hands, it reveals a blush, whose cause, "son solitaire exercice," has frankly erotic undertones, later to be reinforced with that curious reflection on the priest's gown. Further, "la tentation d'un regard porté en arrière," to which the persona on the narrative level does not succumb, has somewhat diabolical connotations, "tentation" by definition being a "sollicitation au mal par la suggestion du diable," preparing for "l'apparition quasi-diabolique." This temptation, moreover, not only brings to mind "Hérodiade," but also that other biblical story, of the wife of Lot and her forbidden backward glance upon the depravation of the Sodomites who had no wives. [5]

The poem's important turning point, then, is the literal one of the persona, away from the factual scene toward that of his imagination, "*me figurer en esprit* l'apparition quasi diabolique qui continuait à froisser le renouveau de ses côtes, à droite, à gauche," terminating with the most unpoetic "ventre." In "chaste frénésie" the poem's juxtaposition of antithetical elements reaches its climax, with the former a moral and the latter again a physiological-medical term, the one implying both a moral quality as well as the control of reason, while the latter designates its opposite: lack of control, a state of delirium due to mental derangement. The process of accumulation, "de ses côtes, à droite, à gauche et du ventre," is repeated with "se frictionner ... jeter, se rouler, glisser," whose boisterous hilarity culminates with the sudden bewildered cessation of the agitation, due to the tickling of a flower. Thus, as spring invades the ecclesiastic's body, his outer trappings, too, appear defeated by the mere force of flowers. And "cette robe," denoting

---

[5] Mallarmé's obsession with the forbidden glance manifests itself already in his translation of Tennyson's *Godiva*. Carl Paul Barbier, *Documents Stéphane Mallarmé* (Paris: Nizet, 1970), p. 4, suggests that it was probably begun in 1874. Though following Tennyson closely, Mallarmé certainly does not refrain from elaborating the following section (p. 24):

> Elle revint alors à cheval, vêtue de seule chasteté:
> Et un seul rustre vil, un composé de fange ingrat
> La fatale risée de tous les ans futurs
> Perçant un petit trou pour voir, avec crainte,
> Regarda — mais ses yeux avant de satisfaire leur volonté
> Se séchèrent, aveuglés, au fond de sa tête
> Et tombèrent devant lui. Ainsi les Pouvoirs, qui veillent
> Sur les nobles faits, lui ôtèrent un sens dont il avait abusé —

the cassock but suggesting a woman's dress and thus seemingly uniting the two, strangely befits the celibate, that "solitaire" whose androgynous aspect was already suggested above.

In the following sentence, a curious inversion takes place; for, while the ecclesiastic appears to have become a natural phenomenon, nature is personified and thus humanized, and it is the latter which the persona now addresses directly with "Solitude, froid silence épars dans la verdure, ... vous connûtes les claquements furibonds d'une étoffe..." Nature's impassible cold silence contrasts sharply here with the cloth's furious clappings, that frenzy, paradoxically, of something usually inanimate, and a synecdoche, moreover, which further dehumanizes the priest. "Silence épars dans la verdure," by the way, which echoes "vierge absence éparse en cette solitude" of the "Nénuphar," points to the movement of these prose poems into an open, natural setting. The ecclesiastic's "sens moins subtils qu'inquiets" once more reinforces the contrast of a calm flora witnessing an "individu fait pour la spiritualité" subjected to his troubled senses. Throughout the poem, the cassock — "sombre agitation basse," "cette robe spéciale portée avec l'apparence qu'on est pour soi tout même sa femme," "claquements furibonds d'une étoffe" — has something sinister about it, an effect created by the shocking surprise of seeing this traditional symbol of dignity literally "par le démon secoué." [6] And "la nuit absconse en ses plis" finally shaken out of it, culminates that accumulation of the dark, the mysterious, and the hidden suggested by that "robe spéciale" which, like a shroud, hid a skeleton whose bizarre "heurts sourds contre la terre" evoke an almost Bertrand-like *tableau macabre*. "Mais l'énergumène n'avait point à vous contempler" again stresses the difference between the poet-persona, mentally beholding and communicating with nature, and the priest who lets himself be possessed by her diabolic forces, "énergumène," a "terme de théologie," literally designating the priest as "qui est possédé du démon."

The absolute-like "hilare," however, saves the passage from sliding into the Gothically-horrible; the hilarious ecclesiastic is

---

[6] "L'Ecclésiastique" here echoes the grotesque note of the early "Une Négresse par le démon secouée," originally entitled "Image Grotesque," which could well be the title of our prose poem.

content to find the source of his agitation within himself, that demon hardly to be accounted for by the life he had furtively escaped. And this life is now evoked and contrasted to the "souffle vernal," a seminarian's life with "les immuables textes" inscribed in his flesh, making the poor priest appear somewhat like the branded chattel of the Church, a suggestion later reinforced with his mirthful comparison to "un âne." And though both poet-persona and ecclesiastic seem to move from refusal toward acceptance of the world, the distance between the two figures — the one an ideal, the other burlesque — is immense, so that we can associate the two only as contrasting figures, the prose poem continually stressing their difference. "Lui aussi" certainly points back to the poem's beginning, where the poet-persona had confessed his own escape to a contact with Nature. But while it has led the ecclesiastic to roll on the ground "dans la béatitude de sa simplicité native," it has inspired the poet artistically, a point strongly emphasized in the conclusion. While the ecclesiastic's response to spring is sterile, the poet's is creative.

The anecdote proper terminates with the humorous accumulation of "obédience," "canons," "interdits" and "censures," a list of that formidable array of constraints of organized spirituality to protect its own from that "immédiat, net, violent, positif" contact with Nature which the ecclesiastic has succumbed to. His subsequent "béatitude" is on the literal level the simple and animalistic bliss of an ass, while ironically suggestive of its mystical designation of the elect.

Thus, far from likening poet and priest, "L'Ecclésiastique" consistently contrasts them. In some of the later prose poems, and especially the last two, "La Déclaration Foraine" and "Le Nénuphar Blanc," we have been tracing the development of the theme of the poetic vocation which imposes a renunciation of life in the service of a higher mission. This theme prepares the image of the poet-priest, already suggested in the *recueil,* and with which the cycle will culminate. And the function of "L'Ecclésiastique," which also justifies its precise position in the cycle, is to prepare his consecration. For Mallarmé, the atheist poet, seems to feel the need of explicitly exorcising the socially-sanctioned priest figure before the poet-priest, who will be consecrated in the following piece, "La Gloire," can take his place.

It is somewhat surprising that the remaining portion of the piece is not set off by paragraphing like the introduction, for there occurs a marked break in the last two sentences, where the poet-persona returns to himself and his role as creator of the poem, thus not merely stepping out of the anecdote, but almost out of the poem itself. "Le héros de ma vision" points back to that moment in the anecdote, when the persona had abandoned the description of the observed to paint the image of his mind, "me figurer en esprit l'apparition." At the same time "héros" is a final ironic designation of this anti-hero, whose real-life model must no doubt by now have returned "inaperçu dans la foule, et les habitudes de son ministère." But in resolutely rejecting the trite and "real" conclusion from the adventure, the poet-persona underlines once again the artificial, artistic, and burlesque character of this "ecclésiastique," whose furtive embrace with spring is once more evoked with the suggestive "pistils" and "sucs" attached to his person.

The final sentence again alludes to the poet's fundamental bargain with his destiny: the deliberate renunciation of life for the rewards of art. "Ma discrétion ... n'a-t-elle pas pour récompense," is reminiscent of "sans compensation à cette secousse qu'un besoin d'explication figurative" of the "Déclaration," or "mon imaginaire trophée" of the "Nénuphar." In each case, the poet turns away from the encounter with reality's fleeting phenomena, to give them permanence by "fixing" them in a harmonic image. Nothing is more fugitive, in fact, than the eruption of nature's spring, or the temporary divagations of man under its influence, but lasting is this "image marquée d'un sceau mystérieux de modernité, à la fois baroque et belle," the poet's definition of our prose poem. The "rêverie d'un passant" designates poetry and poet, he the perishable and mortal creator of the permanent. [7]

It is not the adventure, but its image, the poem, which is mysteriously signed and sealed, for its beauty is hidden, by a

---

[7] "Fixer à jamais," however, expresses an optimism most unusual for Mallarmé. The hero of the "Toast Funèbre" was similarly designated "Quelqu'un de ces passants," in a poem celebrating both the mortal and immortal aspect of the poet, and the poet-hero of "Conflit" will say of himself: "quelque singulier instinct de ne rien posséder et de seulement passer."

modernity — which may well be that of the form of the prose poem itself — rendering it both baroque and beautiful. "Baroque et belle," those melodious last words, which constitute the confident master poet's judgment of his own work, once more underline the antithetical tension which permeates "L'Ecclésiastique," in which the fantastic and the bizarre are molded into artistic harmony.

LA GLOIRE

"La Gloire" appeared for the first time in 1886, composed that year for Verlaine's *Les Hommes d'aujourd'hui,* where it carried the subtitle "Notes de mon Carnet," which it retained in one of its subsequent publications. The *Pléiade* edition closes the *recueil* of "Poèmes en Prose" with this piece, although it is the penultimate one of the "Anecdotes ou Poèmes" cycle in *Divagations.*

The anecdote is about the poet-persona's autumn visit to the forest of Fontainebleau, from his departure by train from the city to his arrival before the festive forest, which he does not approach until he is alone, a solitary "royal intruder" into Nature's splendor.

The title, passionately echoed in the first word, has by its superposition of multiple references, as well as its sound-look beauty, something of the many-faceted sparkle and fire of the whole prose poem. For all the meanings of glory are simultaneously suggested here: renown, fame, honor, but above all *éclat* and superhuman *splendeur,* thus a magnificence not only royal but divine, which is that of the Poet.[1] "La Gloire!" bursts forth like a

---

[1] The term "gloire" is frequent throughout the verse poetry, where it always refers to the poet's renown as well as his magnificence, both aim and reward of his quest. Cf. "Las de l'amer repos où ma paresse offense" of 1864; "Toast Funèbre" of 1873; "Quelle soie aux baumes de temps" of 1885.

In the early correspondence, Mallarmé distinguishes already, as he does in the first paragraph of our prose poem, between true and false glory. Cf. Mondor, *Propos,* p. 71, and *ibid.,* p. 94. Cf. also OC p. 873, where, as well as in many a *tombeau,* Mallarmé links the notions of glory and death. Cf. also Naumann, *Sprachgebrauch,* p. 70. Finally, the notions of royalty and splendor, the poet's "gloire," are beautifully expressed in Mallarmé's commemorative discourse on Villiers, for him the ideal poet, whom he quotes in the passage:

beam of light caught in a diamond's flare — not unlike the brilliant apparition of "Le Phénomène Futur" which left poets "le cerveau ivre un instant d'une gloire confuse" — its afterglow then slowly dying in the remainder of the sentence.

On the anecdotal level, this opening sentence-paragraph introduces a first-person narrator who emphasizes his deliberate isolation from "the others." But at the same time it reveals another contrast, a stylistic one created by the juxtaposition of a highly lyrical and lofty tone: "La Gloire! je ne la sus qu'hier, irréfragable," with a narrative manner tending toward the ironic: "et rien ne m'intéressera d'appelé par quelqu'un ainsi." And this double tension already intimated here, between the solitary poet-persona with his vision and the blind masses of humanity, as well as that between an elevated language and an ironic vein, is characteristic of the whole poem, much of whose anecdote is dominated by irony, while the theme which it conveys constitutes a sublime elevation.[2] These tensions reflect, in fact, the fundamental antithesis of ideality and reality inherent in the very notion of apotheosis — deification in death — which is celebrated in "La Gloire."

The second sentence-paragraph, relating the narrator's departure from the city and announcing the forest, both describes the surrounding phenomena and evokes the moment's special ambiance, in a language as beautiful as it is economically functional. For by its tonality the sentence establishes the poem's *éclairage,* while also pointing to its theme and to several subordinate ideas suggested by it. "Cent affiches s'assimilant l'or incompris des jours" juxtaposes the city's banal advertising posters with that peculiar golden glow

---

Ce qu'il voulait, ce survenu, en effet, je pense sérieusement que c'était: régner. Aussi ce candidat à toute majesté survivante, d'abord élut-il domicile, chez les poëtes; cette fois, décidé, il le disait, assagi, clairvoyant "avec l'ambition d'ajouter à l'illustration de ma race la seule gloire vraiment noble de nos temps, celle *d'un grand écrivain.*" La devise est restée (OC p. 489).

[2] Cf. Royère, *Mallarmé,* pp. 268-69:
Mais l'antinomie fondamentale de l'Idéal et du Réel porte le poète qui les pense simultanément à un double paroxysme de mysticité et d'ironie, et la distance entre ces deux pôles de l'univers mallarméen est telle qu'il semble impossible qu'un même homme passe, comme il fait, d'une sorte de délire esthétique au tact sceptique des réalités humaines.

of autumn days, [3] whose symbolic significance is hidden from the crowd, again emphasizing the poet-persona's solitude. The autumn sun is appropriated by the signs which reflect it, those publicity posters which betray the higher function of letters, thus reintroducing the theme developed in "Un Spectacle Interrompu," of the profanation of *écriture* in a journalistically-oriented civilization unaware of this defillment. While the signs are rushing past the train, the persona's eyes, a fitting synecdoche for him as beholder, try to pass beyond the immediate, to the distant horizon, recalling Mallarmé's designation of himself as "lecteur d'horizons" (OC p. 402). And an urgency makes itself felt, the poet being doubly drawn toward horizon and forest, by the train and by his desire "de se recueillir dans l'abstruse fierté que donne une approche de forêt en son temps d'apothéose." He is striving to come to a rest in the forest's calm — "extatique torpeur" — which is heavy with impending motion. Its "fierté" announces "orgueils surhumains," and it is "abstruse" again merely to *la foule,* the adjective at the same time etymologically foreshadowing the poet's role of "intrus royal." The characteristically vague nominal phrase "une approche de forêt," suggestive both of the narrator's approach of the forest and of the forest's approach of its final hour, with "approche" once more emphasizes the urgency and that sense of expectancy tending, both spatially and temporally, toward "apothéose."

The following paragraph vividly recalls the opening passages of "La Déclaration Foraine," where "une vocifération, parmi trop de félicité" of an evening hour was as discordant as here the "discord parmi l'exaltation de l'heure," which shrilly breaks the equilibrium of the moment's inner and outer harmony. [4] For its peace is

---

[3] The phrase "l'or incompris des jours" is an example of that new magic and beauty with which "ordinary" words are endowed by the poet, which Mallarmé discusses in "Crise de Vers":

> Le vers qui de plusieurs vocables refait un mot total, neuf, étranger à la langue et comme incantatoire, achève cet isolement de la parole: niant, d'un trait souverain, le hasard demeuré aux termes malgré l'artifice de leur retrempe alternée en le sens et la sonorité, et vous cause cette surprise de n'avoir ouï jamais tel fragment ordinaire d'élocution, en même temps que la réminiscene de l'objet nommé baigne dans une neuve atmosphère (OC p. 368).

[4] The curious use of the preposition "parmi" before a singular noun, "parmi l'exaltation de l'heure," recalls "parmi trop de félicité" of "La Dé-

shattered by a stationmaster's cry, as the train comes to a stop at the narrator's destination. And there is a double dissonance, both that of the voice interrupting the hour's silent exaltation, and that produced by the "crying out" of the very name, Fontainebleau, itself, "faussé," thus, by an inarticulate bark, which merely conveys their location to the passengers, and thus serves *la foule* while disturbing the poet. This again suggests the theme touched upon above, that of the antithetical double function of language: its every-day use as *parole* and its use by the poet; for while in the former a name is but a designation, so that, once information has been imparted, the word is left to die, the same name in that other realm lives independently by its own vitality. The syntax of our sentence, first introducing the evocations carried by that name, and only then the magic word itself, accentuates this notion and recalls the similar function of "Saxe" in the early "Frisson d'Hiver," where it suggests both temporal and spatial distance. Fontainebleau, "connu pour déployer la continuité de cimes tard évanouies," is a name both historically famous, pointing to "gloire," and evocative of the woods' silhouette on the horizon. And here it suggests further the evening hour hovering over those trees threatened both by impending darkness and the late moment of the year, the fall — "évanouies" — of that splendor. "Cimes tard évanouies" also vaguely intimates Fontainebleau's historical past, represented by its palace, a motif which will later be picked up by the trees, which appear like "torches ... dans une haute garde," with both their "pourpre" and that of the sky evoking the splendor of royalty.

And just as the "interrupteur" had violated peace, so the narrator now mentally resorts to violence, which is not devoid of irony. For the absolute phrase, "la glace du compartiment violentée," a superb concrete image of the inner experience of suddenly interrupted calm, paints but an imaginary breaking of the window in order to reach out and seize that adversary by the throat. This imagined gesture introduces a likewise imaginary, and rather

---

claration" and the same construction in "L'Ecclésiastique," "parmi cette robe spéciale." By an uncommon use of prepositions in general, Mallarmé usually creates a greater vagueness and therewith increases the suggestiveness of the phrase. Those he uses most strikingly are "selon" and "parmi," expressions of envelopment which create a special ambiance around the beings and events of the poems.

one-sided, dialogue. "Tais-toi!" not only calls for quiet, but suggests the verb's secondary meaning "ne pas divulguer un secret," which the narrator develops in entreating the other not to give away to the crowd "l'ombre ici insinuée dans mon esprit," that magic evoked by the name. And the stationmaster's dehumanizing "aboi indifférent" juxtaposed with "l'ombre ici insinuée dans mon esprit," sharply accentuates the clash of outer and inner worlds, with the former again gaining the upper hand by the means of noise, that of the compartment doors' banging. "Les touristes omniprésents vomis" [5] not only marks again the narrator's isolation from *la foule,* but now adds his scorn for them, which is emphasized further by their reification implied in the substitution of the train's doors for its passengers: "ne divulgue pas . . . aux portières."

The station's "vent inspiré et égalitaire," with the ironie juxtaposition of the exceptional and its opposite, contrasts with "une quiétude" of the following sentence, which now introduces the real presence of the forest, so far merely announced by the narrator's anticipatory reflections accompanying his approach. "Une quiétude menteuse de riches bois suspend alentour quelque extraordinaire état d'illusion" accentuates two of the poem's essential ingredients, that of illusion, inherent in the very idea of spectacle and theatre, and that of suspense, which is its atmosphere. The former is reinforced with a vocabulary cluster dispersed throughout the piece — "paraître," "trahison," "fausser," "menteuse," "illusion," "doute," "ombre" — which with "pompeux," "splendeur," "éclat," "exaltation," "ivresse," "orgueil," points to the illusory magnificence of the solar drama. For it is to witness its final act that the poet-persona has left the city; and it is because he alone is capable of appreciating its significance that he must be its solitary spectator. In his "Hamlet" essay, of the same year as "La Gloire," Mallarmé stresses the poet's role of ideal beholder, who alone penetrates the meaning of this spectacle which reflects, however, not only the poet's, but mankind's destiny:

---

[5] This expression of alienation and revulsion is similarly rendered in the early "Les Fenêtres:"

> Mais hélas! ici-bas est maître: sa hantise
> Vient m'écœurer parfois jusqu'en cet abri sur,
> Et le *vomissement* impur de la Bêtise
> Me force à me boucher le nez devant l'azur. (OC p. 33)

> Loin de tout, la Nature, en automne, prépare son Théâtre, sublime et pur, attendant pour éclairer, dans la solitude, de significatifs prestiges, que l'unique œil lucide qui en puisse pénétrer le sens (notoire, le destin de l'homme), un Poëte, soit rappelé à des plaisirs et à des soucis médiocres (OC p. 299).

And while the poet there returns to "des soucis médiocres," the ideal one of our poem leaves a mediocre existence to attend the sublime performance.

But restrained still by that mediocrity he is trying to escape, the poet-persona cannot yet free himself — as his eyes had vainly tried to reach beyond the city toward the horizon — to meditate on that "quiétude menteuse," that deceptive calm, pregnant with its own annihilation and with the storm which will disperse this wealth of flaming trees, a splendor held suspended in an extraordinary illusion of immortality. And so his mind falls back again to the immediate, that proudly dutiful master of his railroad station, "bon employé vociférateur par devoir." "Vociférateur," reminding of "une vocifération, parmi trop de tacite félicité" of "La Déclaration," by its etymology — *vox ferus* — recalls the "aboi indifférent" above and further dehumanizes this man who is later, as is the crowd, *chosifié* as a mere "uniforme inattentif." The persona mentally pleads with him for silence, long enough "de m'isoler de la délégation urbaine," which once more emphasizes his obstinate, but necessary, alienation. He has no intention, however, of hoarding "une ivresse à tous départie par les libéralités conjointes de la nature et de l'Etat," which echoes the tone of the "vent inspiré et égalitaire" above. But in the very concession, even if an ironic one, of the equal right of admission to the others, "les touristes omniprésents," "ces voyageurs," the persona intensifies his separation from them by an accumulation of terms referring to the organized masses of society which swallow up their individualities, "tous," "Etat," "délégation urbaine." All are entitled, certainly, to their holiday outing in the public forest, earned by their labor in the city. But in this poem the poet-persona cannot — as he does in the next and culminating poem of the cycle — linger over their concerns, now mere obstacles to his "isolating himself toward" his aim. Here the deliberately vague verbal construction implies the movement of separation away from the multitude and that toward the solitary vision, physical and mental escape.

Then the ironic tone yields to the lyricism of "l'extatique torpeur de ces feuillages là-bas trop immobilisés pour qu'une crise ne les éparpille bientôt dans l'air," before shifting back to an ironically condescending gesture. And this vibration, even within a single sentence, between elevated and low tonalities, neither destroying the mood created by the other, evidences Mallarmé's complete mastery of the genre; a genre all his own, moreover, and which, as he explained in "Un Spectacle Interrompu," exploits both the factual and the ideal. The tension of "l'extatique torpeur" is that of a dramatic crisis, with opposing forces momentarily interlocked, before that turning point which tips the balance, turning — in this supreme drama — not only the leaves' but the sun's glory into death. The "crise" is both a culmination and annihilation; it brings to mind the "mémorable crise" of the "Coup de Dés," Man's ultimate tragic effort and his *naufrage*. "Trop immobilisés," with its emphasis on the excessive, later accentuated with "ce pompeux octobre *exceptionnel*," "*trop* inappréciable trophée" and culminating with "d'orgueils *sur*humains," contains the moment's threat, and also recalls that elevation-disintegration complex celebrated in "Pauvre Enfant Pâle," which symbolized the poet's drama. [6]

From its lyric height the sentence falls — amusingly the last words of the foregoing phrase are "dans l'air" — back to the immediate scene, where the pleading narrator now wants to resort to

---

[6] Cf. Cohn, *L'Œuvre*, pp. 268-69:

> Le mouvement vers le haut est annulé par le mouvement vers le bas dans le passage que nous étudions. ... ce procédé se trouve à plusieurs reprises chez Mallarmé toujours avec l'idée d'un orgueil enflé aboutissant à une chute: "feuillages là-bas trop immobilisés (cf. notre texte) pour qu'une crise ne les éparpille bientôt" (289); "la tige/Grandissait trop pour nos raisons" (*Prose*, 56); plus subtilement: "trop inappréciable trophée pour paraître" (289); "un éclat triomphal (note l'élément *phal*) trop brusque pour durer" (384), ... La défaite sera complètement indiquée par la *foudre* qui habituellement frappe les projections les plus élevées, les projets les plus ambitieux; "l'honneur d'Erechteus par la foudre frappé" (701) en représente un excellent exemple qui évoque un *hubris* grec.

In our prose poem cycle, it is "Pauvre Enfant Pâle," which first unambiguously elaborates the Icarian theme of excess which contains and demands its own destruction, here implied in "apothéose."

bribery, "suborneur métal." But in a single brief sentence-paragraph the plan, as well as the whole imaginary dialogue, collapses in an anticlimactic "real" confrontation with reality. For the narrator "sans dire mot," which ironically contrasts with all those imagined ones, simply hands over his ticket to the stationmaster, whose inattention and professional politeness remind us that all along he was, of course, completely unaware of the agitation he had caused. "Quelque barrière," literally the station gate, suggests perhaps once more the obstacles of this quest-voyage.

It appears as though the stationmaster had done the narrator's bidding, for no one else gets off the train, and he sees "l'asphalte s'étaler net de pas," the synecdoche for the road suggesting urban civilizations's subjection of nature, while "net de pas" vaguely recalls the stain of the feared "touristes omniprésents *vomis.*" Mallarmé expresses his "hantise" of asphalt as a symbol of progress similarly in "Bucolique":

> Longs faubourgs prolongés par la monotonie de voies jusqu'au central rien qui soit extraordinaire, divin ou totalement jailli du sol factice en échange des lieues d'asphalte, de nouveau, à piétiner, pour fuir (OC p. 402).

And the very rhythm of this sentence reflects that monotony which the poet flees, in our poem: "une monotonie énorme de capitale." The notion of civilization corrupting nature, which appears to be an inversion of the repeated superimposition of the artificial upon the natural evident throughout these prose poems, indicates the mature poet's acceptance of that nature, toward which we see these later pieces gradually move.[7] But it is an acceptance on the poet's terms, where — in contrast, for example, to the priest's in "L'Ecclésiastique" — nature is spiritualized by being endowed with a symbolic significance accessible to the poet alone. And since it is accessible to the rest of mankind only through poetry, this "orphic explanation" of nature is both the poet's highest task and his obligation toward his fellow man:

---

[7] It is, therefore, surprising to find some critics call Mallarmé "un homme d'intérieur." Cf. Michaud, *Message,* p. 189. While the early autumn poem of our cycle, "Plainte d'Automne," was indeed a poem of the "intérieur," the late autumn piece, "La Gloire," shows the persona's flight from not merely the room, but the city itself, into open nature.

L'explication orphique de la Terre, qui est le seul devoir du poëte et le jeu littéraire par excellence (OC p. 663).

The narrator can hardly believe that only he has heard the calling of "ce pompeux octobre exceptionnel,"[8] but then the very contrast between that exceptional moment in nature and the city's monotony explains the latter's incomprehension of the former, the whole paragraph stressing their difference. For autumn's climactic hour is directly juxtaposed with the empty duration of "millions d'existences étageant leur vacuité," dead lives which make up "une monotonie énorme de capitale." And in this phrase, which syntactically echoes "une approche de forêt" above, "énorme," that is the exceptional, and "monotonie," its opposite, cancel each other, leaving nothing but that emptiness whose obsession will dissipate itself with the whistle blast, like one last shrill, discordant note of progress, vanishing with and in the disappearing locomotive's steam. The poet is suddenly alone to feel "qu'il est, cet an, d'amers et lumineux sanglots, mainte indécise flottaison d'idée désertant les hasards comme des branches, tel frisson et ce qui fait penser à un automne sous les cieux."

"D'amers et lumineux sanglots" paints both the forest's autumnal glow and conveys the bitter funereal grief of its approaching death, which Mallarmé in his "Hamlet" essay calls "l'amertume feuille-morte" (OC p. 299). But the year's imminent death agony is then paradoxically transformed into a magnificent analogy suggesting birth; for the falling of autumnal leaves from the branches is likened to the slowly ripened ideas disengaging themselves from the ramifications of chance, thus achieving their birth and liberation. And so, on the threshold of both death and life, leaf and idea seem to hesitate, "indécise," in this "suspens" which permeates "La Gloire," before floating — Mallarmé again uses "flottaison," a word he loves and which we encountered in the "Nénuphar" — the one out of, the other into, existence. The "idée" becomes manifest in a

---

[8] October is Mallarmé's favorite month, already celebrated in the early "Soupir:"
—Vers l'Azur attendri d'Octobre pâle et pur
and frequently mentioned in the correspondence. Cf. Mondor, *Correspondance* II, p. 248 (to Verlaine).

poem, the hesitating leaves being an image, then, of poetry awaiting its birth. [9] And so it is poetry not yet — perhaps never — written which confers its luminosity on that which exists, its mere dream incandescing and constituting "La Gloire." [10]

Like the preceding one, the poem's last paragraph is a delicate tissue made from a single intricately manipulated thread, beginning with a rich analogy. As the still astonished narrator ascertains that he is, indeed, alone, his arms are raised up, wing-like, in a gesture of surprise, and as though he had "slipped off" doubt. Freed of it now, "les bras de doute envolés," he compares himself to one carrying something high, "comme qui porte aussi un lot d'une splendeur secrète, trop inappréciable trophée pour paraître!" And this invisible trophy recalls "Le Nénuphar Blanc," where the poet's prize was likewise invisible — "mon imaginaire trophée" — because ideal. A trophy, moreover, suggests something won by conquest, that is the poetic quest which issues in conquest, for it conquers reality or experience — and language — to yield the ideal. And so the poet's difference from the others is again stressed, for they — as for example the *ecclésiastique* — instead of conquering experience, undergo it. This proud trophy (we saw how it supports the motif of *hubris* emphasized throughout "La Gloire") is "un lot d'une splendeur *secrète*," that necessarily *solitary* vision, whose wealth can be imparted to the many only in poetry, as for example in this prose poem.

Assured now of solitude, the poet-persona pauses at the edge of the forest, for his serene possession of himself and of the moment is in perfect harmony with its "suspens," that anticipatory arrest of both time and motion. The forest's splendor now reaches its climax, which unites it with that of the sky. In "cette diurne veillée d'immortels troncs," the trees appear to hold a devotional vigil, in

---

[9] In an early letter (1866 to Aubanel), Mondor, *Correspondance* I, p. 222, Mallarmé already likened the way in which an idea, ripened into a poem, detaches itself to a natural process:
> Je travaille à tout à la fois, ou plutôt je veux dire que tout est si bien ordonné en moi, qu'à mesure, maintenant, qu'une sensation m'arrive, elle se transfigure et va d'elle-même se caser dans tel livre et tel poème. Quand un poème sera mur, il se détachera. Tu vois que j'imite la loi naturelle.

[10] Cf. Cohn, *L'Œuvre*, p. 295.

preparation for the rite, "l'universel sacre." They seem immortal as though their stasis, like that of the vision reflecting them, were forever out of time, in a theatrical illusion, "une quiétude menteuse." But this stasis is rich with tension, for the trees are immobilized in a gesture, that of bending down toward "un," the visionary poet, and pouring over him — "déversement" containing both the notions of "bending over" and of "pouring out" — "d'orgueils surhumains." In the forest's apotheosis, its "fierté" is sublimated to the divine, thus also metaphysically linking its trees with the heavens to which they are reaching out, and with which heavenly splendor they will annoint the Poet. For all this pride and glory, it exists only through that vision which authenticates it, "(or ne faut-il pas qu'on en constate l'authenticité?)" Nature simply *is*:

> La Nature a lieu, on n'y ajoutera pas; que des cités, les voies ferrées et plusieurs inventions formant notre matériel (OC p. 647).

But the poet creates its metaphysical significance, which makes him a God himself. However, in his own apotheosis, he, "the royal intruder," celebrates both his divinity and his mortality.

The trees, flaming torches consuming their own substance in a fire reverberating in the sky's imperial purple clouds, evoke the splendid image of a sonnet of those years:

> Tout Orgueil fume-t-il du soir,
> Torche dans un branle étouffée (OC p. 73)

Their consuming "tous rêves antérieurs à leur éclat" points back to the analogy in which the leaves were likened to the ideas of poems at the moment of their birth. The leaves' and dreams' self-consuming fire, then, again suggests poetry unuttered, arrested in a vision — perhaps reflecting a vision of the *œuvre* which Mallarmé frequently alluded to, but which he never wrote.

With the universal stage set for the sublime *solemnitas,* with heaven and earth aflame and waiting for the Hero, he knows that it is awaiting him to celebrate his triumph. And this scene was already the dream of the very young poet of "Symphonie Littéraire III," of which an early version reads:

> J'ai institué dans mon Rêve la cérémonie d'un Triomphe que j'aime évoquer aux heures de gloire et de féerie, et je l'appelle la Fête du Poète. ... Dans une apothéose, il siège sur un trône d'ivoire, couvert de la pourpre que lui seul a le droit de porter, — vous l'entendez, ô laurier de la Turbie. [11]

But our poet-persona waits — celebrating not the realization but the virtuality of his consecration — until the last vestiges of reality, symbolized by the train "emportant du monde quelque part," be reduced to the proportions "d'une chimère puérile." He will celebrate his "Fête" alone.

"La Gloire," then, closes on this note of solitude of the poet and his vision, [12] recalling the advice Mallarmé gives to the artist in "Crayonné au Théâtre": "... peindre une solitude de cloître à la torche de votre immortalité ..." (OC p. 298). But the revelation of the vision, a vision which had carried the Poet to the solitary and sublime heights of idéality, was the destiny of Man; and so the cycle of prose poems will come to a close not with the last word of this poem, "seul," but with a prose poem in which the poet celebrates "l'homme."

---

[11] For this early version of the Théodore de Banville section of "Symphonie Littéraire," cf. Mondor, *Précisions*, p. 32.

[12] Cohn, *Toward the Poems*, p. 122, analyzing "Quand l'ombre menaça de la fatale loi," about its line "Aux yeux du solitaire ébloui de sa foi":

> *solitaire ébloui de sa foi*: this is the central theme of the prose poem *La Gloire*.

And Pierre Beausire, *Mallarmé poésie et poétique* (Lausanne: Mermod, 1949), p. 9, points to that solitude which seems to characterize Mallarmé's poetry itself.

CONFLIT

"Conflit" was chosen by Mallarmé as the thirteenth and closing piece of "Anecdotes ou Poèmes" in *Divagations*,[1] the culmination of the prose-poem cycle. The uneven number of poems is itself significant; for the odd thirteen, like the seven stars of the constellation in the "Coup de Dés," somehow suggests tension rather than rest, and we have seen how each of these prose poems is characterized by tension. The number thirteen also indicates the cyclical structure of the group, a structure frequently apparent in the individual poems themselves, and already suggested by that old Saxony clock of "Frisson d'Hiver," which struck the thirteenth hour. Against the twelve hours of the clock's dial, as against the twelve signs of the zodiac, the thirteen suggests a cyclical return.

Since the original version of "Conflit" is of the poet's very latest period, it did not undergo significant revisions for its publication in *Divagations*.[2] The poem's setting is the narrator's country retreat, that beautiful forest and river region we know already from "Le Nénuphar Blanc," where he has come for a quiet summer. But on his arrival, he finds the ground floor of his vacation house invaded by a team of railroad workers; and the anecdote,

---

[1] In the *Pléiade* edition, "Conflit" is grouped with other prose pieces under "Variations sur un Sujet," as it had appeared under that general title in the series of prose pieces which Mallarmé had published in 1895 in LA REVUE BLANCHE. But the other prose poems of *Divagations* had likewise first come out separately in various publications. Since the 1897 edition of *Divagations*, one year before Mallarmé's death, indicates the author's own grouping and thus his structural determination of his prose work, it would appear prudent to follow that order.

[2] Paxton, who in *The Development* examines the variants of all the REVUE BLANCHE pieces, discusses those of "Conflit" on p. 88.

which is about his encounter with these working men, becomes the vehicle for the theme of the Poet's relationship with the People, a theme already touched upon in some of the earlier prose poems, but developed fully in this closing piece.

The tension of "Conflit" is inherent in its very title, whose kinetic quality, *cum fligere,* is obvious. And as it thus evokes not a resolution, but a clash, hostile encounter even, it is in harmony with a vocabulary cluster of the combative and the belligerent, which is prominent in the poem: "envahie," "injure," "ennemi," "force pure," "défense," "assaillant," "stratégie," "pugilat," "lutte," "tomber," "champ de bataille." The tension in the very concept of conflict is further rendered by the sound-look of the word designating it, the round-lettered "con," suggestive of the female, and "flit," with its dominant "i," high and light sound and pointed letters, suggestive of the male principle, its antithesis — thus already prefiguring the image of "pioche" and "pelle" of the poem.[3] As the male and the female principles stand in antithetical relationship to each other, so do the master-poet and the crowd. And this relationship of the poet to mankind, his position in society, is the principal theme of this poem.

The first word, "longtemps," evokes both human freedom and imprisonment, in that Space and Time are not only the categories of our mind which permit us to order and rule the indeterminate manifold about us, but also the protective modes of understanding beyond which Man — even in his artistic vision — may venture only at the risk of annihilation. And "longtemps" here opens a poem dealing with the persona's secure order of existence, created by himself, threatened from the outside, that is by the unforeseen. This threat of annihilation, a dominant theme in Mallarmé's poetic universe, was celebrated in the dramatic *Igitur,* whose hero, at the point of breaking beyond those mental categories and thus ceasing to exist as an individual mind, overshadowed several of the early prose poems; it was further reflected in some of the early pieces

---

[3] Cf. Cohn, *Toward the Poems,* p. 270:
> o — stasis, circularity ... A corollary of the circularity is evidently the female principle...

And on p. 268:
> i — male principle, hero, light, centripetal...

in the persona's hesitations and fears, imaged, for example, in the trembling spider webs of "Frisson d'Hiver," or the need for the protective shell of rooms. In was finally openly confronted in "Pauvre Enfant Pâle" with its celebration of elevation into death. [4]

For a long time the first-person narrator believed, felt secure, in a certain order of existence created by himself; and the anecdote relates the threatened destruction of this order through the fortuitous, a narrative schema not unlike those of most of the late prose poems. This very difficult first sentence-paragraph reflects that experience, so that to force its syntactical dislocation into a smooth rendition would be to destroy its intention. In the phrase "que s'exempte mon idée d'aucun accident même vrai," "mon idée," that is the mental representation and ordering of phenomena in and by the mind, and that mind itself, are contrasted with "accident," namely the uncontrolled phenomenon confronting it. In this encounter, the intellect's impulse is to free itself from the contingent by rejecting it; and, again, as elsewhere in these last prose poems, in refusing to submit to it, the mind can dominate chance by transforming it into meaning. This Kantian transformation, *als ob — comme si, comme si —* is that of Art, like philosophy a fiction, a sublime fiction which pretends that mind is able to conquer matter, or thought chance. The mind, then, prefers to plunge into and draw from — "puiser" later to be echoed by "puisatiers" — its own principle. And just as "idée" and "accident" were contrasted in the preceding clause, so here "principe" and "hasard." The object of this drawing forth from its own principle is "jaillissement," a bursting forth of idea or thought, reinforcing "puiser," both terms suggestive of creation out of the first origin, water, *fons et origo* of both race and individual, and hence vaguely intimating the poet's kinship with the race. [5]

---

[4] In an early verse poem, "Les Fenêtres," this threat is imaged in a persona who, pushing through the window out into the infinite, risks falling through eternity. And in the late "Prose," quoted already in connection with "Pauvre Enfant Pâle," there is an image most reminiscent of Nerval, that Symbolist precursor who did, in fact, "assume the risk" of poetic vision threatening to destroy the mind.

[5] This "jaillissement," poetic inspiration, was forever latent in the "noble œuf de cygne, tel que n'en *jaillira* le vol" of the "Nénuphar." In an undated letter to Charles Morice, quoted in Mondor, *Propos*, p. 164, Mallarmé writes:

With the second paragraph begins the anecdote, the persona's return for his annual summer visit to his country house, his partaking of the great rhythm of nature. [6] His love for the deserted house results from his disposition to create in its calm the elements of his universe, so in harmony with this quiet, hidden world. But even here once again the unexpected and hated encounter with intruders to his peace, that cherished silence, will occasion a poem. With the regularity of the annual cycle, which infallibly turns the vines on the outside stairway green, the poet expects the same happiness at each return, upon pushing the shutters back against the old walls. "Chaque année" underlines the security of the temporal and spatial laws, that rhythmical cycle in which the earth always takes the same time to travel the same space, and back again to the origin to repeat the same revolution, while the becoming green again of the old stone stairway is a beautiful image for both stability — that of the stone — and rebirth — the new green leaves. [7] As the poet-persona opens the shutters for the customary summer view, he links — "raccorder" points to "accord," "harmony," and thence "re-establishing harmony" — this view to past ones: "l'œillade d'à présent au spectacle immobilisé autrefois." And when "today's glance" is in this way linked to last year's and those of the years before, namely to the recreated, "fixed" mental image of memory, it seems that in this act today's live view is also already "immobilized." Thus the present is rendered stable by being linked to the past, that is by being internalized at once. This is reminiscent of the conclusion of "L'Ecclésiastique," where the poet had likewise "fixed" the fugitive in a permanent image: "... d'en fixer à jamais ... l'image." And nature as "spectacle" for the poet beholder prepares already for the poem's conclusion, where he will, again, become a participant in its drama.

Le chant *jaillit* de source innée, antérieur à un concept, si purement que refléter au dehors mille rythmes d'images. [my italics]

[6] Mallarmé's summer retreat, Valvins, was celebrated by Valéry, *Œuvres* I (Paris: Gallimard, 1957), p. 85, in a poem by that name where even the "Nénuphar"'s *yole* gets its due.

[7] René Ghil, *Les Dates,* p. 25, recalls this outside stairway of Mallarmé's Valvins residence:

Une porte campagnarde, et la cour, d'où parmi des rosiers monte l'escalier de pierre haut et rustique.

By this expedient, the mechanism of instantly connecting the outer view to the inner, mental, view, the poet-persona creates an illusion: "comme si pas d'interruption." For the real world of phenomena is characterized by ruptures, breaks, interruptions, and it is only the poetic mind which creates its form or order, which "fixes" it.

But this year, the operation does not produce the expected reward, the "contentement pareil," for the persona's faithful returns, — and the narrator's term "gage" here is similar to the "récompense" in "L'Ecclésiastique." For now the banging of the old, worm-eaten shutters against the walls "scande un vacarme," utterly unfamiliar to the customary scene. And the term "battement," fitting synecdoche for the shutters whose noise is being emphasized, as an artillery term is equally suited to the military vocabulary cluster mentioned above. "Scander" is used ironically here, for what is scanned is not verse, but clamor and shouts, "refrains" not of song, but of angry fighting from below. The narrator now remembers having been notified that the ground floor of the house was to be rented to railroad construction workers for the summer. And "légende de la malheureuse demeure" personifies the house as a martyr, and prepares for the narrator's resolution to come to its defense. The great age of the house is stressed to contrast with progress, echoing not only the mood of "Plainte d'Automne" and "Frisson d'Hiver," but especially "La Gloire," where one of the symbols of progress was likewise the railroad. "Coin," in the sense of "endroit retiré, peu fréquenté" prepares for "solitude" further on in the sentence, while "intact," *tangere,* suggests undefiled, pure. "*Envahie* par une bande de travailleurs" accentuates the military tone in pointing to occupation by force, reinforced with "bande," an antagonistic group. "Travailleurs" at the same time already vaguely foreshadows the contrast with *bourgeois* to be developed further on. "Offenser le pays" makes the country a victim, particularly vulnerable "parce que tout de solitude," and thus in harmony with its solitary poet inhabitant, and martyrized like the old house. When the unwelcome news about the workers had arrived, the poet had hesitated over coming this year, "irais-je ou non" rendering this conflict of alternatives. But, assuming a knightly stance, that of coming to the rescue of the defenseless, militant in his own turn, he decided "à défendre, comme mien," and even "arbitrairement s'il le faut, le local." This tells us also that the persona does not own this property, but that he merely is, like these itinerant workers, a passing occupant himself, a point developed later on. And so, overcome by a tenderness for the wronged and defenseless house, he assumes his task of "hôte de sa déchéance." And "dans la suppression concernant des sites précieux," with "précieux," points both to the poetic transformation of nature and to the style which accomplishes it.

"Invraisemblablement" is a typically Mallarméan beginning with the elaborate adverb setting the tone of the sentence, or paragraph.[8] The narrator can hardly believe that his house, so loved for its "désuétude" (echoing "abandonnée" above), a place so exceptional, should have been turned into — and what a contrast! — a "cantine d'ouvriers." "Cantine" by association with its secondary meaning, "où l'on vend à boire dans des casernes, les prisons," already foreshadows the workers' drinking which will figure prominently later on, while, once again, intimating a military ambiance. However, "ouvriers" already marks a progression from the above "bande de travailleurs," in suggesting the word's collective use for the whole class of working people, which these men will come more and more to represent for the poet-persona. In fact, the aggressor threatening here is progress, rather than the workers who are merely its instrument. Moreover, the use of progress in the plural, a term which is usually in the singular when it refers to "le progrès: l'évolution de l'humanité, de la civilization," constitutes an ironic fragmentation of the apparent general "mouvement en avant."

But now accepting the feared confrontation, the narrator from his window looks these men over: "terrassiers, puisatiers," and are not earth and water the elements from which the poet also draws — Valvins, loved for its land and river? At the moment, the men are "au repos, dans une tranchée," and this ditch, in which they are stretched out, suggests by association a "terme de

---

[8] This device, which we already mentioned in connection with "Réminiscence," is even more common in Mallarmé's verse than in his prose: "Victorieusement fui..."; "Indifféremment sommeillez..."; "Mais langoureusement longe..."; "Indomptablement a dû..."; "Abominablement quelque idole..."

guerre," the trench which foreshadows the poem's culminating image of the battlefield. Characteristically, this poem's persona, too, meditates on the clothing people wear: "velours hâve aux jambes." Their corduroys thus worn, the project must be going ahead: "le remblai bouge." Their jerseys' blue and white transverse stripes occasion a comparison rendering these humble work clothes deeply symbolic; for they resemble a watery surface, water again reminiscent of first origins — suggested already with "jaillissement" and "puiser" — which notion is reinforced by their lying in the earth. The clothing thus symbolizes the human life cycle, which is in harmony with the evocation of the solar-annual one above. Blue and white further suggest milk as original substance and sustenance, recalling Hérodiade's memories of the "lait bu jadis," and that "blancheur sibylline" of "Don du Poëme." "L'homme est la source qu'il cherche" also points back to the opening where the poetic act was called the mind's drawing from its own principle, the suggestion here being that not only the poet, but the laborers also, that is both physical and spiritual workers, pursue a quest leading back to the origin. [9]

And so gradually a secret kinship of the poet-persona with his unwelcome intruders suggests itself, perhaps even symbolized by "co-locataires." "La rumeur les dit chemineaux," while on the narrative level telling us that reportedly they are railroad workers, connotes, with "rumeur" and the secondary meaning of "chemineaux," "tramp," society's negative attitude toward them, which prepares for the theme of their being victimized by that society, developed later on. The poet sees in the workers the contradiction of weariness and strength. It is not quite clear whether their independence, "en l'absence d'usine," is a chosen or imposed one; "grouillement partout" is somewhat evocative of the crawling workers of an anthill, perhaps reinforced with the ironic "partout où la terre a souci d'être modifié," for at the moment the men appear vanquished both by and in that impassible earth.

---

[9] In a letter of 1889 to Vielé Griffin, quoted in Mondor, *Propos,* p. 142, Mallarmé writes:
> C'est une œuvre comme il en pourrait surgir au début d'une littérature, si tout ne finissait, au contraire, par les commencements.

Cf. also Richard, *L'Univers,* p. 264.

The opening sentence of the following paragraph is characteristic of Mallarmé's latest manner: entirely lacking in verbs, it is tersely difficult. "Les maîtres quelque part," the workers, is again indicative of a certain progression from "bande de travailleurs," to "les ouvriers quelconques par excellence" to this appelation, which designates foremen ("maître ouvrier") while also suggesting that they are now the masters of the region. Their behavior is free of constraint and noisy, where "verbe haut" likewise indicates a progression from the earlier "vacarme" and "altercations." In the "malade des bruits" we recognize (to mention the early prose poems) the narrator of "Plainte d'Automne," who always cherished solitude, that of "Frisson d'Hiver," who loved in his companion a "calme enfant," and the persona of "Le Démon de l'Analogie," who listened only to an inner voice. In the late ones, the clash of silence and harmony with noise and discord opened the anecdotes of "La Déclaration Foraine" and "La Gloire," while "Le Nénuphar Blanc" celebrated silence. [10]

But gradually the narrator becomes accustomed to these workers' lives, whose steady monotony is beautifully rendered in "cette cohue entre, part, avec le manche, à l'épaule, de la pioche et de la pelle," which not only conveys the unchanging, simple rhythm with these one and two-syllable words, but reinforces it with internal alliteration. "Cohue" once more stresses their noisiness so painful to the poet, while "pioche" and "pelle" are introduced here to be picked up again and fully developed later on in inverse order. And this way of life causes the persona to reflect, "inviting in its favor" rather vague emotions, "de derrière la tête," not quite thoughts yet, but impressions forcing him beyond notions of which one says "*c'est de la littérature,*" where the author's italics underline a derogatory intention. The following sentence defines this vague feeling, for seeing in a storage cellar the workers' shovels and picks neatly lined up, the poet is overcome by a "religious" emotion, forcing him to his knees, as he reflects on the basic life-creating force — the sexual one — doubly symbolized here by the workers

---

[10] Richard, *L'Univers*, p. 440:
> Autre grief de Mallarmé contre la matière: sa crudité, son aggression immédiate, par celle surtout exercé, dans le domaine des sons.

who impregnate the earth by their labor, and by their tools, shovel and pick, womb- and phallus-shaped. [11] And this religious emotion is accentuated with the vocabulary cluster "dévot," "crypte," "religion," "m'agenouiller." "Dévot ennemi" conveys the narrator's ambiguous attitude, with its tension of both love and hate for those men, a tension underlying the whole poem, and which is that indicated by its title, "Conflit." "Pénétrant" is richly suggestive, for, while on the literal level referring to the persona's stealing into the tool shed, it has sexual connotations in harmony with other elements of the sentence. As the poet penetrates the cellar, he is in turn penetrated, that is deeply affected by this encounter. The "crypte ou cellier en commun" suggests the workers' forming a kind of spiritual community, the instruments of their labor functioning as a synecdoche for the men; for "crypte" can also refer to a certain kind of church itself, while "en commun" reinforces the communal idea. It is thus as though the poet had stolen into "their" church secretly, where the images before which he bows are the instruments of their toil: "la rangée de l'outil double, cette pelle et cette pioche, sexuels." And in "l'outil double" there is even an intimation of an androgynous quality, vaguely evocative of a first mythical stage of life, before the sexes were divided. The instruments' metal, which itself had to be wrought from deep within the earth, sums up "la force pure du travailleur," the latter now totally redeemed with "pure." For the worker, too, though unlike the farmer who tills and sows, renders the earth fruitful by his labor. The poet's inner conflict of attitudes, then, is one of the simultaneous emotions of "religion" and "mécontentement," making him the workers' "dévot ennemi."

The following sentence has a rich ambiguity suggested by "intrus"; for from the narrator's viewpoint, the intruders are the workers, whom no man of law prides himself in ousting. (The self-importance of this imagined country constable or sheriff is nicely rendered with "se targuer," a verb implying something of the ostentatious pretentiousness of the small official, reminiscent of

---

[11] Though any instrument with which the laborer impregnates the earth is in that sense phallic, I feel that the sexual aspect of the shovel and the pick here refers not only to this figurative sense, but also to the very shape of those instruments themselves, suggestive of "female" and "male."

the stationmaster of "La Gloire.") But "l'intrus," in view of the foregoing, might also refer to the narrator himself who had stolen into the workers' toolshed; and we recall that in the preceding poem, the poet-persona had designated himself "l'intrus royal," the only other use of the noun in these prose poems. Further, some of the rest of the clause could also equally well apply to the workers and to the narrator: both have paid the owner, and both might be there on the basis of a mere verbal agreement customary in the country, "beaux tacites, usages locaux." "Etabli par surprise" could refer to the narrator's surprise at seeing the workers there (he had forgotten the letter telling him about it), while for the workers the narrator's presence might be just as astonishing. And it is this ambiguity which somehow again vaguely intimates a kinship between the poet and the working men, setting them both off against the "propriétaire." The last clause shows the narrator's reaction to the situation as a balancing of alternatives: play along with them, or defend himself against them, which reflects the tension of his conflicting feelings. The "role" he might play is, therefore, equivocal; is it that of "homme de loi" or of "intrus"? He will play it out now in an internal dialogue, like the imaginary one he had held with the stationmaster of "La Gloire." In this role, he will both "restrict" the intruders "à mes droits" but also assume the part of fellow-intruder, "camarades" accentuating his fellowship with the men.

Now he mentally "acts out" his approach, not without misgivings as to a certain disdainful tone of language, should he speak to the men, a tone which would be due not to condescension on his part, but simply to the fact that he has no taste for "promiscuité," a word which intends no value judgment, but accentuates the persona's fear of the disorder of *hasard*. However, might he not, after all, fall into the "note juste"? Now these are terms of music, the former designating intonation and length of sound, the latter conformity to the rules of scale and tonality. And the significance of the musical terminology here lies in its connotation of the formal, the artistic; for as the poet-persona discloses his imaginary address, we recognize in it the language of art, *écriture* rather than parole. The only term the men would have understood, really, is the first word: "Camarades," which continues the progression we have been following from the beginning of the encounter, with the gradually increasing rapprochement of poet and people. But "vous ne supposez pas l'état de quelqu'un épars dans un paysage celui-ci" is formal and distant, so that the preceding "camarades" seems somehow nullified by it. The narrator referring to himself with the very impersonal "quelqu'un" stresses his distance, which is emphasized by the use of the definite article in "l'état." Again, not *this* region, but "un paysage celui-ci" underlines the remoteness not only of the speaker, but also of the setting, from those spoken to. There is, thus, again a tension between a desired rapprochement and a factual distance, the attempt of a personal tone, which is then undercut by the most highly impersonal style possible.

"Epars" here as in the "Nénuphar" and the "Ecclésiastique" refers to something characterizing the natural setting; in the former it was a "vierge absence éparse en cette solitude," and in the latter a "solitude, froid silence épars dans la verdure." In our poem it is "l'état de quelqu'un épars dans un paysage," which accentuates the correspondence between the poet and his chosen *paysage*.[12] And this landscape — "où toute foule s'arrête" — of absence, solitude and silence, is an ambiance protected by the forest's density. The forest protects the land, and the land the still water, recalling the magic and secret landscape of the "Nénuphar," which like ours was evocative of the protective shelter of the womb;[13] and in "Conflit" this landscape gently modulates the motif of the return to the source introduced at the beginning.

"Or mon cas, tel," characteristic by the absence of the verb, suggests by its brevity almost a shyness on the part of the poet, the small one-syllable words expressing his reluctance to tell the

---

[12] This correspondance between *paysage* and poet recalls the early Gide's Symbolist "Le Voyage d'Urien," on which he comments himself in a note: André Gide, *Romans, Récits et Soties; Œuvres Lyriques* (Paris: Gallimard, 1958), pp. 1464-65:

> Il y a là une sorte d'algèbre esthétique: émotion et manifeste forment équation; l'un est l'équivalent de l'autre. Qui dit *émotion* dira donc *paysage*; et qui dit *paysage* devra donc connaître émotion.
> . . . .
> Il n'y a pas d'émotion, si particulière et neuve qu'elle puisse paraître, qui n'ait en la nature *tous ses équivalents*—

[13] Cf. Richard, *L'Univers*, p. 134.

workers that their noisy behavior hurts him, while their activities are being rendered somewhat less offensive by the use of the impersonal pronoun. The enumeration of vulgarities is summed up in "discordance," a discord causing an "intolérable, if invisible rent" in the poet's soul which wants to remain in harmony with the atmosphere, "ce suspens lumineux de l'air." And this ambiance of vibrating airy brightness, a calm only broken by the trembling of light, is reminiscent of that golden equilibrium of "La Gloire."

Though it is clear that the workers would not have understood his language, they might have understood the poet's need for calm instinctively, and certainly better than others more sophisticated than they, which again accentuates the bond between poet and workers. For they are distinguished from the broad bourgeoisie, here represented by "onze messieurs," such as the property owners of the region. The incomprehension of the poet on the part of society — a theme familiar from the early "Le Guignon" to the mature *tombeaux* — is here symbolized by the "rire immédiat," a response as cruel as it is ugly, and which has nothing in common with the idealized working man's innocent, but not unfeeling, lack of understanding. These reflections are confirmed, moreover, by a characteristic of these men's lives, their drinking, both bane and blessing for them. For it is because they have "le sens du merveilleux," that sense which the poet also has and which the materialistic bourgeoisie does not know, that they are "pochards." Is it not by means of their kind of "ivresse" that they turn their back on an unacceptable here and now? And is it not because of their brutish hard toil — "soumis" and "corvée" reminiscent of the soldier's unquestioning performance of his duty — that they have a sense, however vague, "de délicatesses quelque part supérieures?" For this reason, then, might they not perhaps see in the narrator's "douloureux privilège," a life and work condemning him to solitude (where we feel the tension between the privileged calling and the price paid for it), a personal rather than a social distinction and thus not be suspicious and defiant? Might they not, therefore, if but for a short time, try to disturb the poet less? But no, much more "plausiblement," habit would get the upper hand soon; and by its etymology the adverb suggests that the workers would rightfully go back to their own noisy ways. And then the poet's understanding of the necessities of these men, as vital to them as his own to himself, is developed. But we must keep in mind that this dialogue is merely imaginary, an idealized one which will soon clash with a real one. "A moins qu'un ne répondit, tout de suite, avec égalité" intimates that they are now on equal terms with him, with "avec égalité" even suggesting a certain dignified manner of presentation on their part. At this point, then, poet and workers seem to have reached a temporary balance of equality. The imaginary justification of the workers is that for those short periods when work ceases, they need each other's shouting to continue to exist; they need to be encouraged by it, their own and that of the others, like a chain of hands, where each individual is at the same time supported by, and supporting, himself and the whole group. The shouting of a comrade is exhilarating almost like drinking, and costs nothing; and so the poet understands that "leur chœur, incohérent, est en effet nécessaire."

How quickly the persona becomes less firm in his "défense," now as sensitive to their needs as he had been — and still is — to his own! Is he not almost ready to lead the "assaillant" in by the hand? But "défense" and "assaillant," again military terms, suggest that, even now that the poet's attitude has shifted from his former defensive stance, the tension remains insurmountable. For the countryside itself, this small domain exactly right for "l'usage du rêveur," closed off from the outside world by the forest shade — "se clôture, au noir d'arbres" echoing "où toute foule s'arrête, en tant qu'épaisseur de forêt à l'isolement" above — how can it accommodate those intruders? And this land, is it not a symbol for the poet's mind — as had been the room in the early prose poems — jealously closed off from the outside world?

The term "la Propriété" is not the narrator's designation of this spot, but "comme le veut le vulgaire," implying legal possession and ownership which is held, ironically, by absent owners: and their kind of possession has nothing in common with that spiritual affinity of the poet with this land. Here the theme of the narrator's non-ownership of this property, already intimated above, is fully developed. But there is a curious juxtaposition in "il faut que je l'aie manquée, avec obstination," namely the legal acquisition of the place; for "manquer" implies passivity, and "avec obstination" its opposite. At the same time the poet muses on his lack of funds, "omettant le moyen d'acquisition," but then again suggests choice with "pour satisfaire quelque singulier instinct de ne rien posséder et de seulement passer." His poverty at any rate, whether chosen or imposed by circumstances, puts the poet on the side of the working class. Perhaps the poet-persona had refrained from acquiring property so as not to risk a disturbance such as the present one. In other words, in not binding himself to material possessions, he might have hoped to remain free from chance (*hasard* always of the domain of *matière*), "l'aventure." But then, immediately, the meaning of this word is negated, "l'aventure qui n'est pas, tout à fait, le hasard," which shows a most significant shift from the position at the poem's opening, where "idée" and "accident," as well as "principe" and "hasard," were still in diametrical opposition. What really has shifted is the workers' presence as representing "hasard." Not a pure chance encounter this, which draws the poet nearer to the "prolétaires," with whom he feels a growing spiritual kinship.

The following line, one of the most beautiful of the poem, is a restatement of the title, "Conflit." For "alternatives" poses, again, no resolution, but simply balances rapprochement and *éloignement*, attitudes which result in the tension of conflicting feelings: "sympathie" and "malaise." And "je prévois" suggests the poet's function of *voyant* in the widest sense, for this "saison, de sympathie et de malaise" exceeds the sphere of the poem and might well reflect Mallarmé's historical moment, his socially revolutionary nineteenth century, for whose conflicts the poet sees no resolution.[14]

On the anecdotal level, the narrator, who had above leaned toward rapprochement, now suggests the alternative, that is breaking off the connection by means of a quarrel, and the military connotation of "querelle" is reinforced by "stratégie," which, ironically, amounts to closing a garden gate. For this little garden, created "par mon art," is not part of the surrounding land but an artificial creation, set off against the natural setting. And while the poet is almost willing to share the latter with the workers, he jealously protects this garden, a symbol, perhaps, for artistic

---

[14] For Mallarmé's socio-historical consciousness, cf. Robert Greer Cohn, *Mallarmé's Masterwork: New Findings* (Paris: Mouton, 1966), p. 48.

creation, a poem.[15] In fact, "qu'étranger ne passe le seuil" is an exhortation which could well apply to the very poem in which it appears. The poet's "jardinet" is juxtaposed and contrasted with the workers' "cabaret"; as to a tavern, might the men find another way to the workyard; let them cut through the fields.

At this point the internal, imaginary, dialogue ceases; for as the narrator is closing the garden gate, one of the drunken workers angrily reacts with a very real curse, as violent as his gesture is furious. And in "fumier! se profère violemment," the contrast between the curse and the *préciosité* of the phrase is not devoid of humor. As the drunkard leans over the gate shouting his insult, the persona is annoyed despite himself, although he understands that the other through his drunkenness is no more responsible than an angry child, "grand gars." But after the long imaginary encounter with the idealized workingmen, the persona must consider the other his equal; simply another human being. "Est-ce caste, du tout" poses and at the same time answers the question of class distinction as it affects this skirmish: it is purely that of one individual with another. The poet-persona is "en ce moment" still under the spell of the inner and imaginary confrontation, despite the intrusion of outer phenomena: the anger of a vulgar drunkard. Therefore, he cannot quite distinguish yet between the "forcené, titubant et vociférant," who in fact threatens him, and the "homme" of the vision. And "considérer" by its etymology which suggests "looking at the stars" *(cum sidus)* humorously intimates something of the conflict of dream and reality. With "forcené" and "homme" the irrational and the rational are contrasted, "vociférant" recalling the "vociférateur" of "La Gloire." The persistence of the factual is reflected in the short blunt sentence, with its harsh sounds: "Très

---

[15] The analogy of garden and poetry is, moreover, also suggested by Valéry, *Œuvres*, I, p. 657; here in one of his "Variétés" about Mallarmé he says:

> Un poète use à la fois de la langue vulgaire, — qui ne satisfait qu'à la condition de comprehension et qui est donc purement transitive, — et du langage qui s'oppose à celui-ci, — comme s'oppose un jardin soigneusement peuplé d'espèces bien choisies à la campagne toute inculte où toute plante vient, et d'où l'homme prélève ce qu'il y trouve de plus beau pour le remettre et le choyer dans une terre exquise.

raide, il me scrute avec animosité," while "impossible de l'annuler mentalement" admits the mind's defeat by matter.[16]

Earlier the narrator had mused upon the blessing of drunkenness, and here its bane confronts him in fact, in the form of "ce colosse tout à coup grossier et méchant," whom he can't overcome mentally. "Le coucher en la poussière," reminiscent of traditional epic combat, again already foreshadows the final scene. But the persona won't yield to his adversary's further "provocations," or the fistfight, which would illustrate the class struggle: the notion of "caste" is being reintroduced here, but ironically, for "la lutte des classes" is undercut with the mundane phrase "sur le gazon." Moreover, are these men not already condemned by their vice? Now the poet feels guilty at silently beholding this man's and his brothers' fate — for does his indifference not make him an accomplice of it? And this is a rare, but clear, indication of Mallarmé's social conscience, for under the poet's merely apparent indifference lies not only sympathy, but compassion for the people, whom he will serve in his own way, that is by celebrating them.

Now "un énervement d'états..." interposes itself into the flow of the narrative, the whole sentence by its lack of verbs accentuating a moment where all action, external and internal, stops; for the persona is himself now victimized by the continual tension of clashing feelings and states of mind, to the point where he seems contaminated by "le mal" surrounding him, that is as though intoxicated himself by debilitating and enfeebling confusion.

Yet, at times there is also tranquillity, "le calme ... jusqu'au silence," in windstill evening hours, in this "région d'échos, ... cette contrée de luxe sonore." "Comme on y trempe" — the pronoun referring both to the calm and the country, that is the *état d'âme* and its corresponding symbol in nature — means that the *moi* participates in the privileged moment by immersing itself in it, "tremper" pointing back to the water motif of the opening. "Soirs de dimanche" suggests both the poet's favorite hour of

---

[16] The "méchanceté" of the railroad workers at Valvins is reflected in a letter by Mallarmé to "ses Dames," of 1896, Barbier, *Documents*, p. 77:
> Un désastre, les chemineaux, en partant, ont cassé d'un coup de bêche, exprès, pour qu'on se souvienne d'eux, le plus beau des deux mauviers, proche de l'arbre.

declining day and the notion of *fête: Feierabend*. As in "La Gloire," the holy moment is that instant of "suspens lumineux de l'air," a timelessness where everything becomes transparent in evening's glow, before flowing "lucide vers quelque profondeur." And "lucide" describes both the luminosity of the sunset hour and the poet's state of heightened consciousness, as "profondeur" the shades of the oncoming night as well as those of the mind. Again, as in "La Gloire," this momentary equilibrium between the forces of light and darkness is "la crise," symbolic of the human drama: "may it claim kinship with someone."

"Les compagnons" appreciate the instant in their own way, by ceasing to fight, "se concerter" implying at least some degree of harmony. Yet, "en le décor vautrés" brings out a contrast of the animal-like in the men and the art-like in nature — nature spiritualized by the poet — as they "wallow" in its "decor." Though the narrator does not leave his window to go outside and talk with the workers, this very passage being about the impossibility of communication, he cannot isolate himself from them mentally. And yet he remains "exclus." For "Conflit," though about Poet and People, like the other prose poems continues to stress the poet's isolation and solitude. And as the window looks out from the old house, which had already been personified earlier, "sur l'endroit qu'elle sait," the poet-persona becomes a pure "regard moi," the desire for communication definitely frustrated now: "sans effet." Not only the poet, but Man is condemned to solitude: "un contact peut ... n'intervenir entre des hommes." [17]

As the narrator overhears their talk, he mentally — perhaps in a whisper even — corrects their misconceptions: not only do they labor for the profit of others — a motif already prepared for above

---

[17] This is also the conclusion of one of Mallarmé's essays, significantly entitled "Solitude":

> J'attribue à la conscience de ce cas, dans un temps que deux hommes ne se sont, peut-être, malgré la grimace à le faire, entretenus, plusieurs mots durant, du même objet exactement, la restriction qui garde des interlocuteurs de rien livrer à fond et de prêter souci; mais les persuade, par ruse mutuelle avec de la bravade, reliquat des surannés combats d'esprit généreux et baroques ou conformément au monde dont les lettres sont le direct affinement — de soustraire autant que révéler sa pensée, le premier; le second, de saisir, obstinément, autre chose — pour réserver leur intégrité, quand un besoin cordial les leurre à se rencontrer (OC pp. 408-9).

— but they even sell themselves. "Afin qu'on vous paie et d'être légalement" means that they not only sell themselves for the profit of others, but that they "legally" buy their very existence, their right to be, from their oppressors. And here again a kinship, but also a difference, suggests itself between poet and working man: both work "au profit d'autres," but the poet cannot sell himself, cannot buy his right to exist. All is silenced finally by the magic of the starry sky: "quelle pierrerie, ce ciel fluide," the adjective suggestive not merely of the flow of water, but also that of sound, evocative of the revolving spheres of the ancient heavens with their music, and the stars fixed in each sphere as in an immense precious piece of jewelry.

The men ("bouches ordinaires" a synecdoche for the workers and their banal talk) are now silenced by the night and stretched out on the ground like dead men, sleeping open-mouthed after having vomited their empty bombast. And as the poet beholds them thus finally come to rest after hard work and hard talking, he again feels drawn to them, to the point of having to justify himself to them: "peut-être, moi, aussi, je travaille..." With the workers now distanced from him by their sleep (a distance which paradoxically makes this rapprochement possible), the persona again creates their idealized response: yes, they appreciate that some work with their minds rather than with their muscles. And though "à cause de comptables" adds some irony, the dominant note is that of simplicity on the part of these men who unquestionably accept this age-old division of human labor. But for the poet this imaginary dialogue culminates in a question of conscience: "à quoi?" For of what use, "parmi l'échange général," is the poet's work? For these men at least, he sadly feels, his production remains "par essence, comme les nuages au crépuscule ou des étoiles, vaine."

Looking down upon the men, the poet-persona sees the familiar lawn turned into a battlefield strewn with the bodies of its victims. And the poem's war imagery reaches its greatest concentration here, "l'escouade du labeur" also being a military term, and "gésir" recalling the formula of epitaphs, while "vaincus" is suggestive of "qui a succombé en guerre, en combat." Now the poet narrates the end of the battle, how they have, one after another, "fallen"; how, as though hit by a "projectile," they stagger before sinking onto the grass, "cet étroit champ de bataille." And "étroit" here not only designates the smallness of the lawn on which the men are resting but intimates that their "battlefield" has none of the historical grandeur extending its modest limits beyond time. "Quel sommeil de corps" again likens this sleep to death, and "la motte sourde," evoking the dull sound of bodies falling to the ground, points to the impassibility of the earth to which Man must inevitably return, once more recalling the motif of the return to the origin.

And with the intruders thus finally vanquished by their human fate, is the one intruded upon at last free? As the poet, "lecteur d'horizons," raises his eyes toward the horizon — the glance we remember from "La Gloire" — to admire and abandon himself to the sunset, the open window does not set him free. For he could liberate himself only by — the American idiom puts it most aptly — "walking over their dead bodies," that is at their expense. He would be repaying the men their lack of understanding for him "avec manque d'égard et de convenance à mon tour," were he to abandon them now, reduced to "cette jonchée d'un fléau." But "en ma qualité," as poet, it is his duty to "comprendre le mystère et juger le devoir," "comprendre" here meaning more than mere intellectual understanding, literally "prendre en soi," the fallen workers thus becoming part of him. Now the poet sets forth "le devoir," their life earned by their labor: "ils ont peiné une partie notable de la semaine pour l'obtenir." But "semaine" is also that "payement" by which they have bought their escape. And this is their "mystery," which the poet understands, and knows in his own way — "ma vue ne peut ... *s'échapper*" — this escape which the bourgeois does not need. Thus once again the narrator tightens the bond between himself and the working people; for as widely as their needs may differ, nothing sums up better wherein they agree than: "le pain ne lui a pas suffi."

Again the monotony of the workers' lives is stressed: how they have toiled upon the earth on which their bodies are now resting, knowing nothing of tomorrow but that they shall toil again, "rampent par le vague et piochent sans mouvement." "Rampent" (as the earlier "grouillement") again likens theirs to an animal existence close to and even in the earth, and "le vague" is the apparent emptiness of those lives, their daily blind and aimless digging without going anywhere, "piochent sans mouvement." With this wearisome work, day after day, they are digging a hole not only in the earth, but in their very existence and life. Yet, as they thus undermine and spend their "sort," are they not setting the foundations of temples, "fondation ... de temple" having both physical and metaphysical implications. The poet is again overcome by a religious emotion: not only is it their labor which allows civilization to erect its monuments on the face of the earth, but it is their labor alone which even makes possible the very civilization of which these monuments are the symbol. These men, then, are the founders and fathers of the culture which produced the poet. The kinship of the persona and the working men in our poem thus grows in complexity; for while the poet-persona assumes, on the one hand, the paternalistic role of shepherd of the sleeping flock, and further that of celebrant of a rite for them, he at the same time, paradoxically, stands in a filial relationship to the workers. [18]

And these men, though again unconscious of it, honor the sacred in human existence by their brief repose from toil, unknowing participants in the human tragedy, whose symbolic reflection in nature (as we saw in "La Gloire") is accessible to the poet alone. Thus they celebrate through the poet's consciousness the "fête" which their sleeping eyes cannot see, and whose symbolic significance they would not comprehend. Their deep sleep, moreover, that "momentané suicide" reflected in the sunset, and which they have chosen by their drinking, recalls Mallarmé's meditations on suicide elsewhere; for example the voluntary death dramatized in *Igitur*, which we discussed in connection with "Le Démon de l'Analogie." There is here a suggestion, then, that the men have in their own way, by their chosen "momentary suicide," this only "free" act possible, negated chance. [19]

---

[18] Robert Greer Cohn develops this motif of "the hardy ancestor" as it is reflected in the "Coup de Dés" (the "Maître" and "l'ombre puérile"). Moreover, he points to its reappearance in both "Conflict" and "Confrontation." This motif had already been suggested in "Un Spectacle interrompu" with the bear, the "terrible parent" or "dark brother" figure. Cf. pp. 108-9.

[19] Cf. Richard, *L'Univers*, p. 240:

On sait que l'idée de son propre suicide occupa longtemps Mallarmé ... C'est que, comme le dit Mallarmé dans *la Fausse Entrée*

"Une colonnade de futaie," which recalls the "immortels troncs" of "La Gloire," would symbolize for these men the resplendent feeling of pride in their work, if fate permitted. But this ideal "connaissance" contrasts, in fact, with their dull sleep, like "resplendirait" with the actual darkness in their minds.[20] And instead of standing upright and proudly like those trees,[21] they have followed "quelque instinct" which has victimized them, so that their drinking is paradoxically both their escape from, and their victimization by, chance. The twisted posture of their bodies ("déjeter" lexically refers both to the human body and to trees) contrasts with the ideal upright position of that "colonnade de futaie," while accentuating the poem's circularity. For this image of the men lying on the ground asleep recalls the opening one, where they were "au repos, dans une tranchée." The workers' physical condition, moreover, reflects their metaphysical one: they are victimized by and for humanity, just as they are "victimes" rather than "officiants" in the drama celebrated here by the poet-priest (also in his own way a victim), whose consecration was the theme of "La Gloire." The solar drama symbolizes the human one, and the poet-officiant's regular observance of it ("avec l'absolu d'un accomplissement rituel") endows it with the ritual of a religious ceremony. This is the ideal theatre — already announced in "Un Spectacle Interrompu" — where the workers figure and represent

---

(OC p. 348), tuer est "le seul acte en soi surnaturel commis à la disposition de l'homme." Se tuer est peut-être alors le seul moyen d'accéder à la fois à soi, à l'esprit et au sacré. C'est bien le sens que Mallarmé donne, dans *Conflit* (OC p. 359), à ce "momentané suicide," cette fulguration mineure, d'ivresse.

[20] This last reference to trees in these prose poems reveals a significant progression, perhaps a reflection of the poet-persona's growth. In "Le Phénomène Futur," we encountered "les arbres... leur feuillage blanchi (de la poussière du temps)"; in "Plainte d'Automne," "des peupliers dont les feuilles me paraissent mornes même au printemps"; in "La Pipe," "ces arbres malades du square." But the nocturnal trees of "La Déclaration Foraine" had a nourishing quality, while in the "Nénuphar" the "buée d'argent glaçant des saules" became the idealized woman's limpid glance. The magnificently proud trees of both "La Gloire" and "Conflit," finally, become symbols of human pride and strength.

[21] "Se montrer debout" is a gesture symbolizing control and even defiance; this was clearly developed in the "debout dans les rues" of "Pauvre Enfant Pâle," and its opposite in the ecclesiastic's position "contre la terre."

the sacrifice paid by human labor, their role in the drama assigned to them by fate.

Now the sun has died, and "les constellations s'initient à briller," the verb "s'initier" with "briller" and the repetition of high and bright "i" sounds rendering the sparkling in the sky. Significantly the earlier "étoiles" have become "constellations," no longer the fortuitous and random points of luminosity appearing arbitrarily on the night sky, but those configurations of fixed stars upon which imaginary connecting lines confer their special significance, and which symbolize the poet's new insight which endows his world with greater meaning. "Le hasard" has, thus, been encountered and transformed into order by the poetic mind. The workers having partaken of the evening ritual unknowingly, the poet now wishes that they might share in this light. But "l'obscurité qui court sur l'aveugle troupeau" once more likens the men to animals, to sheep, with the poet as their shepherd, while the darkness is both that of the surrounding night and that of their minds. Their blindness, later reinforced with "ces yeux scellés," contrasts with the lucidity of the poet who had become a "regard." And he wants his wish (that the stars' light also enlighten them) to be uttered, not merely for the sake of justice but for his own peace of mind, reminding us that an article in which Mallarmé likewise deals with the poet's relationship to the people ("Confrontation") was originally entitled "Cas de Conscience."

Of them alone will he think, of "les importuns," who have cut him off from "le lointain vesperal," this evocation of the penultimate of the canonical hours accentuating the poet's priestly function, prepared by his "religious" emotion above. He maintains, in fact, a vigil for these men, whose designation of "artisans" again points to their secret kinship with the artist. The "il m'est loisible" has something of the tone of the *dignum et justum est* of the Mass, while the workers' individualities (like those of the faithful in the ritual) are annihilated and magnified as they are taken up in the flow of humanity, a flow "unbroken" as that of the river by their side, inevitable death and rebirth into which they have poured their toil and their lives.

In the conclusion of "Conflit," some of its themes are echoed once more, as in a coda: these working men with their toil, though "sans l'intermédiaire du blé," render the earth fruitful, and with their "intelligence robuste" they, too, have an understanding — though not the poet's high consciousness — of the human condition which they alone make even possible by their labor, "le miracle de vie qui assure la présence."

The "défrichements passés," as well as the work of generations to come, are part of them, and they, in turn, part of past and future, "les mêmes." Aqueducts and provinces establish the historical dimension, linking the present to antiquity and "tous les siècles," *saecula saeculorum*. Whatever their individual names or their lives, they flow into the stream of humanity anonymously, like the ideal Poet, who is ultimately subsumed in his creations:

> ... mon travail personnel qui, je crois, sera anonyme, le Texte y parlant de lui-même et sans voix d'auteur (OC p. 663).

Their sleep on the earth symbolizes the return to the common origin, and the earth, "la génératrice," on which they are resting — and which they have also rendered fruitful — is that giant womb from which all life springs (after its embrace by the sun), and the giant tomb to which all must return. The workers, then, sink into the stream of time and, "autant cela possible," of eternity.

Though their "étroit champ de bataille" has denied these men historical grandeur, the Poet in celebrating them with this poem confers upon them an immortality only art can give: "Conflit" is their *tombeau*.

CONCLUSION

Our detailed reading has indicated, then, that the thirteen prose poems of "Anecdotes ou Poèmes" constitute a unified cycle, centering about a two-fold theme: the poet's relation to the raw data of human experience, and the transformation of that experience into an ordered artistic universe through the poetic vision. I have already noted the exaggerated emphasis which contemporary critical interpretation tends to place on poetry as "poetry about poetry"; yet we must accept Mallarmé's own comment in *Divagations* that the entire book treats that single subject.[1] All of Mallarmé's work, indeed — his lyric poetry and his prose, including these prose poems — is literature about literature, reflexive-reflective like the figure of Narcissus and his beloved image.

At one point Mallarmé appears to belittle the "Anecdotes ou Poèmes," — "ces riens," as he calls them — explaining that their appearance in *Divagations* results only from the poet's obligation to his public. We know that he could at some times be as modest about his poetry as he was bold at others, though neither attitude was ever completely free of that irony which so suffuses his entire work, and which is apparent in the very title of *Divagations*. At one time this great poet could describe his entire poetic output as mere "exercises"[2] while at another he could call himself one of

---

[1] Mallarmé, *Divagations*, p. 1.
[2] Cf. his famous "biographical" letter to Verlaine:
> Rien de si simple alors que je n'aie pas eu hâte de recueillir les mille bribes connues, qui m'ont, de temps à autre, attiré la bienveillance de charmants et excellents esprits, vous le premier! Tout cela n'avait d'autre valeur momentanée pour moi que de m'entretenir la main: et quelque réussi que puisse être quelquefois un des [un mot manque] à eux tous, c'est bien juste s'ils composent un album, mais pas un livre (OC p. 663).

his own favorite poets.[3] In the end we must judge his own evaluation of the prose poems not by the possibly ironic "riens," but by his deliberate inclusion of them in his final book.

Moreover, in placing these poems in a definitive order, Mallarmé clearly suggests a particular perspective from which they are to be viewed, and creates a whole which must influence our reading of each of its parts. This retrospective grouping of pieces written over a period of more than thirty years does not imply that Mallarmé was fully conscious of their developing thematic unity, even at the end of his life; it does, however, indicate to the reader a structure and an attitude, evolving and yet self-consistent, a harmonious part of Mallarmé's poetic universe. As we have followed the poet's lead in our exploration of the prose poems, the structure which has gradually revealed itself, and which has in turn enlightened each poem, is that of a cyclical progression. The ascending spiral is the most convenient spatial and physical figure for the temporal and metaphysical development of the cycle. "Anecdotes ou Poèmes" reflects the development of the poet, and the distance from "Montreur" to Poet-Priest is temporal; to experience it is to *move* through this evolution, a process of change in time and in the style which creates it.

By way of elucidation let us retrace briefly the major movement of the cycle — the development of the poet from his artistic birth to his maturity — as it is reflected thematically in each piece, and in the developing style of the *recueil*. In this we will be conforming to the structure imposed on the cycle by Mallarmé himself.

The cycle opened with "Le Phénomène Futur," a vision of Beauty: Venus at the moment of her birth out of the primeval sea, preserved "par la science souveraine," that is, the magic of language. Only the "boniment" of the "Montreur" can describe what humanity is no longer capable of comprehending: a memory of Eden, the vision of which will, for a privileged moment, intoxicate poets alone with an overhelming glory. The role of the "Montreur"-poet, which we found also echoed in the verse poetry, is progressively developed in the cycle, that is the role of the poet as a performer before and for the crowd. And the image of the

---

[3] Cf. OC p. x.

poet-persona as showman before the uncomprehending crowd also symbolizes the poet's isolation from and in the society of man, a society without which, however, he would cease to be.

"Plainte d'Automne," laden with the memories of the poet's sister Maria and her death, celebrated one of the Orphic functions of poetry, the quest which leads "out of this world"; but the persona — from here on and throughout the remainder of the cycle a first-person narrator — hesitated at this point before the double calling: the descent into the crepuscular realm of the mind, and the ascent toward the ideal, his vocation. He was a reader of decadent literature and a listener to old-fashioned airs, that is, romantic poetry; he appreciated a moment of art characterized by refusal of the now, as death-directed as the very hour he preferred: "chute." In this piece we saw only the sunset, not the constellations, while only the last words vaguely suggest the first stirrings of song.

The third poem, bounded by the imagery of the poet's parlor, moved us into Winter, the "saison de l'art sereine," haunted by the ennui of sterility — pure and white as the page on which the poem cannot be born. The key images of "Frisson d'Hiver" are the room, the mirror, the window, the spider's lace, and the clock. This room, so jealously protected, emerged as a symbol of the poet's mind, with its familiar objects, cherished and old. But the persona still hesitated to look deep into the Venetian mirror, profound and mysterious fountain of the soul — what unfamiliar phantoms might it not reveal? The other threat was from without: from those windows, at once shielding and exposing the meditations of this calm, pale solitude, the narcissistic fragility of which was imaged in the trembling spider webbing. In his correspondence of those years, Mallarmé says: "Ma chambre est si grande, si haute, que j'y suis encore un étranger et ne l'ai pas peuplée de ma pensée et de mes paroles." [4] And just a few years later, as we saw, with the plan of his *œuvre* beginning to take shape in his mind, he adds

— centre de moi-même, où je me tiens comme une araignée sacrée, sur les principaux fils déjà sortis de mon

---

[4] Mondor, *Correspondance* I, p. 176, letter to Eugene Lefébure from Tournon, dated "octobre-novembre 1865" by the editor.

esprit, et à l'aide desquels je tisserai aux points de rencontre de merveilleuses dentelles, que je devine...[5]

To the same correspondent: "... et j'ai besoin de la plus silencieuse solitude de l'âme, et d'un oubli inconnu, pour entendre chanter en moi certaines notes mystérieuses."[6] "Frisson d'Hiver" marks this moment of withdrawal from the outside, so that the poet may hear the melody within.

This "chant intérieur" and the poet's enslavement to it was the theme of "Le Démon de l'Analogie," whose dominant vocabulary is that of rhetoric and music, and whose key symbols are those of poetry: the traditional lyre, the lute, the wing and bird, and "palme" and "plume." But this *engagement* is at the cost of a death — of a former self — and this poem is at once a poetic rendition of the creative process and a monody, celebrating thus both a becoming and a dying. The general feeling of the poem was that of the persona controlled by, rather than controlling, his inspiration, the *furor poeticus*. He is now driven to look into the mirror, which reflects his own image: a poet caressing the voice; and, as the mirror turns into a window, it reveals to him the symbols of his art.

The poet's sacrificial death, Promethean and Orphic, was the theme of "Pauvre Enfant Pâle," which I do not consider an expression of Mallarmé's compassion for the unfortunate of society. Rather, it is the poet projecting himself into the pale singer who sings "fatalement," that is, who is fated to sing, and "qui s'en va seul par la vie." The poem foreshadows the "Cantique de Saint Jean" and its decapitation theme. Now the poet-singer is "outside" the windows: his vision — the nudity of Hérodiade? — sets him apart, and as his head rises higher and higer, his voice strains to the breaking point, just as that string of the lyre of "Lé Démon de l'Analogie." In both the prose poem and the "Cantique," death is the punishment of a crime — as in the myths — committed "pour moi, pour ceux qui valent moins que moi."

The last of the early prose poems, "La Pipe," whose title plays with both the instrument of the privileged moment — its *madeleine* as it were — and by association with the instrument which sings

---

[5] *Ibid.*, p. 225.
[6] *Ibid.*, p. 181.

it, was the objectification of an epiphany aroused by the mechanism of involuntary memory. The poet now knows "l'art d'évoquer les minutes heureuses," that is, he has now mastered the art of traditional poetry. And it is precisely here that a break with tradition occurs in these prose poems, "La Pipe" constituting the last of the "early," the traditional, pieces of the cycle.

For the seventh poem marked a decisive change: Mallarmé has now forged a new language of art: he no longer distinguishes, in the traditional way, between a language of verse and one of prose, but between one of art and one of communication:

> Dans le genre appelé prose, il y a des vers, quelquefois admirables, de tous rythmes. Mais, en vérité, il n'y a pas de prose; il y a l'alphabet et puis des vers plus ou moins serrés; plus ou moins diffus. Toutes les fois qu'il y a effort au style, il y a versification (OC p. 867).

The language of art, "écriture," means for Mallarmé a closed system of artistic (symbolic) expression, which would have to be mastered like the fundamentals of the other arts, and the example he himself suggests is that of music. "Un Spectacle Interrompu" discussed and demonstrated the distinction between "écriture" and "parole," between the literary art and journalism, the poem's anecdote being the vehicle for its demonstration. But that anecdote at the same time touched upon a satellite theme: that of the evolution of the human race. Artistic vision was set apart from the common one, and "mon regard de poëte" contrasted with that of the "reporters." And the style of the poem is, precisely, the objectification of this artistic vision. The first "late" prose poem also clearly expressed the calm serenity of the mature poet "... car ma façon de voir, après tout, avait été supérieure, et même la vraie."

A comparison of "Réminiscence," the eighth poem of the cycle, with "L'Orphelin," a much earlier version of the same piece, strikingly shows the difference between the early and the mature style of the prose poems. Where it stands in the *recueil,* "Réminiscence" is indeed a remembrance of things past, an evocation of the poet's youth, this "orphelin ... en noir et l'œil vacant de famille," the archetypal, solitary Hamlet:

...l'adolescent évanoui de nous aux commencements de la vie et qui hantera les esprits hauts ou pensifs par le deuil qu'il se plaît à porter (OC p. 299).

And the fairground to which the child felt drawn already presaged, with its ambiance of "fête," "chœurs," "drame," "heure sainte," and its allusion to the poet of the Divine Comedy, something of the sacredness of the ideal ritual theatre, where the Poet will finally celebrate his mysterious office with and for his fellow man.

We found the same setting in the following poem, "La Déclaration Foraine," where an anonymous poet rose out of the crowd to celebrate Beauty for the crowd and before it: "... improviser ici, comme les voiles dans tous les temps et les temples, l'arcane!" The poet-showman's "boniment" has become a formal love poem. But *Minne* — and we recognized in this piece a courtly love poem, where the "old" sonnet form inserted in the prose is thus in harmony with an "old" tradition — is not a way of love, but a way of art, and his Lady was for the *Minnesänger* but the occasion of his song. This poem is not, then, about a woman, but about art, and the only absolute power which it appeals to is that of "Métaphore." The tension between the poet's love and hate for the crowd — his fear of it even — pervades the piece:[7] not only would he never have proclaimed his poem without *la foule,* but the Lady could not have understood it without its reverberation from the many. In this manner the piece develops the subordinate theme of a work of art's need to create its audience. Moreover, "La Déclaration Foraine" reaches back to the cycle's opening piece, "Le Phénomène Futur," with its "Montreur" who needed the crowd to exist, while also pointing ahead to its close, "Conflit," where the theme of Poet and People receives its full development.

The magical opening of "Le Nénuphar Blanc" was an awakening from Lethean oblivion into the light of a midsummer day, the emergence and separation of an individual consciousness from the timeless *Urelement.* A self is born, and the poem's theme is its quest through the magic forest. Since this is an artistic quest, nature

---

[7] Mallarmé's attitude toward *la foule,* an attitude whose complexity is reflected in the prose poems, is lucidly discussed in an article by Paul Bénichou, "Mallarmé et le public," *Cahiers du Sud,* 30 (1969), 272-90.

is transformed, and sublimated: the fountain becomes a mirror, the forest a park, and woman the lustral ideal evoked by the poet, who sacrifices the experience of life to art, in order to reduce life to order and form, a fiction: "... le délice empreint de généralité qui permet et ordonne d'exclure tous visages ..." The poet-hero chooses to remain the master of his ideal world, his artistic universe, rather than becoming the slave of that other, the "real" and contingent one, and his mastery is symbolized by the rower's control over his boat. The tension throughout the piece arose from the juxtaposition of the erotic and its sublimation, culminating in the "rapt de mon idéale fleur." At the same time the white "Nénuphar" symbolizes that poetry of true absence and absolute purity — unheard melodies — and finally the poet's silence.

The poetic vocation which imposes a renunciation of life in the service of a higher mission leads to and prepares for the image of the poet-priest, already suggested in some of the earlier poems, with which the cycle culminates. But this new priest is ordained in the religion of art, and the atheist poet seems to feel the need of explicitly exorcising the socially-sanctioned priest-figure before he, the poet — who will be consecrated in "La Gloire" — can take his place. "L'Ecclésiastique," presented as *reportage* of an event as it struck the poet's glance, fulfills this function in the cycle. It tells how the persona had seen, while strolling in the Bois de Boulogne on a spring day, an ecclesiastic "responding" to the season. The poet-persona steals away unseen to elaborate on the bizarre scene in his imagination. Not only does the poet's role as a beholder of nature differ sharply from the ecclesiastic's — "sombre agitation basse" — but the poet's, in contrast to the other's sterile response to Physis, is creative. For the creation of "L'Ecclésiastique," the only spring-time poem in the cycle, constitutes the poet's victory over the enemy season, as well as the poet-priest's victory over a competing ecclesiastical priesthood. The final sentence again underlines the poet's fundamental bargain with life, which had been consistently implied and sometimes stated in these poems: the poet turns away from the encounter with reality's fleeting phenomena by "fixing" them in a harmonious image. For what is more fugitive than those temporary divagations under the influence of the season, which the poet has now transformed into the permanent, the "image marquée d'un sceau mystérieux de modernité, à la fois baroque et belle?" And in those closing words again appears the confident judgment of his own work by the master poet, and a restatement of the definition of the prose poem: "l'image marquée d'un sceau mystérieux de modernité."

Not only confidence, but triumph is expressed in "La Gloire," bursting forth as exultant "jaillissement." The title, reverberating in the first word of the poem, sounds like a trumpet call of victory: the poet has now seen true glory, and the faith in his vision sets him apart from those who do not share it. The anecdote relates the persona's autumn visit to Fontainebleau; and as the forest's splendor reaches its climax, it appears to hold a devotional vigil in preparation for "l'universel sacre." It is for his own consecration in nature's climactic splendor that the poet-persona must withdraw from the others, from the city first, and then his fellow travelers. They cannot hear the magic calling of "Fontainebleau," and so the solitary pilgrim finds himself doubly isolated: abandoned by those whom he has had to escape. Thus he approaches the autumnal forest alone, the stage of the sublime drama waiting for him, the "royal intruder," whose consecration and coronation is the Poet's Glory. This apotheosis, however, celebrates both the poet's splendor and his mortality. And though the poet's vision is solitary, its revelation is the destiny of Man.

Therefore it is to his fellow man that the last and culminating piece of the *recueil* is devoted, a cycle whose final note is not that of the poet's solitude in the stasis of vision, but that of his return from the solitary mountain top into the community of his fellow man. Having received his sacerdotal ordination in "La Gloire," the poet-priest descends as celebrant for the people. And here the structural circularity of "Anecdotes ou Poèmes" becomes most evident. For did not the "Montreur" of "Le Phénomène Futur" celebrate before the people, his audience, uncomprehending like those of the closing piece? But this circularity, as we said, is that of an ascending progression; for as the style of the poetry has progressed, the poet-persona has also progressed through the *recueil,* from "saltimbanque" to the consecrated officiant of a rite for his fellow man.

"Anecdotes ou Poèmes" reveals, then, a unifying progression, especially in the development of the poet-persona. He has gradually evolved from entertainer — reminiscent of Poe's "literary histrio" — to priest, with the former's humble fairground stage evolving into the universal stage of Nature. The "show" has grown into a ritual drama, just as the banal "act" of "Un Spectacle Interrompu" had been transformed by the poetic vision into a setting of eternity and the infinite. In this the cycle reflects the evolution of Mallarmé's notion of the theatre: "la maison de toile" has become the stage of the world, *theatrum mundi.* This is the final image of "Conflit," of the prose poem cycle and its hero: a solitary celebrant of a ritual, the meaning of whose language — the late hermetic style of the prose poems — like that of the Latin of the Christian Mass of Mallarmé's day, is mysteriously veiled from those for whom it is intoned:

> La nef avec un peuple je ne parle d'assistants, bien d'élus: quiconque y peut de la source la plus humble d'un gosier jeter aux voûtes le répons en latin incompris, mais exultant, participe entre tous et lui-même de la sublimité se reployant vers le chœur (OC p. 396).

For language had to die before being reborn for the sacred purpose, and we have witnessed its death and resurrection — analogous to that of the poet himself — in the cycle.

In the closing piece, once again chance enounter has been transformed into meaning, the intruders becoming the heroes celebrated in the *tombeau,* erected for them by the poet, who discovers here his own highest function and fulfillment. And the evolution of the poet-persona reflects that of the function of poetry itself: whereas it initially replaced the young poet's lost faith, fulfilling his spiritual needs and aspirations, it gradually evolved from art to religion, not only for himself, but — as Mallarmé hoped — for Mankind.

The persona's growth is reflected in the cycle, moreover, by a progression in setting, already mentioned, from indoors to outdoors, a development which seems to parallel the poet's growing independence. For as the early prose poems were overshadowed by the influence of Baudelaire, so the persona in those pieces was still protected by the shell of the room shielding him from the world. [8]

---

[8] Significantly, Mallarmé's adolescent poetry collection, of course strongly influenced by his masters, was entitled "Entre Quatre Murs." (Mondor, *Lycéen,* p. 121).

This shell was celebrated especially in "Frisson d'Hiver," which is the very prose poem in which the young Mallarmé quotes a phrase from his prose tribute to Baudelaire. With the crisis reflected in "Le Démon de l'Analogie" the poet attained his deepest descent and his liberation. From this moment early in the cycle, both his independence of literary influences and his movement out and into open nature progress to a culmination in the closing poem: in "Conflit" Nature is the poet's stage. And this movement into nature clearly reflects the poet's growing acceptance of the world, — always, as we have noted, on his own terms.

One of the satellite themes whose evolution is reflected in the cycle is that of the Woman celebrated by the poet-persona. The Muse of the early poems, the dead sister, and then the silent companion who so much resembles her, is in the second part of the cycle replaced by a full-blown beauty, that "flamme" (and Mallarmé certainly plays with the phonetic doublet "flamme-femme") which inspires the passion which the poet renounces for the sake of art. But her maddening attraction pervades both "La Déclaration Foraine" and "Le Nénuphar Blanc." At the same time, woman's symbolic adornment evolves from the virginal crown of white roses, merely suggested in "Plainte d'Automne," to the enigmatic diamond brooch (or necklace) of "une contemporaine de nos soirs," to the diamond-buckled belt which does not protect the secret charms of the Nénuphar Lady from the hidden explorer.

At the time of the early projection of his *œuvre,* in 1871, shortly after his metaphysical crisis — from which he emerged both an atheist and a committed poet — and its purgation in *Igitur,* Mallarmé wrote to his friend, Cazalis:

> Je redeviens un littérateur pur et simple. Mon œuvre n'est plus un mythe. (Un volume de Contes, rêvé. Un volume de Poésies, entrevu et fredonné. Un volume de Critique, soit ce qu'on appelait hier l'Univers, considéré du point de vue strictement littéraire). [9]

---

[9] Mondor, *Correspondance* I, p. 342.

And, as Robert Greer Cohn notes, this passage is "remarkably prophetic."[10] For the "Contes" have become our "Anecdotes ou Poèmes," and in each prose poem we find a "conte" or anecdote, which is the vehicle of the major theme and its lesser satellites. In this structural characteristic, "Conflit" likewise reveals its kinship with the other twelve pieces commonly considered "Mallarmé's prose poems"; for its anecdote relates the poet-persona's encounter with the unforeseen (the intruding railroad workers) and his coming to terms with it, which serves as the vehicle for the theme of the Poet and the People. But poet and poetry are inextricably linked: while his poetry at the beginning alienated the persona from the crowd, it now leads him to serve it; like the priest, the poet must first leave that humanity to which he returns later as its servant:

> La foule, à qui l'on ne cèle rien, vu que tout émane d'elle, se reconnaîtra, une autre fois, dans l'œuvre accumulée...
> (OC p. 700)

"Conflit," moreover has in common with the other pieces of the collection its tension, which we found forcefully evident in its very title. Tension and the predominance of a specific vocabulary cluster characterized almost every prose poem. In the opening piece, the tension was that of the contrast between the blindingly bright vision of "Le Phénomène Futur" and the decrepit and dull civilization in which it appeared; in "Plainte d'Automne" it was that of a simultaneously ascending and descending movement still so reminiscent of Baudelaire's "double postulation." But most notable, in this respect, among the "early" prose poems was "Le Démon de l'Analogie" with its celebration of the birth-and-death theme. In the second half of the cycle, "Un Spectacle Interrompu" achieved this tension by its juxtaposition of the poetic vision with that of *la foule,* represented by the theatre audience and the reporters; while the paradoxically ambiguous relationship of the poet and audience, his contempt for them as well as his need of them,

---

[10] Cohn, *L'Œuvre,* pp. 475-76:
> Ce passage est remarquablement prophétique. Les *Contes* sont devenus les *Poèmes en prose,* les poèmes ont été écrits ainsi que les *Divagations.*

was one of the most important themes of "La Déclaration Foraine." In "Le Nénuphar Blanc," the tone was set throughout by eroticism and its sublimation, while in the late "La Gloire," a most remarkable tension was achieved by the feat of closely juxtaposing the ironic and the elevated manners in a totally unprecedented way.

The tension which characterizes each of the prose poems, this somewhat Hegelian play of opposites, invites the question of their philosophic nature, an aspect implicit throughout our reading of these poems. Do they convey any particular philosophic thought in a formal sense, or do they suggest, at least, a philosophic stance on the part of the author? Though the Hegelian hero of *Igitur* overshadowed some of the early pieces of the cycle, there is no Hegelianism apparent in these prose poems, other than a dialectical turn of mind, where the play of opposites creates the living tension which structures the poem. Steland, as we have seen earlier, found not Hegelian dialectics, but "Dialektische Gedanken" in some of the critical pieces of *Divagations*.[11] And though we found in the "Nénuphar" a vaguely Hegelian movement which synthesized the individual woman by "negating" her, as it were, into her ideal Pure Notion, yet this could equally well and equally loosely be said to reflect Platonism.[12]

Mallarmé invites an association with Hegel by his frequent use of Hegelian terms in *Divagations*; and he was, of course, at least indirectly acquainted with that philosophy through his close friendship with Villiers de l'Isle-Adam, about whom he said:

> ... Saint-Bernard, Kant, le Thomas de la Somme, principalement un désigné par lui le Titan de l'Esprit Humain, Hegel, dont le singulier lecteur semblait aussi se revendiquer ... (OC p. 491).

In his poetry, it is principally *Igitur* which reflects Hegel, as its hero moves through the Triad, by first divorcing his consciousness from phenomena, in order to reach a pure consciousness of the self, and finally rising up to the dissolution of that individual conscious-

---

[11] Cf. our discussion of "Un Spectacle Interrompu."
[12] This, as a matter of fact, has been said. Cf. Thibaudet, *La Poésie,* p. 108.

ness in the Absolute Spirit. And as for Hegel this pure self-thinking thought would actualize itself in the final stage of the historical process, so for Mallarmé, Igitur, "the last of his line," symbolized the *aboutissement* of the human spirit where it merges into the *Weltgeist*. And surely, the young Mallarmé was haunted by this temptation, which was at the same time a threat, of "losing his mind" in a spiritual self-annihilation.[13] Since *Igitur* was a most important stage in Mallarmé's development, its hero's image is reflected in some of the early prose poems.

But at the foundation of Hegel's philosophy lies the belief that the rational is the real and the real the rational, and I do not think that Mallarmé shared that optimistic faith. Nor do I believe that Mallarmé ever considered the phenomenological world — the domain of "la matière" — to be the manifestation of infinite reason. We have witnessed throughout the cycle the persona's *lutte contre la matière,* and its spiritualization; the Absolute for Mallarmé, as we have noted, was "le Rien," which reappears in the "Coup de Dés." A thinker who seems to me much more profoundly akin to the poet is Kant. For just as he constructed his entire Idealistic system, that intricate *Critique of Pure Reason,* in the face of Hume's radical empiricism, so Mallarmé built the equally intricate fabric

---

[13] We have discussed this fear and temptation earlier; it is reflected in the correspondence; here indeed it is often dressed in Hegelian terms. Already in 1864, Mallarmé wrote to Cazalis, Mondor, *Correspondance* I, p. 152:

> ... et je passe des heures à observer dans les glaces l'envahissement de la bêtise qui éteint déjà mes yeux, aux cils pendants et laisse tomber mes lèvres.

This crisis then becomes acute in 1867, when he writes again to Cazalis, and this time in Hegelian terms, *ibid.,* p. 242:

> C'est t'apprendre que je suis maintenant impersonnel et non plus Stéphane que tu as connu, — mais une aptitude qu'a l'Univers spirituel à se voir et à se développer, à travers ce qui fut moi.
> Fragile comme est mon apparition terrestre, je ne puis subir que les développements absolument nécessaires pour que l'Univers retrouve, en ce moi, son identité. Ainsi je viens à l'heure de la Synthèse, de délimiter l'œuvre qui sera l'image de ce développement.

And though this seems to announce "Hegelian poetry," if such a phenomenon is possible, only *Igitur,* the fragment of purgation of this same crisis, really is.

of his symbolist and poetic universe in the face of the reigning naturalism and positivism of his day; and we recall, in this connection, his words to one of his disciples: "Non, Ghil, l'on ne peut se passer d'Eden!" Further, just as Kant's "Copernican Revolution" made the human mind the center of the world, so for Mallarmé the poet's mind is the center, that "sacred spider" of the web. Repeatedly Mallarmé's answer to chaos and *hasard* was to construct *comme si* — as if a poetic cosmos and order could be imposed on reality. And it is this tendency, which becomes more and more evident in the later prose poems, which points ahead to the "Coup de Dés."

Here again a profound kinship with Kant comes to light. For is not the entire *Critique of Practical Reason* based on *als ob?* The categorical imperative itself orders human conduct through the fundamental clause, "*as if* the maxim of your action were to . . ." And as Kant on the one hand demolishes systematically the traditional proofs for the existence of God, he founds on the other an entire religious philosophy on those two small Mallarméan words: *comme si — als ob*. Both the greatest Idealist philosopher and the greatest Idealist poet are heroically constructing each his own system, his world-order — the one a philosophical, the other a poetic, *fictional* Cosmos — against the Chaos which they know to be the truth.

Though some may doubt that a personal perception of ultimate chaos lay behind Kant's epistemology, no one can doubt that it lay behind Mallarmé's meticulously structured poetic universe. Indeed, as we have repeatedly insisted in this book, the Chaos which we call reality is the very *raison d'être* for Mallarmé's great poetic construct, the artist's resplendant shoring for the human spirit, with its insistent dream of the immutable, against the withering blasts of contingency. Mallarmé lived all his mature life on the rim of the metaphysical abyss and from this experience created his art. In one of his letters to Odilon Redon, [14] describing the latter's lithograph, "Dans mon rêve, je vis au ciel un visage de mystère," he expresses his sympathy with an image in which he recognized himself:

---

[14] Mondor, *Correspondance* II, p. 280.

... mais mon admiration tout entière va droit au grand Mage inconsolable et obstiné chercheur d'un mystère qu'il sait ne pas exister, et qu'il poursuivra, à jamais pour cela, du deuil de son lucide désespoir, car *c'eût été* la vérité! Je ne connais pas un dessin qui communique tant de peur intellectuelle et de sympathie affreuse, que ce grandiose visage.

Appendix *

LE PHÉNOMÈNE FUTUR

Un ciel pâle, sur le monde qui finit de décrépitude, va peut-être partir avec les nuages: les lambeaux de la pourpre usée des couchants déteignent dans une rivière dormant à l'horizon submergé de rayons et d'eau. Les arbres s'ennuient et, sous leur feuillage blanchi (de la poussière du temps plutôt que celle des chemins), monte la maison en toile du Montreur de choses Passées: maint réverbère attend le crépuscule et ravive les visages d'une malheureuse foule, vaincue par la maladie immortelle et le péché des siècles, d'hommes près de leurs chétives complices enceintes des fruits misérables avec lesquels périra la terre. Dans le silence inquiet de tous les yeux suppliant là-bas le soleil qui, sous l'eau, s'enfonce avec le désespoir d'un cri, voici le simple boniment: "Nulle enseigne ne vous régale du spectacle intérieur, car il n'est pas maintenant un peintre capable d'en donner une ombre triste. J'apporte, vivante (et préservée à travers les ans par la science souveraine) une Femme d'autrefois. Quelque folie, originelle et naïve, une extase d'or, je ne sais quoi! par elle nommé sa chevelure, se ploie avec la grâce des étoffes autour d'un visage qu'éclaire la nudité sanglante de ses lèvres. A la place du vêtement vain, elle a un corps; et les yeux, semblables aux pierres rares, ne valent pas ce regard qui sort de sa chair heureuse: des seins levés comme s'ils étaient pleins d'un lait éternel, la pointe vers le ciel, aux jambes lisses qui gardent le sel de la mer première." Se rappelant leurs pauvres épouses,

---

* The prose poems are reproduced by kind permission of the copyright holders, Editions Gallimard (*Œuvres Complètes de Stéphane Mallarmé*, Paris: 1945).

chauves, morbides et pleines d'horreur, les maris se pressent: elles aussi par curiosité, mélancoliques, veulent voir.

Quand tous auront contemplé la noble créature, vestige de quelque époque déjà maudite, les uns indifférents, car ils n'auront pas eu la force de comprendre, mais d'autres navrés et la paupière humide de larmes résignées se regarderont; tandis que les poëtes de ces temps, sentant se rallumer leurs yeux éteints, s'achemineront vers leur lampe, le cerveau ivre un instant d'une gloire confuse, hantés du Rythme et dans l'oubli d'exister à une époque qui survit à la beauté.

The Future Marvel

A pale sky, over the world which is coming to an end of senile decay, is perhaps going to depart with the clouds: the shreds of the worn purple of sunsets are fading in a river sleeping at the submerged horizon of rays and water. The trees are weary and, under their foliage bleached (from the dust of time rather than that of the roads), rises the tent of the Showman of things of the Past: many a street-lamp is waiting for the evening dusk and revives the faces of a wretched crowd, vanquished by the immortal sickness and the sin of centuries, of men beside their sickly accomplices pregnant with the miserable fruit together with which the earth will perish. In the troubled silence of all the eyes imploring the sun yonder, which plunges beneath the water with a cry's despair, here is the simple salespitch: "No sign treats you to the show inside, for there exists no painter these days capable of rendering even a sad shadow of it. I am bringing, alive (and preserved over the years by the supreme science) a Woman of yore. Some madness, primordial and ingenuous, an ecstasy of gold, I don't know what! called by her her hair, folds itself with the grace of silk around a face illuminated by the bloody nudity of her lips. In place of vain apparel, she has a body; and her eyes, similar to rare stones, do not equal this look which springs from her happy flesh: from breasts raised as though they were full of an eternal milk, the nipples toward the sky, to smooth legs on which still is the salt of the first sea." Remembering their wretched spouses, bald-headed, sickly, and full of horror, the husbands come forward: the wives too, out of curiosity, dejected, want to see.

When all have contemplated the noble creature, a vestige of some already cursed age, some indifferent, for they will not have the strength to understand, but others, woe-begone and their eyelids moist with resigned tears, will look at one another; while the poets of those times, feeling their dull eyes light up again, will make their way towards their lamp, their minds for a moment intoxicated with a dim glory, haunted by the Rhythm and forgetting that they exist in an era which has outlived beauty.

PLAINTE D'AUTOMNE

Depuis que Maria m'a quitté pour aller dans une autre étoile — laquelle, Orion, Altaïr, et toi, verte Vénus? — j'ai toujours chéri la solitude. Que de longues journées j'ai passées seul avec mon chat. Par *seul,* j'entends sans un être matériel et mon chat est un compagnon mystique, un esprit. Je puis donc dire que j'ai passé de longues journées seul avec mon chat, et seul, avec un des derniers auteurs de la décadence latine; car depuis que la blanche créature n'est plus, étrangement et singulièrement j'ai aimé tout ce qui se résumait en ce mot: chute. Ainsi, dans l'année, ma saison favorite, ce sont les derniers jours alanguis de l'été, qui précèdent immédiatement l'automne et, dans la journée, l'heure où je me promène est quand le soleil se repose avant de s'évanouir, avec des rayons de cuivre jaune sur les murs gris et de cuivre rouge sur les carreaux. De même la littérature à laquelle mon esprit demande une volupté sera la poésie agonisante des derniers moments de Rome, tant, cependant, qu'elle ne respire aucunement l'approche rajeunissante des Barbares et ne bégaie point le latin enfantin des premières proses chrétiennes.

Je lisais donc un de ces chers poëmes (dont les plaques de fard ont plus de charme sur moi que l'incarnat de la jeunesse) et plongeais une main dans la fourrure du pur animal, quand un orgue de Barbarie chanta languissamment et mélancoliquement sous ma fenêtre. Il jouait dans la grande allée des peupliers dont les feuilles me paraissent mornes même au printemps, depuis que Maria a passé là avec des cierges, une dernière fois. L'instrument des tristes, oui, vraiment: le piano scintille, le violon donne aux fibres déchirées la lumière, mais l'orgue de Barbarie, dans le crépuscule du souvenir, m'a fait désespérément rêver. Maintenant qu'il murmurait un air joyeusement vulgaire et qui mit la gaîté au cœur des faubourgs, un air suranné, banal: d'où vient que sa ritournelle m'allait à l'âme et me faisait pleurer comme une ballade romantique? Je la savourai lentement et je ne lançai pas un sou par la fenêtre de peur de me déranger et de m'apercevoir que l'instrument ne chantait pas seul.

Autumn Lament

Since Maria left me to go to another star — which one, Orion, Altaïr, and you, green Venus? — I have always cherished solitude. How many long days I have spent alone with my cat. By alone, I mean without a material being, and my cat is a mystic companion, a spirit. So I can say that I have spent long days alone with my cat, and alone with one of the last authors of the Latin decadence; for since the white creature is no more, strangely and oddly I have loved all that which was summed up in the word: fall ["chute"]. Thus, of the year, my favorite season is the last languid days of summer, which immediately precede autumn and, during the day, the hour when I go for a walk is when the sun rests before fading away, with beams of yellow copper on the gray walls and of red copper on the window panes. In the same way, the literature of which my spirit asks pleasure will be the agonizing poetry of Rome's last moments, so long, however, as it breathes in no way the rejuvenating approach of the Barbarians and does not stammer the childish Latin of the first Christian prose sequences.

I was reading, then, one of these beloved poems (whose patches of cosmetic cast more of a spell over me than the rosiness of youth) and plunging my hand into the pure animal's fur, when a barrel organ started to sing with languorous melancholy beneath my window. It was playing in the wide avenue of poplars whose leaves seem dreary to me even in spring, ever since Maria passed by there with candles, a last time. The instrument of the sad, yes, truly: the piano sparkles, the violin gives light to the torn fibers, but the barrel organ, in the twilight of memory, made me desperately dream. Now that it was murmuring a tune joyfully commonplace and which cheered the heart of the suburbs, an old-fashioned, banal tune: why is it that its refrain went to my soul and made me weep like a romantic ballad? I savored it slowly and I did not throw a penny from the window for fear of destroying my mood and perceiving that the instrument was not singing alone.

FRISSON D'HIVER

Cette pendule de Saxe, qui retarde et sonne treize heures parmi ses fleurs et ses dieux, à qui a-t-elle été? Pense qu'elle est venue de Saxe par les longues diligences d'autrefois.

(De singulières ombres pendent aux vitres usées.)

Et ta glace de Venise, profonde comme une froide fontaine, en un rivage de guivres dédorées, qui s'y est miré? Ah! je suis sûr que plus d'une femme a baigné dans cette eau le péché de sa beauté; et peut-être verrais-je un fantôme nu si je regardais longtemps.

—Vilain, tu dis souvent de méchantes choses.

(Je vois des toiles d'araignées au haut des grandes croisées.)

Notre bahut encore est très vieux: contemple comme ce feu rougit son triste bois; les rideaux amortis ont son âge, et la tapisserie des fauteuils dénués de fard, et les anciennes gravures des murs, et toutes nos vieilleries? Est-ce qu'il ne te semble pas, même, que les bengalis et l'oiseau bleu ont déteint avec le temps?

(Ne songe pas aux toiles d'araignées qui tremblent au haut des grandes croisées.)

Tu aimes tout cela et voilà pourquoi je puis vivre auprès de toi. N'as-tu pas désiré, ma sœur au regard de jadis, qu'en un de mes poëmes apparussent ces mots "la grâce des choses fanées"? Les objects neufs te déplaisent; à toi aussi, ils font peur avec leur hardiesse criarde, et tu te sentirais le besoin de les user, ce qui est bien difficile à faire pour ceux qui ne goûtent pas l'action.

Viens, ferme ton vieil almanach allemand, que tu lis avec attention, bien qu'il ait paru il y a plus de cent ans et que les rois qu'il annonce soient tous morts, et, sur l'antique tapis couché, la tête appuyée parmi tes genoux charitables dans ta robe pâlie, ô calme enfant, je te parlerai pendant des heures; il n'y a plus de champs et les rues sont vides, je te parlerai de nos meubles... Tu es distraite?

(Ces toiles d'araignées grelottent au haut des grandes croisées.)

Winter Shiver

This Dresden china clock, which loses time and strikes the thirteenth hour amidst its flowers and gods, to whom did it belong? Consider that it came from Saxony by the slow stagecoaches of olden times.

(Curious shadows are hanging on the worn window panes.)

And your Venetian mirror, deep as a cold fountain, framed by a shore of heraldic serpents who have lost their gilding, who is it who contemplated himself in it? Ah! I am sure that more than one woman has bathed the sin of her beauty in this water; and perhaps I would see a naked phantom if I looked for a long time.

—Vilain, you often say wicked things.

(I see spider webs at the top of the tall casement windows.)

Our traveling chest is also very old: see how this fire reddens its sad wood; the subdued curtains are equally old, and the tapestry of the armchairs whose color is faded, and the ancient engravings on the walls, and all our old things? Does it not seem to you even that the Bengal birds and the blue bird have faded with time?

(Do not think about the spider webs trembling high up on the tall casement windows.)

You love all those things, and that is why I can live by your side. Did you not desire, my sister with the look of olden times, that in one of my poems should appear these words "the grace of faded things"? New things displease you; they frighten you as they do me with their discordant boldness, and you would feel the need to wear them out, which is very difficult to do for those who do not enjoy action.

Come, close your old German almanac, which you are reading attentively, although it appeared more than a hundred years ago and the kings it announces are all dead, and, stretched on the old rug, my head resting on your charitable knees in your faded dress, o calm child, I shall speak to you for hours; there are no longer any fields and the streets are empty, I shall speak to you of our things ... Your mind is wandering?

(Those spider webs are shivering with cold high up on the big casement windows.)

LE DÉMON DE L'ANALOGIE

Des paroles inconnues chantèrent-elles sur vos lèvres, lambeaux maudits d'une phrase absurde?

Je sortis de mon appartement avec la sensation propre d'une aile glissant sur les cordes d'un instrument, traînante et légère, que remplaça une voix prononçant les mots sur un ton descendant: "La Pénultième est morte," de façon que

La Pénultième

finit le vers et

Est morte

se détacha de la suspension fatidique plus inutilement en le vide de signification. Je fis des pas dans la rue et reconnus en le son *nul* la corde tendue de l'instrument de musique, qui était oublié et que le glorieux Souvenir certainement venait de visiter de son aile ou d'une palme et, le doigt sur l'artifice du mystère, je souris et implorai de vœux intellectuels une spéculation différente. La phrase revint, virtuelle, dégagée d'une chute antérieure de plume ou de rameau, dorénavant à travers la voix entendue, jusqu'à ce qu'enfin elle s'articula seule, vivant de sa personnalité. J'allais (ne me contentant plus d'une perception) la lisant en fin de vers, et, une fois, comme un essai, l'adaptant à mon parler; bientôt la prononçant avec un silence après "Pénultième" dans lequel je trouvais une pénible jouissance: "La Pénultième" puis la corde de l'instrument, si tendue en l'oubli sur le son *nul*, cassait sans doute et j'ajoutais en manière d'oraison: "Est morte." Je ne discontinuai pas de tenter un retour à des pensées de prédilection, alléguant, pour me calmer, que, certes, pénultième est le terme du lexique qui signifie l'avant-dernière syllabe des vocables, et son apparition, le reste mal abjuré d'un labeur de linguistique par lequel quotidiennement sanglote de s'interrompre ma noble faculté poétique: la sonorité même et l'air de mensonge assumé par la hâte de la facile affirmation étaient une cause de tourment. Harcelé, je résolus de laisser les mots de triste nature errer eux-mêmes sur ma bouche, et j'allai murmurant avec l'intonation susceptible de condoléance: "La Pénultième est morte, elle est morte, bien morte, la désespérée Pénultième," croyant par là satisfaire l'inquiétude, et non sans le secret espoir de l'ensevelir en l'amplification de la psalmodie quand, effroi! — d'une magie aisément déductible et nerveuse — je sentis que j'avais ma main réfléchie par un vitrage de boutique y faisant le geste d'une caresse qui descend sur quelque chose, la voix même (la première, qui indubitablement avait été l'unique).

Mais où s'installe l'irrécusable intervention du surnaturel, et le commencement de l'angoisse sous laquelle agonise mon esprit naguère seigneur c'est quand je vis, levant les yeux, dans la rue des antiquaires instinctivement suivie, que j'étais devant la boutique d'un luthier vendeur de vieux instruments pendus au mur, et, à terre, des palmes jaunes et les ailes enfouis en l'ombre, d'oiseaux anciens. Je m'enfuis, bizarre, personne condamnée à porter probablement le deuil de l'inexplicable Pénultième.

The Demon of Analogy

Did unknown words ever sing on your lips, accursed shreds of an absurd phrase?

I left my apartment with the peculiar feeling of a wing, gliding over the strings of an instrument, languid and light, which was replaced by a voice pronouncing with a descending intonation the words: "The Penultimate is dead," so that

The Penultimate

ended the line and

Is dead

detached itself from the fateful suspension more uselessly in the void of meaning. I took some steps in the street and recognized in the sound nul *the taut string of the musical instrument, which had been forgotten and which glorious Memory had certainly just touched with its wing or a palm branch and, my finger on the mystery's artifice, I smiled and implored a different speculation with intellectual vows. The phrase, virtual, released from an anterior fall of a feather or a branch came back henceforth heard through the voice, until finally it articulated itself alone, living of its own personality. I went along (no longer satisfied with a perception) reading it at the end of a line of verse, and, once, as though testing it, adapting it to my speech; soon pronouncing it with a silence after "Penultimate" in which I found a painful pleasure: "The Penultimate" then the instrument's string, so stretched in forgetfulness over the sound* nul, *probably broke and I added in the fashion of a prayer: "Is dead." I did not cease to attempt a return to thoughts of my predilection, alleging, to calm myself, that, surely, penultimate is the lexical term signifying the next-to-last syllable of utterances, and its appearance could be explained as the poorly renounced remains of linguistic labors on account of which my noble poetic faculty daily weeps to be broken off: the very sonority and the appearance of falsehood assumed by the haste of the facile affirmation were a cause of torment. Harried, I resolved to let the words of sad nature wander of their own accord over my lips, and I walked murmuring with an intonation susceptible of expressing condolence: "The Penultimate is dead, it is dead, dead indeed, the desperate Penultimate," believing thus to satisfy my anxiety, and not without the secret hope of burying it in the chant's amplification when, horror! — by an easily deductible and nervous magic — I felt that I had, my hand being reflected by a shop window there making the gesture of a caress coming down on something, the very voice (the first, which had undoubtedly been the only one).*

But the moment at which the irrefutable intervention of the supernatural, and the beginning of the anguish, under which my mind, not long ago lord and master, agonizes, establishes itself, that was when I saw, raising my eyes, in the street of the antique dealers which I had instinctively taken, that I was in front of a lute maker's shop, a vendor of old musical instruments which hung on the wall, and, on the ground, some yellow palms and ancient birds, their wings hidden in shadow. I fled, singular person probably condemned to wear mourning for the inexplicable Penultimate.

PAUVRE ENFANT PÂLE

Pauvre enfant pâle, pourquoi crier à tue-tête dans la rue ta chanson aiguë et insolente, qui se perd parmi les chats, seigneurs des toits? car elle ne traversera pas les volets des premiers étages, derrière lequels tu ignores de lourds rideaux de soie incarnadine.

Cependant tu chantes fatalement, avec l'assurance tenace d'un petit homme qui s'en va seul par la vie et, ne comtlant sur personne, travaille pour soi. As-tu jamais eu un père? Tu n'as pas même une vieille qui te fasse oublier la faim en te battant, quand tu rentres sans un sou.

Mais tu travailles pour toi: debout dans les rues, couvert de vêtements déteints faits comme ceux d'un homme, une maigreur prématurée et trop grand à ton âge, tu chantes pour manger, avec acharnement, sans abaisser tes yeux méchants vers les autres enfants jouant sur le pavé.

Et ta complainte est si haute, si haute, que ta tête nue qui se lève en l'air à mesure que ta voix monte, semble vouloir partir de tes petites épaules.

Petit homme, qui sait si elle ne s'en ira pas un jour, quand, après avoir crié longtemps dans les villes, tu auras fait un crime? un crime n'est pas bien difficile à faire, va, il suffit d'avoir du courage après le désir, et tels qui... Ta petite figure est énergique.

Pas un sou ne descend dans le panier d'osier que tient ta longue main pendue sans espoir sur ton pantalon: on te rendra mauvais et un jour tu commettras un crime.

Ta tête se dresse toujours et veut te quitter, comme si d'avance elle savait, pendant que tu chantes d'un air qui devient menaçant.

Elle te dira adieu quand tu paieras pour moi, pour ceux qui valent moins que moi. Tu vins probablement au monde vers cela et tu jeûnes dès maintenant, nous te verrons dans les journaux.

Oh! pauvre petite tête!

Poor Pale Child

Poor pale child, why do you yell at the top of your lungs in the street your shrill and insolent song, which fades out among the cats, the lords of the roofs? for it will not penetrate the second-story shutters, behind which you do not imagine the heavy curtains of faded scarlet silk.

However you sing inexorably, with the tenacious assurance of a little man who goes through life alone and, counting on no one, works for himself. Have you ever had a father? You do not even have an old woman to make you forget your hunger by beating you, when you come home without a penny.

But you work for yourself: standing in the streets, covered with faded clothes made like those of a grown man, prematurely thin and too tall for your age, you sing in order to eat, relentlessly, without lowering your evil eyes toward the other children playing on the pavement.

And your lament is so high, so high, that your bare head, rising in the air as your voice rises, seems to want to leave your little shoulders behind.

Little man, who knows whether it is not going to come off one day, when after having yelled for a long time in the cities, you have committed a crime? a crime is not very difficult to commit, believe me, it is enough to have courage after the desire, and some who ... your little face is energetic.

Not a penny falls into the wicker basket which your long hand, hanging without hope over your trousers, is holding: they will make you evil and one day you will commit a crime.

Your head is still raised up and wants to leave you, as if it knew in advance, while you are singing in a way that becomes threatening.

It will say good-bye to you when you pay for me, for those who are worth less than I. You probably came into the world for that and you are fasting from now on, we will see you in the papers.

Oh! poor little head!

LA PIPE

Hier, j'ai trouvé ma pipe en rêvant une longue soirée de travail, de beau travail d'hiver. Jetées les cigarettes avec toutes les joies enfantines de l'été dans le passé qu'illuminent les feuilles bleues de soleil, les mousselines et reprise ma grave pipe par un homme sérieux qui veut fumer longtemps sans se déranger, afin de mieux travailler: mais je ne m'attendais pas à la surprise que préparait cette délaissée, à peine eus-je tiré la première bouffée, j'oubliai mes grands livres à faire, émerveillé attendri, je respirai l'hiver dernier qui revenait. Je n'avais pas touché à la fidèle amie depuis ma rentrée en France, et tout Londres, Londres tel que je le vécus en entier à moi seul, il y a un an, est apparu; d'abord les chers brouillards qui emmitouflent nos cervelles et ont, là-bas, une odeur à eux, quand ils pénètrent sous la croisée. Mon tabac sentait une chambre sombre aux meubles de cuir saupoudrés par la poussière du charbon sur lesquels se roulait le maigre chat noir; les grands feux! et la bonne aux bras rouges versant les charbons, et le bruit de ces charbons tombant du seau de tôle dans la corbeille de fer, le matin — alors que le facteur frappait le double coup solennel, qui me faisait vivre! J'ai revu par les fenêtres ces arbres malades du square désert — j'ai vu le large, si souvent traversé cet hiver-là, grelottant sur le pont du steamer mouillé de bruine et noirci de fumée — avec ma pauvre bien-aimée errante, en habits de voyageuse, une longue robe terne couleur de la poussière des routes, un manteau qui collait humide à ses épaules froides, un de ces chapeaux de paille sans plume et presque sans rubans, que les riches dames jettent en arrivant, tant ils sont déchiquetés par l'air de la mer et que les pauvres bien-aimées regarnissent pour bien des saisons encore. Autour de son cou s'enroulait le terrible mouchoir qu'on agite en se disant adieu pour toujours.

THE PIPE

Yesterday I found my pipe while dreaming of a long evening of work, of fine winter work. The cigarettes with all the childish joys of summer thrown into the past, which the leaves blue from the sun, the muslins, illuminate, and my grave pipe taken up again by a responsible man who wants to smoke for a long time without stirring, in order to work better: but I did not expect the surprise which this forsaken one was preparing, I had hardly drawn the first puff, when I forgot my great books waiting to be written; amazed, touched, I inhaled the last winter which was coming back to me. I had not touched the faithful friend since my return to France, and all of London, London as I lived it all for myself, a year ago, appeared; first the dear fogs which envelop our brains as if with a muff and have, yonder, a smell of their own, when they seep under the casement windows. My tobacco smelled of a dark room with leather furniture sprinkled with coal dust on which the skinny black cat used to curl up; the big fires! and the maid with red arms pouring coals, and the noise of these coals falling from the sheet-iron bucket into the iron basket, in the morning — while the mailman gave his solemn double knock, which made me live! I saw again through the windows those sickly trees of the deserted square — I saw the open sea, crossed so often that winter, shivering on the steamer's deck soaked from the drizzle and grimy from smoke — with my poor wandering beloved in traveling clothes, a long faded dress the color of highway dust, a coat that stuck damply to her cold shoulders, one of those straw hats with no feather and almost no ribbons, which the rich ladies throw away upon arrival, they are so frayed from the sea air and which poor beloved ones refurbish for many a season more. Around her neck was wound the fearsome kerchief which one waves when saying good-bye forever.

UN SPECTACLE INTERROMPU

Que la civilisation est loin de procurer les jouissances attribuables à cet état! on doit par exemple s'étonner qu'une association entre les rêveurs, y séjournant, n'existe pas, dans toute grande ville, pour subvenir à un journal qui remarque les événements sous le jour propre au rêve. Artifice que la *réalité,* bon à fixer l'intellect moyen entre les mirages d'un fait; mais elle repose par cela même sur quelque universelle entente: voyons donc s'il n'est pas, dans l'idéal, un aspect nécessaire, évident, simple, qui serve de type. Je veux, en vue de moi seul, écrire comme elle frappa mon regard de poëte, telle Anecdote, avant que la divulguent des *reporters* par la foule dressés à assigner à chaque chose son caractère commun.

Le petit théâtre des PRODIGALITÉS adjoint l'exhibition d'un vivant cousin d'Atta Troll ou de Martin à sa féerie classique *la Bête et le Génie;* j'avais, pour reconnaître l'invitation du billet double hier égaré chez moi, posé mon chapeau dans la stalle vacante à mes côtés, une absence d'ami y témoignait du goût général à esquiver ce naïf spectacle. Que se passait-il devant moi? rien, sauf que: de pâleurs évasives de mousseline se réfugiant sur vingt piédestaux en architecture de Bagdad, sortaient un sourire et des bras ouverts à la lourdeur triste de l'ours: tandis que le héros, de ces sylphides évocateur et leur gardien, un clown, dans sa haute nudité d'argent, raillait l'animal par notre supériorité. Jouir comme la foule du mythe inclus dans toute banalité, quel repos et, sans voisins où verser des réflexions, voir l'ordinaire et splendide veille trouvée à la rampe par ma recherche assoupie d'imaginations ou de symboles. Étranger à mainte réminiscence de pareilles soirées, l'accident le plus neuf! suscita mon attention: une des nombreuses salves d'applaudissements décernés selon l'enthousiasme à l'illustration sur la scène du privilège authentique de l'Homme, venait, brisée par quoi? de cesser net, avec un fixe fracas de gloire à l'apogée, inhabile à se répandre. Tout oreilles, il fallut être tout yeux. Au geste du pantin, une paume crispée dans l'air ouvrant les cinq doigts, je compris, qu'il avait, l'ingénieux! capté les sympathies par la mine d'attraper au vol quelque chose, figure (et c'est tout) de la facilité dont est par chacun prise une idée: et qu'ému au leger vent, l'ours rythmiquement et doucement levé interrogeait cet exploit, une griffe posée sur les rubans de l'épaule humaine. Personne qui ne haletât, tant cette situation portait de conséquences graves pour l'honneur de la race: qu'allait-il arriver? L'autre patte s'abattit, souple, contre un bras longeant le maillot; et l'on vit, couple uni dans un secret rapprochement, comme un homme inférieur, trapu, bon, debout sur l'écartement de deux jambes de poil, étreindre pour y apprendre les pratiques du génie, et son crâne au noir museau ne l'atteignant qu'à la moitié, le buste de son frère brillant et surnaturel: mais qui, lui! exhaussait, la bouche folle de vague, un chef affreux remuant par un fil visible dans l'horreur les dénégations véritables d'une mouche de papier et d'or. Spectacle clair, plus que les tréteaux vaste, avec ce don, propre à l'art, de durer longtemps: pour le parfaire je laissai, sans que m'offusquât l'attitude probablement fatale prise par le mime dépositaire de notre orgueil, jaillir tacitement le discours interdit au rejeton des sites arctiques: "Sois bon (c'était le sens), et plutôt que de manquer à la charité, explique-moi la vertu de cette atmosphère de splendeur, de poussière et de voix, où tu m'appris à me mouvoir. Ma requête, pressante, est juste, que tu ne sembles pas, en une angoisse qui n'est que feinte, répondre ne savoir, éclancé aux regions de la sagesse, âiné subtil! à moi, pour te faire libre, vêtu encore du séjour informe des cavernes où je replongeai, dans la nuit d'époques humbles ma force latente. Authentiquons, par cette embrassade étroite, devant la multitude siégeant à cette fin, le pacte de notre réconciliation." L'absence d'aucun souffle unie à l'espace, dans quel lieu absolu vivais-je, un des drames de l'histoire astrale élisant, pour s'y produire, ce modeste théâtre! La foule s'effaçait, toute, en l'emblème de sa situation spirituelle magnifiant la scène: dispensateur moderne de l'extase, seul, avec l'impartialité d'une chose élémentaire, le gaz, dans les hauteurs de la salle, continuait un bruit lumineux d'attente.

Le charme se rompit: c'est quand un morceau de chair, nu, brutal, traversa ma vision dirigé de l'intervalle des décors, en avance de quelques instants sur la récompense, mystérieuse d'ordinaire après ces représentations. Loque substituée saignant auprès de l'ours qui, ses instincts retrouvés antérieurement à une curiosité plus haute dont le dotait le rayonnement théâtral, retomba à quatre pattes et, comme emportant parmi soi le Silence, alla de la marche étouffée de l'espèce, flairer, pour y appliquer les dents, cette proie. Un soupir, exempt presque de déception, soulagea incompréhensiblement l'assemblée: dont les lorgnettes, par rangs, cherchèrent, allumant la netteté de leurs verres, le jeu du splendide imbécile évaporé dans sa peur; mais virent un repas abject préféré peut-être par l'animal à la même chose qu'il lui eût fallu d'abord faire de *notre image,* pour y goûter. La toile, hésitant jusque-là à accroître le danger ou l'émotion, abattit subitement son journal de tarifs et de lieux communs. Je me levai comme tout le monde, pour aller respirer au dehors, étonné de n'avoir pas senti, cette fois encore, le même genre d'impression que mes semblables, mais serein: car ma façon de voir, apres tout, avait été supérieure, et même la vraie.

An Interrupted Performance

How far civilization is from procuring the enjoyments attributable to that state! it is surprising, for example, that there exists no association of dreamers living in every big city, to support a journal observing events with the viewpoint peculiar to dreams. What an artifice reality is, suitable only to fix the attention of the average intellect in the mirages of a fact; but it rests by that very fact on some universal understanding: let us see, then, if there is not, in the ideal, a necessary, evident, simple aspect, which might serve as a type. I want to write, for the benefit of myself alone, a certain Anecdote, as it struck my poet's gaze, before reporters, set up by the crowd to assign each thing its common character, divulge it.

The little theatre of the PRODIGALITÉS adds the exhibition of a living cousin of Atta Troll or Martin to its classic fairy tale The Beast and the Genius; *I had, in order to acknowledge the invitation of the double ticket yesterday strayed to my house, placed my hat in the empty seat at my side, a friend's absence there bearing witness to the general taste for avoiding this naive entertainment. What was happening in front of me? nothing, except that from evasive palenesses of muslin taking refuge on twenty pedestals of Bagdad style, a smile and open arms were going out to the bear's sad heaviness; while the hero, the conjurer and guardian of these sylphs, a clown, in his tall, silvery nakedness, was bantering the animal by our superiority. To enjoy like the crowd the myth enclosed in every banality, what a relaxation for the mind and, without neighbors to whom to pour out reflections, to behold the ordinary and splendid vigil found at the footlights by my search appeased with imaginings or symbols. Foreign to many a recollection of similar evenings, the most novel happenstance! aroused my attention: one of the numerous bursts of applause bestowed according to the enthusiasm for Man's authentic privilege illustrated on the stage, had, broken by what? just come to a dead stop, with a fixed din of glory at the peak, unable to spread. All ears, one had to be all eyes. At the puppet's gesture, a fist clenched in the air opening its five fingers, I understood that he, the ingenious one, had won the sympathies by the appearance of catching something in flight, a figure (and that is all) of the ease with which an idea is taken up by everyone: and that, set in motion by the light breeze, the bear, risen rhythmically and gently, was interrogating this exploit, one claw placed on the ribbons of the human shoulder. No one who did not breathe hard, such grave consequences did this situation bear for the honor of the race: what was going to happen? The other paw came down, supple, against the arm hanging against the tights; and one saw, a couple united in a secret coming-together, something like an inferior, squat, and good man, standing on two spread-out, furry legs, embrace, in order to learn there the practices of genius, and his skull with the black muzzle only half reaching it, the bust of his brilliant and supernatural brother: but who! himself was raising, his mouth foolish with vagueness, a frightful head moving by a thread visible in the horror the true denials of a paper and gold fly. Bright spectacle, vaster than the stage, with this gift, proper to art, of lasting for a long time: in order to complete it, I let, without being shocked by the probably fatal attitude taken on by the mime, the depository of our pride, tacitly pour forth the discourse forbidden to the descendant of arctic sites: "Be kind (that was the meaning), and rather than be wanting in charity, explain to me the quality of this atmosphere of splendor, of dust and voices, in which you have taught me to move. My urgent request is just, which you do not seem, in an anguish which is only feigned, to know not how to answer, launched into the regions of wisdom, subtle elder! me, in order to make you free, still dressed in the crude abode of the caves where I have plunged again, in the night of humble epochs, my latent strength. Let us authenticate, by this tight embrace, before the multitude assembled for this purpose, the pact of our reconciliation." The absence of any breath united to space, in what absolute place was I living, one of the dramas of astral history choosing, in order to produce itself there, this modest stage! The crowd was fading away completely, magnifying the stage as the emblem of its spiritual situation: modern dispenser of ecstasy, the gas, alone, with the impartiality of a thing elemental, was continuing, in the heights of the house, a luminous noise of expectancy.*

The spell was broken: that was when a naked, brutal piece of flesh, directed from the space between the stage settings, crossed my vision, some moments in advance of the usually mysterious reward after these shows. A rag substituted bleeding near the bear who, having rediscovered his instincts previous to a higher curiosity with which the theatrical radiance was endowing him, fell back on his four paws and, as if carrying Silence away with him, went with the muted step of the species to scent, in order to put his teeth to it, this prey. A sigh, almost exempt of disappointment, incomprehensibly relieved the assembly: whose opera glasses, in rows, sought, lighting up the cleanness of their lenses, the acting of the splendid imbecile giddy in his fear; but saw an abject meal preferred perhaps by the animal to the same thing which it would first have been necessary for him to make of our *image, in order to enjoy it. The curtain having hesitated until then to increase the danger or the emotion, suddenly lowered its announcements of prices and commonplaces. I got up like everyone else, to go outside to take a breath of air, astonished not to have felt, once again, the same kind of impression as my fellow man, but serene: for my way of seeing, after all, had been superior, and even the true one.*

RÉMINISCENCE

Orphelin, j'errais en noir et l'œil vacant de famille: au quinconce se déplièrent des tentes de fête, éprouvai-je le futur et que je serais ainsi, j'aimais le parfum des vagabonds, vers eux à oublier mes camarades. Aucun cri de chœurs par la déchirure, ni tirade loin, le drame requérant l'heure sainte des quinquets, je souhaitais de parler avec un môme trop vacillant pour figurer parmi sa race, au bonnet de nuit tarillé comme le chaperon de Dante; qui rentrait en soi, sous l'aspect d'une tartine de fromage mou, déjà la neige des cimes, le lys ou autre blancheur constitutive d'ailes au-dedans: je l'eusse prié de m'admettre à son repas supérieur, partagé vite avec quelque aîné fameux jailli contre une proche toile en train des tours de force et banalités alliables au jour. Nu, de pirouetter dans sa prestesse de maillot à mon avis surprenante, lui, qui d'ailleurs commença: "Tes parents? —Je n'en ai pas. —Allons, si tu savais comme c'est farce, un père... même l'autre semaine que bouda la soupe, il faisait des grimaces aussi belles, quand le maître lançait les claques et les coups de pied. Mon cher!" et de triompher en élevant à moi la jambe avec aisance glorieuse, "il nous épate, papa," puis de mordre au régal chaste du très jeune: "Ta maman, tu n'en as pas peut-être, que tu es seul? la mienne mange de la filasse et le monde bat des mains. Tu ne sais rien, des parents sont des gens drôles, qui font rire." La parade s'exaltait, il partit: moi, je soupirai, déçu tout à coup de n'avoir pas de parents.

Reminiscence

An orphan, I was wandering, in black and my eye vacant of family; at the quincunx festive tents were spreading; did I experience the future and that I would be like that? I loved the smell of the vagabonds, drawn toward them forgetting my companions. No cry of the chorus through the tent's rent, nor distant tirade, the drama requiring the holy hour of the footlights, I wanted to speak to an urchin too unsteady to appear among his people, with a nightcap cut like Dante's hood; who was getting inside himself, in the form of a slice of bread with soft cheese, already the snow of the mountain peaks, the lily or other whiteness constituting wings within: I would have begged him to admit me to his superior meal, quickly shared with some illustrious elder suddenly sprung up against a nearby tent engaged in feats of strength and banalities compatible with the day. He pirouetted naked in the to me surprising nimbleness of his tights and began moreover: "Your parents? —I do not have any. —Go on, if you knew how funny that is, a father... even the other week when he was off his food, he made faces just as beautiful as ever, when the boss was flinging slaps and kicks. My dear fellow!" and he triumphed raising his leg toward me with glorious ease, "he amazes us, papa," then he bit into the chaste meal of the very young one: "Your mom, perhaps you don't have one, you're alone? mine eats tow, and everybody claps their hands. You have no idea, what funny people parents are, who make one laugh." The parade was stirring to life, he left: I sighed, disappointed suddenly not to have parents.

LA DÉCLARATION FORAINE

Le Silence! il est certain qu'à mon côté, ainsi que songes, étendue dans un bercement de promenade sous les roues assoupissant l'interjection de fleurs, toute femme, et j'en sais une qui voit clair ici, m'exempte de l'effort à proférer un vocable: la complimenter haut de quelque interrogatrice toilette, offre de soi presque à l'homme en faveur de qui s'achève l'après-midi, ne pouvant à l'encontre de tout ce rapprochement fortuit, que suggérer la distance sur ses traits aboutie à une fossette de spirituel sourire. Ainsi ne consent la réalité; car ce fut impitoyablement, hors du rayon qu'on sentait avec luxe expirer aux vernis du landau, comme une vocifération, parmi trop de tacite félicité pour une tombée de jour sur la banlieue, avec orage, dans tous sens à la fois et sans motif, du rire strident ordinaire des choses et de leur cuivrerie triomphale: au fait, la cacophonie à l'ouïe de quiconque, un instant écarté, plutôt qu'il ne s'y fond, auprès de son idée, reste à vif devant la hantise de l'existence.

"La fête de..." et je ne sais quel rendez-vous suburbain! nomma l'enfant voiturée dans mes distractions, la voix claire d'aucun ennui; j'obéis et fis arrêter.

Sans compensation à cette secousse qu'un besoin d'explication figurative plausible pour mes esprits, comme symétriquement s'ordonnent des verres d'illumination peu à peu éclairés en guirlandes et attributs, je décidai, la solitude manquée, de m'enfoncer même avec bravoure en ce déchaînement exprès et haïssable de tout ce que j'avais naguères fui dans une gracieuse compagnie: prête et ne témoignant de surprise à la modification dans notre programme, du bras ingénu elle s'en repose sur moi, tandis que nous allons parcourir, les yeux sur l'enfilade, l'allée d'ahurissement qui divise en écho du même tapage les foires et permet à la foule d'y renfermer pour un temps l'univers. Subséquemment aux assauts d'un médiocre dévergondage en vue de quoi que ce soit qui détourne notre stagnation amusée par le crépuscule, au fond, bizarre et pourpre, nous retint à l'égal de la nue incendiaire un humain spectacle, poignant: reniée du chassis peinturluré ou de l'inscription en capitales une baraque, apparemment vide.

A qui ce matelas décousu pour improviser ici, comme les voiles dans tous les temps et les temples, l'arcane! appartînt, sa fréquentation durant le jeûne n'avait pas chez son possesseur excité avant qu'il le déroulât comme le gonfalon d'espoirs en liesse, l'hallucination d'une merveille à montrer (que l'inanité de son famélique cauchemar); et pourtant, mû par le caractère frérial d'exception à la misère quotidienne qu'un pré, quand l'institue le mot mystérieux de fête, tient des souliers nombreux y piétinant (en raison de cela poind aux profondeurs des vêtements quelque unique velléité du dur sou à sortir à seule fin de se dépenser), lui aussi! n'importe qui de tout dénué sauf de la notion qu'il y avait lieu pour être un des élus, sinon de vendre, de faire voir, mais quoi, avait cédé à la convocation du bienfaisant rendez-vous. Ou, très prosaïquement, peut-être le rat éduqué à moins que, lui-même, ce mendiant sur l'athlétique vigueur de ses muscles comptât, pour décider l'engouement populaire, faisait défaut, à l'instant précis, comme cela résulte souvent de la mise en demeure de l'homme par les circonstances générales.

"Battez la caisse!" proposa en altesse Madame... seule tu sais Qui, marquant un suranné tambour duquel se levait, les bras décroisés afin de signifier inutile l'approche de son théâtre sans prestige, un vieillard que cette camaraderie avec un instrument de rumeur et d'appel, peut-être, séduisit à son vacant dessein; puis comme si, de ce que tout de suite on pût, ici, envisager de plus beau, l'énigme, par un bijou fermant la mondaine, en tant qu'à sa gorge le manque de réponse, scintillait! la voici engouffrée, à ma surprise de pitre coi devant une halte du public qu'empaume l'éveil des ra et des fla assourdissant mon invariable et obscur pour moi-même d'abord. "Entrez, tout le monde, ce n'est qu'un sou, on le rend à qui n'est pas satisfait de la représentation." Le nimbe en paillasson dans le remerciment joignant deux paumes séniles vidé, j'en agite les couleurs, en signal, de loin, et me coiffai, prêt à fendre la masse debout en le secret de ce qu'avait su faire avec ce lieu sans rêve l'initiative d'une contemporaine de nos soirs.

A hauteur du genou, elle émergeait, sur une table, des cent têtes.

Net ainsi qu'un jet égaré d'autre part la dardait électriquement, éclate pour moi ce calcul qu'à défaut de tout, elle, selon que la mode, une fantaisie ou l'humeur du ciel circonstanciaient sa beauté, sans supplément de danse ou de chant, pour la cohue amplement payait l'aumône exigée en faveur d'un quelconque; et du même trait je comprends mon devoir en le péril de la subtile exhibition, ou qu'il n'y avait au monde pour conjurer la défection dans les curiosités que de recourir à quelque puissance absolue, comme d'une Métaphore. Vite, dégoiser jusqu'à l'éclaircissement, sur maintes physionomies, de leur sécurité qui, ne saisissant tout du coup, se rend à l'évidence, même ardue, impliquée en la parole et consent à échanger son billon contre des présomptions exactes et supérieures, bref, la certitude pour chacun de n'être pas refait.

Un coup d'œil, le dernier, à une chevelure où fume puis éclaire de fastes de jardins le pâlissement du chapeau en crêpe de même ton que la statuaire robe se relevant, avance au spectateur, sur un pied comme le reste hortensia.

Alors:

>   La chevelure vol d'une flamme à l'extrême
>   Occident de désirs pour la tout déployer
>   Se pose (je dirais mourir un diadème)
>   Vers le front couronné son ancien foyer
>
>   Mais sans or soupirer que cette vive nue
>   L'ignition du feu toujours intérieur
>   Originellement la seule continue
>   Dans le joyau de l'œil véridique ou rieur
>
>   Une nudité de héros tendre diffame
>   Celle qui ne mouvant astre ni feux au doigt
>   Rien qu'à simplifier avec gloire la femme
>   Accomplit par son chef fulgurante l'exploit
>
>   De semer de rubis le doute qu'elle écorche
>   Ainsi qu'une joyeuse et tutélaire torche

Mon aide à la taille de la vivante allégorie qui déjà résignait sa faction, peut-être faute chez moi de faconde ultérieure, afin d'en assoupir l'élan gentiment à terre: "Je vous ferai observer, ajoutai-je, maintenant de plain-pied avec l'entendement des visiteurs, coupant court à leur ébahissement devant ce congé par une affectation de retour à l'authenticité du spectacle, Messieurs et Dames, que la personne qui a eu l'honneur de se soumettre à votre jugement, ne requiert pour vous communiquer le sens de son charme, un costume ou aucun accessoire usuel de théâtre. Ce naturel s'accommode de l'allusion parfaite que fournit la toilette toujours à l'un des motifs primordiaux de la femme, et suffit, ainsi que votre sympathique approbation m'en convainc." Un suspens de marque appréciative sauf quelques confondants "Bien sûr!" ou "C'est cela!" et "Oui" par les gosiers comme plusieurs bravos prêtés par des paires de mains généreuses, conduisit jusqu'à la sortie sur une vacance d'arbres et de nuit la foule où nous allions nous mêler, n'était l'attente en gants blancs encore d'un enfantin tourlourou qui les rêvait dégourdir à l'estimation d'une jarretière hautaine.

—Merci, consentit la chère, une bouffée droit à elle d'une constellation ou des feuilles bue comme pour y trouver sinon le rassérènement, elle n'avait douté d'un succès, du moins l'habitude frigide de sa voix: j'ai dans l'esprit le souvenir de choses qui ne s'oublient.

—Oh! rien que lieu commun d'une esthétique...

—Que vous n'auriez peut-être pas introduit, qui sait? mon ami, le prétexte de formuler ainsi devant moi au conjoint isolement par exemple de notre voiture — où est-elle — regagnons-la: —mais ceci jaillit, forcé, sous le coup de poing brutal à l'estomac, que cause une impatience de gens auxquels coûte que coûte et soudain il faut proclamer quelque chose fût-ce la rêverie...

—Qui s'ignore et se lance nue de peur, en travers du public; c'est vrai. Comme vous, Madame, ne l'auriez entendu si irréfutablement, malgré sa réduplication sur une rime du trait final, mon boniment d'après un mode primitif du sonnet*, je le gage, si chaque terme ne s'en était répercuté jusqu'à vous par de variés tympans, pour charmer un esprit ouvert à la compréhension multiple.

—Peut-être! accepta notre pensée dans un enjouement de souffle nocturne la même.

---

* Usité à la Renaissance anglaise.

The Fairground Declaration

Silence! it is certain that stretched by my side, like dreams, in the cradling swaying of the ride, assuaging the interjection of flowers under the wheels, any woman, and I know of one who understands this, excuses me from the effort of uttering a word: to compliment her aloud on some interrogatory costume, almost an offer of herself to the man in whose favor the afternoon draws to a close, being able in opposition to all this fortuitous conjunction of circumstances only to suggest the distance which on her features ends in the dimple of an intelligent smile. Reality does not allow it so; for there was mercilessly, outside the sunbeam which one felt expiring extravagantly on the landau's gloss, something like an outcry, amongst too much tacit bliss for a nightfall on the outskirts of town, with a storm, everywhere at the same time and without cause, of the shrill common laughter of things and their triumphal brassiness: taking everything into consideration, a cacophony to the ears of whoever, having withdrawn for a moment next to his idea, rather than melting into it, remains alert before the obsession of existence.

"The festival of . . ." and I do not know what sort of suburban get-together! indicated the girl-child transported in my distractions, with her clear voice devoid of dismay; I obeyed and ordered a stop.

Without compensation for this shock, but a need for a figurative explanation plausible for my mind, like lamps, lit up little by little, which arrange themselves symmetrically in garlands and emblems, I decided, having lost the opportunity for solitude, to plunge, with daring even, into this express and detestable outburst of all that I had erstwhile fled in gracious company: ready, and giving no evidence of surprise at the change in our plans, she relies on me with ingenuous arm while we go down, our eyes upon the rows, the lane of confusion which divides the fairgrounds into an echo of the same din and permits the crowd to enclose in it for a time the universe. Subsequent to the onslaughts of a mediocre licentiousness with a view to anything whatever which diverts our stagnation entertained by the dusk, like the firebrand cloud in the background, strange and purple, a heart-gripping human spectacle detained us: a shanty, apparently empty, repudiated by the many-colored frame or the inscription in capital letters.

APPENDIX 239

He to whom this mattress ripped apart in order to improvise here, like the veils in all times and temples, the mystery! belonged, its frequentation during the fast had not excited in its possessor before he unrolled it like the banner of hopes in rejoicing, the hallucination of a marvel to show (except the inanity of his famished nightmare); and yet, stirred by the fraternal character of exception to daily misery which a meadow, when the mysterious word of feast initiates it, holds from numerous shoes trampling on it (for this reason sprouts at the depths of clothing some unique stray impulse of the hard penny to come out for the sole end of being spent) he too! anyone at all, destitute of all except the notion that there was every ground to be one of the elect, if not to sell, then to show, but what? had yielded to the summons of the kindly rendezvous. Or, very simply, perhaps the trained rat, unless the beggar was himself counting on the athletic vigor of his muscles, to determine the popular craze, was at the precise moment absent, as that often results from man's summons by general circumstances.

"Beat the drum!" proposed haughtily Madame... you alone know Who, pointing to an old-fashioned drum whence rose, his arms unfolded in order to indicate as useless the approach of his theatre without illusions, an old man whom this companionship with an instrument of noise and summons seduced perhaps to her unknown project; then, as if, from what at once could be envisaged here the most beautiful, the riddle sparkled, closing the mundane one with a jewel, like the lack of an answer, at her throat! there she is engulfed, at my nonplussed clown's surprise before the public's coming to a stop, whom the call of the drum's ruff and flam catches, deafening my at first unchanging and obscure for myself: "Everybody enter, it's only a penny, it will be returned to whoever is not satisfied with the show." The straw halo in(to) gratitude joining two senile palms emptied, I wave its colors, as a signal, from afar, and covered my head, ready to cut through the crowd standing in the secret of what the initiative of a contemporary of our evenings had known to make of this dreamless place.

Knee-high she was emerging, on a table, from a hundred heads.

Clear, as a beam strayed from somewhere darted her forth electrically, this calculation bursts forth for me, that, for want of everything, she, according as fashion, a fantasy, or the mood of heaven were giving full details of her beauty, was amply paying, without the addition of dance or song, the crowd for the alms exacted in favor of someone; and in the same flash I understand my duty in the peril of the subtle exhibition, or that one had, in order to exorcise the desertion in the curiosities, to have recourse only to some absolute power in the world, as to a Metaphor. Quickly, expound until the elucidation upon many features, of their freedom from apprehension which, not grasping everything all at once, renders itself to the evidence, even though with difficulty, implied in the word and consents to exchanging its cheap coin for exact and superior presumptions, in short, the certainty for everyone of not being cheated.

A glance, the last, at hair where smokes and then lights up with the ostentations of gardens the pallidness of the crepe hat of the same shade as the statuesque dress, rising over a foot hydrangea-colored like the rest, and which advances to the spectator.

Then:

> *The hair, flight of a flame to the extreme*
> *Occident of desires, to be spread all out*
> *Places itself (I would think of a diadem dying)*
> *Toward the crowned forehead, its former seat*
>
> *But without sighing for gold other than this living cloud*
> *The ignition of the always internal fire*
> *Originally the only one, continues*
> *In the jewel of the veracious or laughing eye*
>
> *A nakedness of a tender hero defames*
> *Her who moving neither star nor fires on her finger*
> *Nothing but to simplify with glory the woman*
> *Accomplishes flashingly with her head the feat*
>
> *Of sowing with rubies the doubt which she flays*
> *Like a joyful and tutelary torch.*

My aiding the waist of the living allegory, in order gently to soften its downward bound, who was already giving up her post, perhaps because of a failing on my part of an ulterior flow of words: "I shall have you note, I added, now on a level with the understanding of the visitors, cutting short their astonishment before this dismissal by an affectation of a return to the authenticity of the show, Ladies and Gentlemen, that the person who has had the honor of submitting herself to your judgment does not need, to convey the sense of her charm to you, a costume nor any other customary theatre accessory. This naturalness makes the best of the perfect allusion which dress always furnishes one of woman's primordial incentives, and suffices, as your kindly approbation convinces me." A suspense of appreciation, except for some confounding "O sure!" or "That's it!" and "Yes" from the throats as several bravos lent by pairs of generous hands, led the crowd, with which we were going to mingle, to the exit upon an emptiness of trees and the night, were it not for the waiting still of a childish soldier boy in white gloves who was dreaming of unstiffening them at the assessment of a haughty garter.

"Thank you," *the dear one consented, a gust of a constellation or leaves come straight at her drunk as if to find in it if not the recovery of her equanimity, she had not doubted of success, at least the customary coolness of her voice: I have in mind the memory of things which are unforgettable.*

"Oh, nothing but the commonplace of an aesthetic..."

"Which you might perhaps not have introduced, who knows? my friend, the pretext of thus formulating before me in the conjunct isolation, for example, of our car — where is it — let us get back to it: "but it burst forth, forced out by the brutal blow in the stomach caused by the impatience of people to whom at any price and suddenly one must proclaim something, be it dreams even...

"Which do not know themselves and dash, naked with fear, across the public; it's true. As you, Madam, would not have heard so irrefutably, despite its reduplication on one rhyme of the final stroke, my flattery according to a primitive kind of sonnet, * I wager, if each term had not had its repercussion to you over various tympans to charm a mind open to multiple comprehension."

"Perhaps!" *accepted our thought the same in the playfulness of nocturnal breath.*

---

* Current in the English Renaissance.

LE NÉNUPHAR BLANC

J'avais beaucoup ramé, d'un grand geste net assoupi, les yeux au-dedans fixés sur l'entier oubli d'aller, comme le rire de l'heure coulait alentour. Tant d'immobilité paressait que frôlé d'un bruit inerte où fila jusqu'à moitié la yole, je ne vérifiai l'arrêt qu'à l'étincellement stable d'initiales sur les avirons mis à nu, ce qui me rappela à mon identité mondaine.

Qu'arrivait-il, où étais-je?

Il fallut, pour voir clair en l'aventure, me remémorer mon départ tôt, ce juillet de flamme, sur l'intervalle vif entre ses végétations dormantes d'un toujours étroit et distrait ruisseau, en quête des floraisons d'eau et avec un dessein de reconnaître l'emplacement occupé par la propriété de l'amie d'une amie, à qui je devais improviser un bonjour. Sans que le ruban d'aucune herbe me retînt devant un paysage plus que l'autre chassé avec son reflet en l'onde par le même impartial coup de rame, je venais échouer dans quelque touffe de roseaux, terme mystérieux de ma course, au milieu de la rivière: où tout de suite élargie en fluvial bosquet, elle étale un nonchaloir d'étang plissé des hésitations à partir qu'a une source.

L'inspection détaillée m'apprit que cet obstacle de verdure en pointe sur le courant, masquait l'arche unique d'un pont prolongé, à terre, d'ici et de là, par une haie clôturant des pelouses. Je me rendis compte. Simplement le parc de Madame..., l'inconnue à saluer.

Un joli voisinage, pendant la saison, la nature d'une personne qui s'est choisi retraite aussi humidement impénétrable ne pouvant être que conforme à mon goût. Sûr, elle avait fait de ce cristal son miroir intérieur à l'abri de l'indiscrétion éclatante des après-midi;

elle y venait et la buée d'argent glaçant des saules ne fut bientôt que la limpidité de son regard habitué à chaque feuille.

Toute je l'évoquais lustrale.

Courbé dans la sportive attitude où me maintenait de la curiosité, comme sous le silence spacieux de ce que s'annonçait l'étrangère au commencement d'esclavage dégagé par une possibilité féminine: que ne signifiaient pas mal les courroies attachant le soulier du rameur au bois de l'embarcation, comme on ne fait qu'un avec l'instrument de ses sortilèges.

"—Aussi bien une quelconque..." allais-je terminer.

Quand un imperceptible bruit me fit douter si l'habitante du bord hantait mon loisir, ou inespérément le bassin.

Le pas cessa, pourquoi?

Subtil secret des pieds qui vont, viennent, conduisent l'esprit où le veut la chère ombre enfouie en de la batiste et les dentelles d'une jupe affluant sur le sol comme pour circonvenir du talon à l'orteil, dans une flottaison, cette initiative par quoi la marche s'ouvre, tout au bas et les plis rejetés en traîne, une échappée, de sa double flèche savante.

Connaît-elle un motif à sa station, elle-même la promeneuse: et n'est-ce, moi, tendre trop haut la tête, pour ces joncs à ne dépasser et toute la mentale somnolence où se voile ma lucidité, que d'interroger jusque-là le mystère.

"—A quel type s'ajustent vos traits, je sens leur précision, Madame, interrompre chose installée ici par le bruissement d'une venue, oui! ce charme instinctif d'en dessous que ne défend pas contre l'explorateur la plus authentiquement nouée, avec une boucle en diamant, des ceintures. Si vague concept se suffit: et ne transgressera le délice empreint de généralité qui permet et ordonne d'exclure tous visages, au point que la révélation d'un (n'allez point le pencher, avéré, sur le furtif seuil où je règne) chasserait mon trouble, avec lequel il n'a que faire."

Ma présentation, en cette tenue de maraudeur aquatique, je la peux tenter, avec l'excuse du hasard.

Séparés, on est ensemble: je m'immisce à de sa confuse intimité, dans ce suspens sur l'eau où mon songe attarde l'indécise, mieux que visite, suivie d'autres, l'autorisera. Que de discours oiseux en comparaison de celui que je tins pour n'être pas entendu, faudra-t-il, avant de retrouver aussi intuitif accord que maintenant, l'ouïe au ras de l'acajou vers le sable entier qui s'est tu!

La pause se mesure au temps de ma détermination.

Conseille, ô mon rêve, que faire?

Résumer d'un regard la vierge absence éparse en cette solitude et, comme on cueille, en mémoire d'un site, l'un de ces magiques nénuphars clos qui y surgissent tout à coup, enveloppant de leur creuse blancheur un rien, fait de songes intacts, du bonheur qui n'aura pas lieu et de mon souffle ici retenu dans la peur d'une apparition, partir avec; tacitement, en déramant peu à peu sans du heurt briser l'illusion ni que le clapotis de la bulle visible d'écume enroulée à ma fuite ne jette aux pieds survenus de personne la ressemblance transparente du rapt de mon idéale fleur.

Si, attirée par un sentiment d'insolite, elle a paru, la Méditative ou la Hautaine, la Farouche, la Gaie, tant pis pour cette indicible mine que j'ignore à jamais! car j'accomplis selon les règles la manœuvre; me dégageai, virai et je contournais déjà une ondulation du ruisseau, emportant comme un noble œuf de cygne, tel que n'en jaillira le vol, mon imaginaire trophée, qui ne se gonfle d'autre chose sinon de la vacance exquise de soi qu'aime, l'été, à poursuivre, dans les allées de son parc, toute dame, arrêtée parfois et longtemps, comme au bord d'une source à franchir ou de quelque pièce d'eau.

THE WHITE WATER-LILY

I had rowed much, with a big, clean, drowsy motion, my eyes turned inward fixed on the entire forgetfulness of the journey, as the hour's laughter was gliding round about. So much motionlessness idled away the time that, brushed by a dull sound into which the skiff slipped halfway, I only verified the stop by the steady glittering of initials on the bared oars, which recalled my worldly identity to me.

What was happening, where was I?

To understand the adventure, I had to recall my early departure, in this flaming July, on the bright interval between its sleeping vegetation of an ever narrow and listless stream, in quest of water flowers and with the intention of exploring the site occupied by the property of a lady friend's lady friend, for whom I was to improvise a "Good day." Without any strip of grass detaining me before one landscape more than another chased away with its reflection in the water by the same impartial oar stroke, I had just run aground in some clump of reeds, mysterious end of my cruise, in the middle of the stream: where all at once the stream, widened into a fluvial grove, displays the apathy of a pond creased by a spring's hesitations to depart.

A detailed inspection revealed to me that this tapering obstacle of greenery in the current masked the single arch of a bridge prolonged, on land, on either side, by a hedge enclosing lawns. I understood. Merely the park of Madame..., the unknown one I was to greet.

An attractive neighborhood, during the vacation season; the nature of a person who has chosen herself a retreat so humidly impenetrable could only conform to my taste. Surely, she had made of this crystal her interior mirror sheltered from the brilliant indiscretion of the afternoons; she would come there and the cool silvery vapor of the willows was soon only the limpidity of her glance accustomed to each leaf.

I evoked her all lustral.

Leaning forward in the sportive attitude in which curiosity held me, as if beneath the spacious silence with which the strange one would announce herself, I smiled at the beginning of the servitude emanating from a feminine possibility: which the straps attaching the rower's shoes to the wood of the boat symbolized quite well, as one is but one with the instrument of one's enchantments.

"As well any woman whosoever..." I was going to terminate.

When an imperceptible noise made me doubt whether the inhabitant of the shore was haunting my leisure, or, contrary to all hope, the pond.

The step ceased, why?

Subtle secret of feet that go, come, lead the mind where she wills, the dear shadow, buried in batiste and the lace of a skirt flowing on the ground as if to surround, from heel to toe, floatingly, this initiative by which her steps move forth, very low with the folds thrown back in a train, with their clever double arrow.

Does she know a reason for her standing still, the stroller herself; and would I not be holding my head too high if I raised it in order to see over these reeds and over all that mental drowsiness in which my lucidity is veiled, to interrogate so far as that, the mystery?

"—To whatever type your features may adjust themselves, I feel their precision, Madame, interrupt something installed here by the rustling of an arrival, yes! this instinctive charm of something beneath, which the most authentically tied of sashes, with a buckle of diamonds, does not defend against the explorer. So vague a concept suffices: and will not transgress the delight imprinted by generality, which permits and demands the exclusion of all faces, to the point where the revelation of one (do not bend it, authenticated, over the furtive threshold where I reign) would chase away my emotions, with which it has no business."

My introduction, in this pirate's outfit, I can attempt it with the excuse of chance.

Separated, one is together: I permeate her obscure intimacy, in this suspense on the water where my dream delays the undecided one, better than any visit, followed by others, will allow it. How many trifling conversations, in comparison with the one which I made in order not to be heard, will be necessary before so intuitive an accord as now can be found again, my ear at the level of the mahogany toward all the sand which has become silent!

The pause is measured by the time of my determination.

Advise, o my dream, what to do?

Sum up in a glance the virgin absence scattered in this solitude and, as one picks, in memory of a site, one of those magical closed water-lilies which suddenly rise up there, enveloping with their hollow whiteness a nothing, made of untouched dreams, of the happiness that will not take place and of my breath held here in the fear of an apparition, leave with it; silently, rowing away little by little without breaking the illusion by a shock, and so that the splashing of the visible bubble of foam coiled up in my flight does not throw the transparent resemblance of the abduction of my ideal flower at the feet of someone arrived.

If, attracted by the feeling of something unusual, she appeared, the Meditative one or the Haughty one, the Wild one, the Gay one, too bad for that indescribable face forever unknown to me! for I accomplished the maneuver according to the rules: got myself free, *turned, and was already passing round an undulation of the stream, carrying away, like a noble swan's egg, such that flight will never burst forth from it, my imaginary trophy, swollen with nothing except the exquisite emptiness of self which every lady, in the summer, loves to pursue, along the walks of her park, delayed sometimes and for a long time, as if on the edge of a spring to cross or some body of water.*

L'ECCLÉSIASTIQUE

Les printemps poussent l'organisme à des actes qui, dans une autre saison, lui sont inconnus et maint traité d'histoire naturelle abonde en descriptions de ce phénomène, chez les animaux. Qu'il serait d'un intérêt plus plausible de recueillir certaines des altérations qu'apporte l'instant climatérique dans les allures d'individus faits pour la spiritualité! Mal quitté par l'ironie de l'hiver, j'en retiens, quant à moi, un état équivoque tant que ne s'y substitue pas un naturalisme absolu ou naïf, capable de poursuivre une jouissance dans la différentiation de plusieurs brins d'herbes. Rien dans le cas actuel n'apportant de profit à la foule, j'échappe, pour le méditer, sous quelques ombrages environnant d'hier la ville: or c'est de leur mystère presque banal que j'exhiberai un exemple saisissable et frappant des inspirations printanières.

Vive fut tout à l'heure, dans un endroit peu fréquenté du bois de Boulogne, ma surprise quand, sombre agitation basse, je vis, par les mille interstices d'arbustes bons à ne rien cacher, total et des battements supérieurs du tricorne s'animant jusqu'à des souliers affermis par des boucles en argent, un ecclésiastique, qui à l'écart de témoins, répondait aux sollicitations du gazon. A moi ne plût (et rien de pareil ne sert les desseins providentiels) que, coupable à l'égal d'un faux scandalisé se saisissant d'un caillou du chemin, j'amenasse par mon sourire même d'intelligence, une rougeur sur le visage à deux mains voilé de ce pauvre homme, autre que celle sans doute trouvée dans son solitaire exercice! Le pied vif, il me fallut, pour ne produire par ma présence de distraction, user d'adresse; et fort contre la tentation d'un regard porté en arrière, me figurer en esprit l'apparition quasi diabolique qui continuait à froisser le renouveau de ses côtes, à droite, à gauche et du ventre, en obtenant une chaste frénésie. Tout, se frictionner ou jeter les membres, se rouler, glisser, aboutissait à une satisfaction: et s'arrêter, interdit du chatouillement de quelque haute tige de fleur à de noirs mollets, parmi cette robe spéciale portée avec l'apparence qu'on est pour soi tout même sa femme. Solitude, froid silence épars dans la verdure, perçus par des sens moins subtils qu'inquiets, vous connûtes les claquements furibonds d'une étoffe; comme si la nuit absconse en ses plis en sortait enfin secouée! et les heurts sourds contre la terre du squelette rajeuni; mais l'énergumène n'avait point à vous contempler. Hilare, c'était assez de chercher en soi la cause d'un plaisir ou d'un devoir, qu'expliquait mal un retour, devant une pelouse, aux gambades du séminaire. L'influence du souffle vernal doucement dilatant les immuables textes inscrits en sa chair, lui aussi, enhardi de ce trouble agréable à sa stérile pensée, était venu reconnaître par un contact avec la Nature, immédiat, net, violent, positif, dénué de toute curiosité intellectuelle, le bien-être général; et candidement, loin des obédiences et de la contrainte de son occupation, des canons, des interdits, des censures, il se roulait, dans la béatitude de sa simplicité native, plus heureux qu'un âne. Que le but de sa promenade atteint se soit, droit et d'un jet, relevé non sans secouer les pistils et essuyer les sucs attachés à sa personne, le héros de ma vision, pour rentrer, inaperçu, dans la foule, et les habitudes de son ministère, je ne songe à rien nier; mais j'ai le droit de ne point considérer cela. Ma discrétion vis-à-vis d'ébats d'abord apparus n'a-t-elle pas pour récompense d'en fixer à jamais comme une rêverie de passant se plut à la compléter, l'image marquée d'un sceau mystérieux de modernité, à la fois baroque et belle?

The Ecclesiastic

The spring seasons impel the organism to acts which, in another season, are unknown to it, and many a treatise of natural history abounds in descriptions of this phenomenon, among the animals. Of how much more plausible interest it would be to gather some of the changes which the climacteric moment brings about in the demeanor of individuals destined for spirituality! The irony of winter hardly having left me, I retain of it, for my own part, an equivocal state as long as it is not replaced by a naive or absolute naturalism, capable of pursuing enjoyment in the differentiation of several blades of grass. Nothing in the present case bringing profit to the crowd, I escape, in order to meditate on it, beneath some shades surrounding the city as of late: now it is from within their almost banal mystery that I shall exhibit a tangible and striking example of vernal insprirations.

Keen was my surprise just now, in a seldom-frequented spot of the Bois de Boulogne, when I saw, somber low agitation, through the thousand interstices of bushes good for hiding nothing, entire and from the upper palpitations of the tricorn hat animating himself down to the shoes fastened by silver buckles, an ecclesiastic who, far from witnesses, was responding to the solicitations of the lawn. Far be it from me (and nothing similar serves the designs of providence) that, guilty as a scandalized hypocrite seizing a stone from the road, I should bring, by my smile even of understanding, a blush upon this poor man's face covered with both hands, other than that doubtless found in his solitary exercise! Fast of foot, I had to use some skill in order not to produce a distraction by my presence; and steeled against the temptation of a backward glance, imagine in my mind the quasi-diabolical apparition who went on rubbing spring with his sides, on the right, on the left, and with his stomach, while achieving a chaste frenzy. Everything, rubbing himself or throwing his limbs about, rolling, sliding, led to a satisfaction: and stopping, bewildered by some tall flower stem tickling his black calves, amid that special gown worn with the appearance that one is everything for oneself, even one's own wife. Solitude, cold silence scattered in the greenery, perceived by senses less subtle than troubled, you have known a cloth's furious clappings; as if the night hidden in its folds came finally shaken out of it! and the dull thuds against the earth of the rejuvenated skeleton; but the possessed one did not have to contemplate you at all. It was enough to seek in himself mirthfully the cause of a pleasure or a duty, which hardly excused a return to the capers of the seminary confronted with a lawn. The influence of the spring-time breath gently expanding the immutable texts inscribed in his flesh, he too, emboldened by this confusion agreeable to his sterile thought, had come to acknowledge the general well-being by an immediate, clear, violent, positive contact with Nature, free of any intellectual curiosity; and candidly, far from the servitudes and constraints of his occupation, from canons, interdicts or censures, he was rolling, in the beatitude of his native simplicity, happier than a donkey. That, the object of his walk attained, the hero of my vision got up straight at once, not without shaking off the pistils and wiping off the sap clinging to his person, in order to return unnoticed into the crowd and the habits of his ministry, I do not dream of denying it; but I have the right not to take that into consideration. My discretion with regard to erstwhile manifest frolics does it not receive for its reward to fix thereof forever, as a passer-by's reverie pleased itself to complete it, the image marked with a mysterious seal of modernity, at once baroque and beautiful?

LA GLOIRE

La Gloire! je ne la sus qu'hier, irréfragable, et rien ne m'intéressera d'appelé par quelqu'un ainsi.

Cent affiches s'assimilant l'or incompris des jours, trahison de la lettre, ont fui, comme à tous confins de la ville, mes yeux au ras de l'horizon par un départ sur le rail traînés avant de se recueillir dans l'abstruse fierté que donne une approche de forêt en son temps d'apothéose.

Si discord parmi l'exaltation de l'heure, un cri faussa ce nom connu pour déployer la continuité de cimes tard évanouies, Fontainebleau, que je pensai, la glace du compartiment violentée, du poing aussi étreindre à la gorge l'interrupteur: Tais-toi! Ne divulgue pas du fait d'un aboi indifférent l'ombre ici insinuée dans mon esprit, aux portières de wagons battant sous un vent inspiré et égalitaire, les touristes omniprésents vomis. Une quiétude menteuse de riches bois suspend alentour quelque extraordinaire état d'illusion, que me réponds-tu? qu'ils ont, ces voyageurs, pour ta gare aujourd'hui quitté la capitale, bon employé vociférateur par devoir et dont je n'attends, loin d'accaparer une ivresse à tous départie par les libéralités conjointes de la nature et de l'Etat, rien qu'un silence prolongé le temps de m'isoler de la délégation urbaine vers l'extatique torpeur de ces feuillages là-bas trop immobilisés pour qu'une crise ne les éparpille bientôt dans l'air; voici, sans attenter à ton intégrité, tiens, une monnaie.

Un uniforme inattentif m'invitant vers quelque barrière, je remets sans dire mot, au lieu du suborneur métal, mon billet.

Obéi pourtant, oui, à ne voir que l'asphalte s'étaler net de pas, car je ne peux encore imaginer qu'en ce pompeux octobre exceptionnel du million d'existences étageant leur vacuité en tant qu'une monotonie énorme de capitale dont va s'effacer ici la hantise avec le coup de sifflet sous la brume, aucun furtivement évadé que moi n'ait senti qu'il est, cet an, d'amers et lumineux sanglots, mainte indécise flottaison d'idée désertant les hasards comme des branches, tel frisson et ce qui fait penser à un automne sous les cieux.

    Personne et, les bras de doute envolés comme qui porte aussi un lot d'une splendeur secrète, trop inappréciable trophée pour paraître! mais sans du coup m'élancer dans cette diurne veillée d'immortels troncs au déversement sur un d'orgueils sur-humains (or ne faut-il pas qu'on en constate l'authenticité?) ni passer le seuil où des torches consument, dans une haute garde, tous rêves antérieurs à leur éclat répercutant en pourpre dans la nue l'universel sacre de l'intrus royal qui n'aura eu qu'à venir: j'attendis, pour l'être, que lent et repris du mouvement ordinaire, se réduisit à ses proportions d'une chimère puérile emportant du monde quelque part, le train qui m'avait là déposé seul.

Glory

Glory! I did not know it until yesterday, irrefragable, and nothing thus called by anyone will interest me.

    A hundred signs assimilating the days' misunderstood gold, treason of letters, have fled, as to all the confines of the city, my eyes drawn to the level of the horizon by a departure on the rails before plunging in meditation in the abstruse pride which the approach of a forest gives in its time of apotheosis.

    So in discord amidst the hour's exaltation, a cry falsified this name known to unfold the continuity of late vanished tree tops, Fontainebleau, that I thought, the glass of the compartment having been outraged with my fist, also of seizing the interruptor by the throat: Be quiet! Do not divulge by means of an indifferent barking the shadow here insinuated in my mind, to the carriage doors banging under an inspired and egalitarian wind, the omnipresent tourists having been spewed out. A deceptive calm of rich woods suspends roundabout some extraordinary state of illusion, what do you answer me? that they, these travelers, have left the capital for your station today, good employee vociferating out of duty, and of whom I expect, far from hoarding an intoxication dispensed to all by the joint liberalities of nature and of the State, nothing but a silence prolonged for the time it takes to isolate myself from the urban delegation toward the ecstatic torpor of those leaves yonder, too still but that a crisis will not soon disperse them in the air; see, without making an attempt upon your integrity, take it, a coin.

An inattentive uniform inviting me to some barrier, I hand over, without saying a word, instead of the bribing metal, my ticket.

Obeyed however, yes, in seeing only the asphalt spread out clear of foot-steps, for I cannot yet imagine that in this pompous exceptional October, of the million existences ranging their vacuity so much like an enormous monotony of the capital, whose obsession is going to become obliterated here with the blast of the whistle in the mist, no one but I stealthily escaped should have felt that there are, this year, bitter and luminous sobs, many a doubtful floating of ideas deserting chance like branches, a certain shiver and which makes one think of an autumn beneath the skies.

No one, doubt's arms flown away as one who also carries a portion of secret splendor, too inappreciable a trophy to appear! but without dashing at once into this diurnal vigil of immortal tree trunks to the pouring out upon one of superhuman prides (for must one not ascertain its authenticity?) nor passing the threshold where torches consume, in a high guard, all dreams anterior to their bursting, reverberating in purple in the clouds the universal consecration of the royal intruder who will only have had to come: I waited, in order to be he, that the train, slowly and taken up by its ordinary motion, should be reduced to its proportions of a childish fancy carrying people somewhere, having deposited me there alone.

CONFLIT

Longtemps, voici du temps — je croyais — que s'exempta mon idée d'aucun accident même vrai; préférant aux hasards, puiser, dans son principe, jaillissement.

Un goût pour une maison abandonnée, lequel paraîtrait favorable à cette disposition, amène à me dédire: tant le contentement pareil, chaque année verdissant l'escalier de pierres extérieur, sauf celle-ci, à pousser contre les murailles un volet hivernal puis raccorder comme si pas d'interruption, l'œillade d'à présent au spectacle immobilisé autrefois. Gage de retours fidèles, mais voilà que ce battement, vermoulu, scande un vacarme, refrains, altercations, en dessous; je me rappelle comment la légende de la malheureuse demeure dont je hante le coin intact, envahie par une bande de travailleurs en train d'offenser le pays parce que tout de solitude, avec une voie ferrée, survint, m'angoissa au départ, irais-je ou pas, me fit presque hésiter — à revoir, tant pis! ce sera à défendre, comme mien, arbitrairement s'il faut, le local et j'y suis. Une tendresse, exclusive dorénavant, que c'ait été lui qui, dans la suppression concernant des sites précieux, reçût la pire injure; hôte, je le deviens, de sa déchéance: invraisemblablement, le séjour chéri pour la désuétude et de l'exception, tourné par les progrès en cantine d'ouvriers de chemin de fer.

Terrassiers, puisatiers, par qui un velours hâve aux jambes, semble que le remblai bouge, ils dressent, au repos, dans une tranchée, la rayure bleu et blanc transversale des maillots comme la nappe d'eau peu à peu (vêtement oh! que l'homme est la source qu'il cherche): ce les sont, mes co-locataires jadis ceux, en esprit, quand je les rencontrai sur les routes, choyés comme les ouvriers quelconques par excellence: la rumeur les dit chemineaux. Las et forts, grouillement partout où la terre a souci d'être modifiée, eux trouvent, en l'absence d'usine, sous les intempéries, indépendance.

Les maîtres si quelque part, dénués de gêne, verbe haut.— Je suis le malade des bruits et m'étonne que presque tout le monde répugne aux odeurs mauvaises, moins au cri. Cette cohue entre, part, avec le manche, à l'épaule, de la pioche et de la pelle: or, elle invite, en sa faveur, les émotions de derrière la tête et force à procéder, directement, d'idées dont on se dit *c'est de la littérature!* Tout à l'heure, dévot ennemi, pénétrant dans une crypte ou cellier en commun, devant la rangée de l'outil double, cette pelle et cette pioche, sexuels — dont le métal, résumant la force pure du travailleur, féconde les terrains sans culture, je fus pris de religion, outre que de mécontentement, émue à m'agenouiller. Aucun homme de loi ne se targue de déloger l'instrus — baux tacites, usages locaux — établi par surprise et ayant même payé aux propriétaires: je dois jouer le rôle ou restreindre, à mes droits, l'empiètement. Quelque langage, la chance que je le tienne, comporte du dédain, bien sûr, puisque la promiscuité, couramment, me déplaît: ou, serai-je, d'une note juste, conduit à discourir ainsi? — Camarades — par exemple — vous ne supposez pas l'état de quelqu'un épars dans un paysage celui-ci, où toute foule s'arrête, en tant qu'épaisseur de forêt à l'isolement que j'ai voulu tutélaire de l'eau; or mon cas, tel et, quand on jure, hoquète, se bat et s'estropie, la discordance produit, comme dans ce suspens lumineux de l'air, la plus intolérable si sachez, invisible des déchirures. —Pas que je redoute l'inanité, quant à des simples, de cet aveu, qui les frapperait, sûrement, plus qu'autres au monde et ne commanderait le même rire immédiat qu'à onze messieurs, pour voisins: avec le sens, pochards, du merveilleux et, soumis à une rude corvée, de délicatesses quelque part supérieures, peut-être ne verraient-ils, dans mon douloureux privilège, aucune démarcation strictement sociale pour leur causer ombrage, mais personnelle — s'observeraient-ils un temps, bref, l'habitude plausiblement reprend le dessus; à moins qu'un ne répondit, tout de suite, avec égalité. —Nous, le travail cessé pour un peu, éprouvons le besoin de se confondre, entre soi: qui a hurlé, moi, lui? son coup de voix m'a grandi, et tiré de la fatigue, aussi est-ce, déjà, boire, gratuitement, d'entendre crier un autre. —Leur chœur, incohérent, est en effet nécessaire. Comme vite je me relâche de ma défense, avec la même sensibilité qui l'aiguisa; et j'introduis, par la main, l'assaillant. Ah! à l'exprès et propre usage, du rêveur se clôture, au noir d'arbres, en spacieux retirement, la Propriété, comme veut le vulgaire: il faut que je l'aie manquée, avec obstination, durant mes jours — omettant le moyen d'acquisition — pour satisfaire quelque singulier instinct de ne rien posséder et de seulement passer, au risque d'une résidence comme maintenant ouverte à l'aventure qui n'est pas, tout à fait, le hasard, puisqu'il me rapproche, selon que je me fis, de prolétaires.

Alternatives, je prévois la saison, de sympathie et de malaise...

—Ou souhaiterais, pour couper court, qu'un me cherchât querelle: en attendant et seule stratégie, s'agit de clore un jardinet, sablé, fleuri par mon art, en terrasse sur l'onde, la pièce d'habitation à la campagne... Qu'étranger ne passe le seuil, comme vers un cabaret, les travailleurs iront à leur chantier par un chemin loué et fauché dans les moissons.

"Fumier!" accompagné de pieds dans la grille, se profère violemment: je comprends qui l'aménité nomme, eh! bien même d'un soûlaud, grand gars le visage aux barreaux, elle me vexe malgré moi; est-ce caste, du tout, je ne mesure, individu à individu, de différence, en ce moment, et ne parviens à ne pas considérer le forcené, titubant et vociférant, comme un homme ou à nier le ressentiment à son endroit. Très raide, il me scrute avec animosité. Impossible de l'annuler, mentalement: de parfaire l'œuvre de la boisson, le coucher, d'avance, en la poussière et qu'il ne soit pas ce colosse tout à coup grossier et méchant. Sans que je cède même par un pugilat qui illustrerait, sur le gazon, la lutte des classes, à ses nouvelles provocations débordantes. Le mal qui le ruine, l'ivrognerie, y pourvoira, à ma place, au point que le sachant, je souffre de mon mutisme, gardé indifférent, qui me fait complice.

Un énervement d'états contradictoires, oiseux, faussés et la contagion jusqu'à moi, par du trouble, de quelque imbécile ébriété.

Même le calme, obligatoire dans une région d'échos, comme on y trempe, je l'ai, particulièrement les soirs de dimanche, jusqu'au silence. Appréhension quant à cette heure, qui prend la transparence de la journée, avant les ombres puis l'écoule lucide vers quelque profondeur. J'aime assister, en paix, à la crise et qu'elle se réclame de quelqu'un. Les compagnons apprécient l'instant, à leur façon, se concertent, entre souper et coucher, sur les salaires ou interminablement disputent, en le décor vautrés. M'abstraire ni quitter, exclus, la fenêtre, regard, moi là, de l'ancienne bâtisse sur l'endroit qu'elle sait; pour faire au groupe des avances, sans effet. Toujours le cas: pas lieu de se trouver ensemble; un contact peut, je le crains, n'intervenir entres des hommes. — "Je dis" une voix "que nous trimons, chacun ici, au profit d'autres." — "Mieux," interrompais-je bas, "vous le faites, afin qu'on vous paie et d'être légalement, quant à vous seuls." — "Oui, les bourgeois," j'entends, peu concerné "veulent un chemin de fer." — "Pas moi, du moins" pour sourire "je ne vous ai pas appelés dans cette contrée de luxe et sonore, bouleversée autant que je suis gêné." Ce colloque, fréquent, en muettes restrictions de mon côté, manque, par enchantement; quelle pierrerie, le ciel fluide! Toutes les bouches ordinaires tues au ras du sol comme y dégorgeant leur vanité de parole. J'allais conclure "Peut-être moi, aussi, je travaille..." — A quoi? n'eût objecté aucun, admettant, à cause de comptables, l'occupation transférée des bras à la tête. A quoi — tait, dans la conscience seule, un écho — du moins, qui puisse servir, parmi l'échange général. Tristesse que ma production reste, à ceux-ci, par essence, comme les nuages au crépuscule ou des étoiles, vaine.

Véritablement, aujourd'hui, qu'y a-t-il?

L'escouade du labeur gît au rendez-vous mais vaincue. Ils ont trouvé, l'un après l'autre qui la forment, ici affalée en l'herbe, l'élan à peine, chancelant tous comme sous un projectile, d'arriver et tomber à cet étroit champ de bataille: quel sommeil de corps contre la motte sourde.

Ainsi vais-je librement admirer et songer.

Non, ma vue ne peut, de l'ouverture où je m'accoude, s'échapper dans la direction de l'horizon, sans que quelque chose de moi n'enjambe, indûment, avec manque d'égard et de convenance à mon tour, cette jonchée d'un fléau; dont, en ma qualité, je dois comprendre le mystère et juger le devoir: car, contrairement à la majorité et beaucoup de plus fortunés, le pain ne lui a pas suffi — ils ont peiné une partie notable de la semaine, pour l'obtenir d'abord; et, maintenant, la voici, demain, ils ne savent pas, rampent par le vague et piochent sans mouvement — qui fait en son sort, un trou égal à celui creusé, jusqu'ici, tous les jours, dans la réalité des terrains (fondation, certes, de temple). Ils réservent, honorablement, sans témoigner de ce que c'est ni que s'éclaire cette fête, la part du sacré dans l'existence, par un arrêt, l'attente et le momentané suicide. La connaissance qui resplendirait — d'un orgueil inclus à l'ouvrage journalier, résister, simplement et se montrer debout — alentour magnifiée par une colonnade de futaie; quelque instinct la chercha dans un nombre considérable, pour les déjeter ainsi, de petits verres et ils en sont, avec l'absolu d'un accomplissement rituel, moins officiants que victimes, à figurer, au soir, l'hébétement de tâches si l'observance relève de la fatalité plus que d'un vouloir.

Les constellations s'initient à briller: comme je voudrais que parmi l'obscurité qui court sur l'aveugle troupeau, aussi des points de clarté, telle pensée tout à l'heure, se fixassent, malgré ces yeux scellés ne les distinguant pas — pour le fait, pour l'exactitude, pour qu'il soit dit. Je penserai, donc, uniquement, à eux, les importuns, qui me ferment, par leur abandon, le lointain vespéral; plus que, naguères, par leur tumulte. Ces artisans de tâches élémentaires, il m'est loisible, les veillant, à côté d'un fleuve limpide continu, d'y regarder le peuple — une intelligence robuste de la condition humaine leur courbe l'échine journellement pour tirer, sans l'intermédiaire du blé, le miracle de vie qui assure la présence: d'autres ont fait les défrichements passés et des aqueducs ou livreront un terre-plein à telle machine, les mêmes, Louis-Pierre, Martin, Poitou et le Normand, quand ils ne dorment pas, ainsi s'invoquent-ils selon les mères ou la province; mais plutôt des naissances sombrèrent en l'anonymat et l'immense sommeil l'ouïe à la génératrice, les prostrant, cette fois, subit un accablement et un élargissement de tous les siècles et, autant cela possible — réduite aux proportions sociales, d'éternité.

Conflict

For a long time, for a time — I believed — that my thought abstained from any accident even a true one; preferring over chance to draw, springing forth, from its own essence.

A predilection for an abandoned house, which would seem to favor this state of mind, leads me to retract myself: so much is the contentment the same, except this time, as each year turns the outside stone stairs green, at pushing the wintry shutters back against the walls, then linking, as though there had been no interruption, today's glance with the scene formerly immobilized. This is the reward for faithful returns; but now the banging of the wormeaten shutters scans a racket, refrains and squabbles from below; I remember now how the legend of the unfortunate abode, of which I frequent the intact corner, having been invaded by a band of workers engaged in offending the country, because it was till now totally secluded, with a railroad, arrived and distressed me at my departure; would I go or not — the news made me almost hesitate — to see it again, what a pity! The premises will have to be defended as mine, despotically if necessary, and here I am. And henceforth there is an exclusive tenderness on my part, to think that it was it which, in the ruining of an area until now preciously beautiful, suffered the greatest wrong; I become the host of its decline: it is hard to believe that the abode loved for its disuse and the exceptional quality about it has ben turned by progress into a canteen for railroad workers.

Diggers, shaftsinkers, with the corduroy on their legs worn out, so the embankment must be going ahead; they line up, at rest in a shelter trench, the blue and white transverse stripes of their jerseys gradually forming what resembles a sheet of water (clothing oh! to think that man is the source which he is seeking): it is they, my co-tenants formerly those, in my mind, when I encountered them on the roads, coddled like very ordinary working men: reportedly they are itinerant workers. Weary and strong, a swarming mass everywhere where the earth is solicitous of being changed, they find in the absence of a factory, and in weather's inclemency, their independence.

The masters, if they are around somewhere, free of constraint, are loud of speech. — I am the invalid of noise and am astonished that almost everyone feels a repugnance to bad odors and less so to shouting. This mob enters and leaves with the handle of the pick and shovel on the shoulder: now it invites in its favor emotions in the back of one's mind and forces one to proceed, directly, from ideas of which one says to oneself that is literature! Just now, making my way, as a devout enemy, into a crypt or common *storage room, before the row of the double tool, this sexual shovel and pick — whose metal, summing up the pure strength of the worker, fecundates the uncultivated soil, I was seized by religion, besides discontent, and moved to the point of kneeling down. No man of law prides himself on ousting the intruder — silent leases, local customs — established by surprise and having even paid the owners: I must play the role or restrict, to my rights, the trespass. No matter what language, assuming I were to speak, would sound disdainful, of course, since promiscuousness, generally, displeases me: or will I be led to speechifying, in the right tone, thus? "Comrades" for example "you cannot imagine the condition of someone dispersed in a landscape such as this, where no crowds penetrate, because of the forest's density, to the isolation which I intended to be the water's guardian; now my position is such, and when there is swearing, hiccuping, fighting and mangling one another, the dissonance produces, as in this luminous uncertainty of the air, the most intolerable, know this, and invisible of rents." Not that I fear the futility, as regards these unsophisticated people, of this avowal, which would strike them, surely, more than it would others in the world and would not command the same immediate laughter that it would of eleven gentlemen, for neighbors: drunkards, they have a sense for the marvelous and, subject to arduous drudgery, for in some sense superior susceptibilities; and they would in my sorrowful privilege perhaps not see any strictly social demarcation at which to take offence, but a personal one — should they be circumspect for a while, shortly, habit plausibly gets the upper hand again; unless one of them answered, at once, on equal terms. "We feel, when work has stopped for a short time, the need to intermingle with each other: who yelled, me, he? his shout has magnified me, and drawn me out of my weariness; also, it is already like drinking for nothing to hear another shouting." Their incoherent chorus is, as a matter of fact, necessary. And I relax my defense as quickly, with the same sensitiveness which had sharpened it; and I introduce the besieger with my own hand. Ah! for the express and proper use of the dreamer lies enclosed, in the trees' shades, in spacious retirement, the Property, as the vulgar would have it: it must be that I let that chance go by, with obstination, in my time — not to mention the means of acquisition — in order to satisfy some peculiar instinct not to possess anything and to merely pass, at the risk of a residence like this one now open to adventure, which is not altogether chance, since it draws me near, according to what I have become, proletarians.*

Alternatives, I foresee the season of sympathy and uneasiness...

—Or would I wish, in order to put an end to this, that someone tried to pick a quarrel: while undecided and as only strategy, it is a question of closing a small garden, graveled, and adorned with flowers by my art, as embanked garden above the water, the country living room... May no stranger pass its threshold, as to a tavern, the workers shall go to their workyard by a rented road, mowed in the fields.

"Heap of manure," accompanied by kicking against the gate bars, someone shouts violently: I understand who calls the compliment and who it is aimed at, well even from a drunkard, a tall guy with his face against the fence railing, it annoys me despite myself; is it class-consciousness? not at all; I do not, at this moment, individual against individual, measure any difference and do not succeed in not considering the staggering and yelling madman as a man, nor do I succeed in denying my resentment toward him. Very stiff, he scrutinizes me with animosity. Impossible to cancel him, mentally: to finish off the work of drink, to bring him down, in advance, into the dust, that he might not be this all at once coarse and malevolent giant. I do not even yield to his new provocations which are brimming over, by a fistfight which would illustrate the class struggle on the lawn. The evil which is his ruin, drunkenness, will take care of that for me, to the point that, knowing it, I suffer from my mutism, having remained indifferent, which makes me an accomplice.

An indolent nervous irritation, due to conflicting states of mind, and the contagion, through the confusion, of some imbecile intoxication, have even gotten to me.

But tranquility also, which is obligatory in a region of echoes, as one becomes part of it, I have it, particularly on Sunday evenings, to the point of silence. I have an apprehension with respect to this hour, which takes on the day's transparency, before the coming of darkness, then disperses it lucidly into some depth. I love to be present, undisturbed, at the crisis, and may it claim kinship with someone. The fellows appreciate the moment in their own way and discuss peacefully between supper and bedtime salaries, or dispute interminably, sprawled in the scenery. I do not remove myself, nor leave, though an excluded one, the window of the ancient house which looks out on a familiar place, in order to make advances to the group, without effect. Always this is the case: there is no way of coming together; I fear that no contact can take place among men. "I say," says a voice, "that we are toiling, everyone here, for the benefit of others." "What's more," I interrupt under my breath, "you do it in order to be paid and to exist, as far as you are concerned, legally." "Yes, the bourgeois," I hear, not much concerned, "want a railroad." "Not me, at least," having to smile, "I did not call you into this sonorous and luxurious region, which is now thrown into as much of a confusion as I myself am inconvenienced." This frequent colloquy, consisting of silent reservations on my part, is silenced, by magic: what a gem, this fluid sky! All common mouths silenced now are flush with the earth, as though they were disgorging their proud oratory there. I was going to conclude: "Perhaps I, too, work . . ." No one would have objected "At what?", admitting, on account of pay-masters, the work transferred from the arms to the head. "At what?", an echo, in the consciousness only, falls silent — that might be useful, at least, in the general exchange. I feel a sadness that my production should remain, for these men here, in essence, vain like the clouds at twilight or stars.

Indeed, what is the matter today?

The work gang lies at the meeting place, but vanquished. They who make it up have found, one after another, here fallen in the grass, hardly the strength, all of them staggering as if shot, to arrive and fall down in this narrow battlefield: what a heavy sleep of bodies on the dull sod.

So I am going to contemplate and muse freely.

No, my view cannot, from the window where I am leaning my elbows, escape in the horizon's direction, without some part of me unduly encroaching on this scourge strewn about, lacking respect and manners in my turn; I must, in my capacity, understand its mystery and judge its task; for, contrary to the majority and more fortunate of men, bread alone was not enough for them — they have toiled a considerable part of the week, in order to obtain it, *first; and now, here they are, they don't know tomorrow and grovel through the indefinite, digging without movement — which in their destiny makes a hole equal to the one dug, up to now, every day, in the reality of plots of ground (a foundation, most certainly, of a temple). They reserve, honorably, without bearing witness to what it is nor that this feast might brighten up, the sacred part of existence, by a cessation, the waiting and the momentary suicide. The knowledge which would become resplendent — of a pride attached to their daily work, to resist, simply and appear standing up — is round about magnified by a colonnade of full-grown trees; some instinct sought it in a considerable number, to twist them thus about, of drinks, and they are from them, with the absoluteness of a ritual consumption, less officiants than victims, occupied in representing, in the evening, the stupefaction of tasks if the observance derives from fatality rather than a will.*

The constellations are beginning to shine: how I would wish that within the darkness which falls over the blind herd, points of brightness also, such a thought just now, should settle, despite these sealed eyes which do not distinguish them — for the sake of the fact, for accuracy's sake, in order that it may be said. I shall, therefore, think of them alone, the intruders, who, by their surrender more than erstwhile by their turmoil, are closing off from me the distant twilight. These artisans of elementary tasks, it is permissible to me, watching over them near a limpid unbroken river, to see in them the people — a healthy understanding of the human condition bends their back daily in order to draw, without the intermediary of wheat, the miracle of life which assures the presence: others have made past land-clearings and aqueducts or shall surrender a strip of land to such and such a machine, the same, Louis-Pierre, Martin, Poitou and the Norman, thus they call each other, when they don't sleep, by their mothers' terms or after their province; but births sank rather into anonymity, and the boundless sleep with their ear to mother earth, exhausting them, this time, undergoes a despondency and an enlargement of all the ages and, as much as that is possible — reduced to the social proportions, of eternity.

A LIST OF WORKS CITED

Mallarmé, Stéphane, *Divagations*. Paris: Bibliothèque Charpentier, 1897.
——. *Œuvres*. (Ed. Henri Mondor et G. Jean-Aubry) Paris: Gallimard, 1945.
——. *Correspondance*. 3 Vols. (I: 1862-1871; II: 1871-1885; III: 1866-1889) (Ed. Mondor & Austin, Mondor & Richard) Paris: Gallimard, 1959, 1965, 1969.
Mondor, Henri. *Mallarmé Lycéen*. Paris: Gallimard, 1954.
——. *Autres précisions sur Mallarmé et inédits*. Paris: Gallimard, 1961.
——. *Mallarmé: Propos sur la poésie*. Monaco: Ed. du Rocher, 1953.
Barbier, Carl Paul. *Documents Stéphane Mallarmé II*. Paris: Nizet, 1970.
Cook, Bradford, ed. and tr. *Mallarmé: Selected Prose Poems, Essays and Letters*. Baltimore: Johns Hopkins Univ. Press, 1956.
Fischer, Carl. *Stéphane Mallarmé Sämtliche Gedichte französisch mit deutscher Übersetzung*. Heidelberg: Lambert Schneider Verlag, 1957.
Hartley, Anthony, ed. and tr. *Mallarmé*. Baltimore: Penguin, 1965.

Ayda, Adile. *Le Drame intérieur de Mallarmé*. Istanbul: Ed. de la Turquie Moderne, 1955.
Bachelard, Gaston. *L'Eau et les rêves*. Paris: Librairie Jose Corti, 1942.
Beausire, Pierre. *Mallarmé poésie et poétique*. Lausanne: Marmod, 1949.
Bernard, Suzanne. *Le Poème en prose de Baudelaire jusqu'à nos jours*. Paris: Nizet, 1959.
Block, Haskell M. *Mallarmé and the Symbolist Drama*. Detroit: Wayne Univ. Press, 1963.
Cellier, Léon. *Mallarmé et la morte qui parle*. Paris: Presses Universitaires de France, 1959.
Chadwick, Charles. *Mallarmé sa pensée et sa poésie*. Paris: Corti, 1962.
Chassé, Charles. *Les Clefs de Mallarmé*. Paris: Aubier, 1954.
Chevalier, Jean. *Dictionnaire des symboles*. Paris: Laffont, 1969.
Chisholm, A. R. *Mallarmé's 'Grand Œuvre'*. London: Univ. of Manchester Press, 1962.
Clayton, Vista. *The Prose Poem in French Literature of the Eighteenth Century*. New York: Columbia Univ., 1936.
Cohn, Robert Greer. *Toward the Poems of Mallarmé*. Berkeley: Univ. of California Press, 1965.
——. *Mallarmé's "Un Coup de Dés": an Exegesis*. New Haven: Yale French Studies, 1949.

Cohn, Robert Greer. *L'Œuvre de Mallarmé: Un Coup de Dés.* Paris: Les Lettres, 1951.
———. *Mallarmé's Masterwork: New Findings.* Paris: Mouton, 1966.
Davies, Gardner. *Mallarmé et le drame solaire.* Paris: Corti, 1959.
———. *Vers une explication rationnelle du "Coup de Dés."* Paris: Corti, 1953.
Doubrovsky, Serge. *Pourquoi la nouvelle critique.* Paris: Mercure de France, 1966.
Eliade, Mircea. *The Sacred and the Profane.* New York: Harcourt, Brace & World, 1959.
Fowlie, Wallace. *Mallarmé.* Chicago: Univ. of Chicago Press, 1962.
Ghil, René. *Les Dates et les œuvres.* Paris: Cros, 1923.
Jean-Aubry, G. *Une Amitié exemplaire: Villiers de l'Isle-Adam et Mallarmé.* Paris: Mercure de France, 1942.
Kahn, Gustave. *Symbolistes et décadents.* Paris: Vannier, 1902.
Kugel, James L. *The Techniques of Strangeness in Symbolist Poetry.* New Haven and London: Yale Univ. Press, 1971.
Mauclair, Camille. *Princes de l'esprit.* Paris: Ollendorf, 1931.
Mauron, Charles. *Introduction to the Psychoanalysis of Mallarmé.* Neuchatel: Griffon, 1950.
Mercier, Alain. *Les Sources ésotériques et occultes de la poésie symboliste (1870-1914). Le Symbolisme français.* Paris: Nizet, 1969.
Michaud, Guy. *Message poétique du symbolisme.* Paris: Nizet, 1966.
Mondor, Henri. *Vie de Mallarmé.* Paris: Gallimard, 1941.
Moreau, Pierre. *La Tradition française du poème en prose avant Baudelaire.* Paris: Lettres Modernes, 1959.
Naumann, Walter. *Der Sprachgebrauch Mallarmés.* Marburg: Hermann Bauer, 1930.
Parent, Monique. *Saint-John Perse et quelques devanciers, étude sur le poème en prose.* Paris: Belles Lettres, 1960.
Paxton, Norman. *The Development of Mallarmé's Prose Style.* Genève: Droz, 1968.
Poulet, Georges. *La Distance intérieure.* Paris: Plon, 1952.
Rauhut, Franz. *Das Französische Prosagedicht.* Hamburg: Friederichson, de Gruyter & Co. m. b. H., 1929.
Richard, Jean-Pierre. *L'Univers imaginaire de Mallarmé.* Paris: Ed. du Seuil, 1961.
Richard, Noel. *Le Mouvement décadent.* Paris: Nizet, 1968.
Robertson, J. F. *A History of German Literature.* Edinburgh: Wm. Blackwell & Sons, 1959.
Royère, Jean. *Mallarmé.* Paris: Simon Kra, 1927.
St. Aubyn, Frederic Chase. *Stéphane Mallarmé.* New York: Twayne Publishers, 1969.
Scherer, Jacques. *L'Expression littéraire dans l'œuvre de Mallarmé.* Paris: Droz, 1947.
Soula, C. *La Poésie et la pensée de Stéphane Mallarmé, essai sur le symbole de la chevelure.* Paris: Champion, 1929.
Spitzer, Leo. *Stilstudien.* München, 1961.
Steland, Dieter. *Dialektische Gedanken in Stéphane Mallarmés "Divagations."* München: Wilhelm Fink Verlag, 1965.
Symons, Arthur. *The Symbolist Movement in Literature.* New York: Dutton, 1919.

Thibaudet, Albert. *La Poésie de Stéphane Mallarmé.* Paris: Gallimard, 1926.
Wais, Kurt. *Mallarmé.* München: Beck'sche Verlagsbuchhandlung, 1952.
Weinberg, Bernard. *The Limits of Symbolism.* Chicago: Univ. of Chicago Press, 1966.
Wicks, Charles Beaumont. *The Parisian Stage.* University: Univ. of Alabama Press, 1961 & 1967.
Williams, Thomas. *Mallarmé and the Language of Mysticism.* Athens: Univ. of Georgia Press, 1970.

Bénichou, Paul. "Mallarmé et le public," CAHIERS DU SUD, no. 297 (1949), 272-290.
Bonniot-Mallarmé, Geneviève. "Mallarmé par sa fille," LA NOUVELLE REVUE FRANÇAISE, XXVII (1926), 516-523.
Chassé, Charles. "Le thème de Hamlet chez Mallarmé," REVUE DES SCIENCES HUMAINES, LXXVII-LXXVIII (1955), 157-169.
Chisholm, A. R. "Le Démon de l'Analogie," ESSAYS IN FRENCH LITERATURE, 1 (Nov. 1964), 106, U. of Western Australia Press.
Davies, Gardner. "The Demon of Analogy," FRENCH STUDIES (1955), 197-211 and 326-347.
Scherer, Edmond. "Hegel et l'hegélianisme," REVUE DES DEUX MONDES, XXXI (1861), 812-856.
Taupin, René. "The Myth of Hamlet in France in Mallarmé's Generation," MODERN LANGUAGE QUARTERLY, XIV (1953), 432-447.

Baudelaire, Charles. *Petits poèmes en prose.* Paris: Garnier, 1962.
———. *Les Fleurs du Mal.* Paris: Garnier, 1961.
Bertrand, Aloysius. *Gaspard de la nuit.* Abbeville: Passeports, 1964.
Gide, André. *Œuvres.* Paris: Gallimard, 1958.
Hugo, Victor. *Les Contemplations.* Paris: Livres de poche, 1965.
Huysmans, J.-K. *A rebours.* Paris: Ed. Fasquelle, 1968.
Poe, E. A. *Representative Selections.* New York: American Writers Series, 1964.
Proust, Marcel. *A la Recherche du temps perdu.* Paris: Gallimard, 1954.
Rimbaud, Arthur. *Œuvres.* Paris: Garnier, 1960.
Staël-Holstein, Anne Louise Germaine baronne de. *De l'Allemagne.* (Ed. J. de Pange, "Les grands écrivains de la France,") Paris: Hachette, 1958-60.
Valéry, Paul. *Œuvres.* Paris: Gallimard, 1957.
Villiers de l'Isle-Adam. *L'Eve future.* Paris: Pauvert, 1960.

NORTH CAROLINA STUDIES IN THE ROMANCE LANGUAGES AND LITERATURES

I.S.B.N. Prefix 0-88438

Recent Titles

FROM VULGAR LATIN TO OLD PROVENÇAL, by Frede Jensen. 1972. (No. 120). *-920-0.*

GOLDEN AGE DRAMA IN SPAIN: GENERAL CONSIDERATION AND UNUSUAL FEATURES, by Sturgis E. Leavitt. 1972. (No. 121). *-921-9.*

THE LEGEND OF THE "SIETE INFANTES DE LARA" (*Refundición toledana de la crónica de 1344* versión), study and edition by Thomas A. Lathrop. 1972. (No. 122). *-922-7.*

STRUCTURE AND IDEOLOGY IN BOIARDO'S "ORLANDO INNAMORATO," by Andrea di Tommaso. 1972. (No. 123). *-923-5.*

STUDIES IN HONOR OF ALFRED G. ENGSTROM, edited by Robert T. Cargo and Emmanuel J. Mickel, Jr. 1972. (No. 124). *-924-3.*

A CRITICAL EDITION WITH INTRODUCTION AND NOTES OF GIL VICENTE'S "FLORESTA DE ENGANOS," by Constantine Christopher Stathatos. 1972. (No. 125). *-925-1.*

LI ROMANS DE WITASSE LE MOINE. *Roman du treizième siècle.* Édité d'après le manuscrit, fonds français 1553, de la Bibliothèque Nationale, Paris, par Denis Joseph Conlon. 1972. (No. 126). *-926-X.*

EL CRONISTA PEDRO DE ESCAVIAS. *Una vida del Siglo XV,* por Juan Bautista Avalle-Arce. 1972. (No. 127). *-927-8.*

AN EDITION OF THE FIRST ITALIAN TRANSLATION OF THE "CELESTINA," by Kathleen V. Kish. 1973. (No. 128). *-928-6.*

MOLIÈRE MOCKED. THREE CONTEMPORARY HOSTILE COMEDIES: *Zélinde, Le portrait du peintre, Élomire Hypocondre,* by Frederick Wright Vogler. 1973. (No. 129). *-929-4.*

C.-A. SAINTE-BEUVE. *Chateaubriand et son groupe littéraire sous l'empire.* Index alphabétique et analytique établi par Lorin A. Uffenbeck. 1973. (No. 130). *-930-8.*

THE ORIGINS OF THE BAROQUE CONCEPT OF "PEREGRINATIO," by Juergen Hahn. 1973. (No. 131). *-931-6.*

THE "AUTO SACRAMENTAL" AND THE PARABLE IN SPANISH GOLDEN AGE LITERATURE, by Donald Thaddeus Dietz. 1973. (No. 132). *-932-4.*

FRANCISCO DE OSUNA AND THE SPIRIT OF THE LETTER, by Laura Calvert. 1973. (No. 133). *-933-2.*

ITINERARIO DI AMORE: DIALETTICA DI AMORE E MORTE NELLA VITA NUOVA, by Margherita de Bonfils Templer. 1973. (No. 134). *-934-0.*

L'IMAGINATION POETIQUE CHEZ DU BARTAS: ELEMENTS DE SENSIBILITE BAROQUE DANS LA "CREATION DU MONDE," by Bruno Braunrot. 1973. (No. 135). *-934-0.*

ARTUS DESIRE: PRIEST AND PAMPHLETEER OF THE SIXTEENTH CENTURY, by Frank S. Giese. 1973. (No. 136). *-936-7.*

JARDIN DE NOBLES DONZELLAS, FRAY MARTIN DE CORDOBA, by Harriet Goldberg. 1974. (No. 137). *-937-5.*

Symposia

LOS NARRADORES HISPANOAMERICANOS DE HOY, edited by Juan Bautista Avalle-Arce. 1973. (No. 1). *-951-0.*

When ordering please cite the *ISBN Prefix* plus the last four digits for each title.

Send orders to:

    University of North Carolina Press
    Chapel Hill
    North Carolina 27514
    U. S. A.

The Department of Romance Studies Digital Arts and Collaboration Lab at the University of North Carolina at Chapel Hill is proud to support the digitization of the North Carolina Studies in the Romance Languages and Literatures series.